FROM RANJI TO ROHAN

A bit of ourselves. With eternal love, [illegible]
Tooting, 29/4/2018

Rohan Kanhai and his wife, Brenda Hague, in London, a few days after their marriage on 11 September 1963

FROM RANJI TO ROHAN

Cricket and Indian Identity in Colonial Guyana 1890s – 1960s

CLEM SEECHARAN

Published by Hansib Publications in 2009

Hansib Publications Limited
P.O. Box 226, Hertford, Hertfordshire, SG14 3WY, UK

Email: info@hansib-books.com
Website: www.hansib-books.com

A catalogue record for this book is
available from the British Library

ISBN: 978-1-906190-27-9

© Clem Seecharan

The right of Clem Seecharan to be identified as
the author of this work has been asserted in accordance with
the Copyright, Designs and Patents Act 1988.

All rights reserved. No part of this publication may be
reproduced, stored in or introduced into a retrieval system,
or transmitted in any form, or by any means, electronic,
mechanical, photocopying, recording, or otherwise,
without the prior permission of the publisher.

Printed and bound in Malta by Melita Press

For Dr Tulsi Singh of
Palmyra Village, Guyana and Midland, Texas
on his 60th birthday and
for the example and inspiration over many decades

CONTENTS

ACKNOWLEDGEMENTS

I am indebted to the following institutions where most of the research was done: the British Library (Newspaper Library), at Colindale, the National Archives (Georgetown, Guyana) and the University of the West Indies Library (St. Augustine, Trinidad).

I am very grateful to my wife, Chris, and our granddaughter, Sophie Vaughan, for their tolerance while this work was in progress: many chores went undone and priceless 'play-time' was lost. But Aja's love is imperishable.

I give special thanks to Saba for her generosity over many decades.

Oscar Ramjeet (Florida) and Dr Tulsi Singh (Texas) have inspired me throughout the project; so, too, Rita Christian (my indefatigable friend and colleague), Phyllis Knight, Ivan Madray and Jonathan Moore. Oscar and Tulsi offered wonderful insights at all stages of the writing. Barry Newton's help by way of stimulating conversation and in providing several pieces from his fine collection of *Wisden* (lacking a few, such as the 1970 issue when Basil Butcher was one of the five) is much appreciated. My former student, Peter Mason, a fine writer and biographer of Learie Constantine, continually challenges me to rethink

I wish to thank many other friends who continue to offer moral support, thus ensuring that I keep my eyes on the ball: Faiyaz Ali, Mike Atherton, Mazrul Bacchus, Jack Balder, Frank Birbalsingh, Bridget Brereton, the late David de Caires and Doreen de Caires, David Dabydeen, Patsy Downey, Peter Fraser, Henry Gulabh, Denis Judd, Raymond Kudrath, Neville Linton, John Mair, Ian McDonald, Chris Marshall, Bob Morgan, Moses Nagamootoo, Roland Quinault, Jaikaran Ramdeo, Jack Ramraj, Eddie Rooney, Brinsley Samaroo, Ron Sanders, Roy Sawh, Royston, Sunil and Tristan Seecharan, Esau Shamshudin, John Smoliniec (JL), Jean Stubbs, Graham Taylor-Russell, Michael Wishart and Andrew Wright.

I wish also to remember a special friendship shared with Dr Latif Ayub (now of Tennessee) who, more than 40 years ago, helped me to survive the privations of my Georgetown sojourn. I even recall our going at midnight to procure sustenance (tennis-roll and cheese with peanut-punch), and the *Guiana Graphic* – to see what J.S. Barker had written about the 'Tiger of Port Mourant'.

I thank Steve Blunt, my university's outstanding photographer, for several of the evocative images in the book. My former vice-chancellor, Brian Roper, was an avid supporter of my cricket projects. This has been very important to my work.

Finally, I am grateful to the pioneer of Caribbean publishing in this country, Arif Ali, for publishing this book; and Richard Painter, the printer, for his fine work and abundant patience.

At the time of going to press, I am saddened to hear that Ivan Madray passed away in Guyana on 23 April 2009. He was buried at his beloved Port Mourant, which still possessed his soul after nearly 51 years of continuous residence in England. I wish to express my deepest sympathy to his great friend and partner, Rohinee Heerah.

Clem Seecharan
Professor of Caribbean History and Head of Caribbean Studies
London Metropolitan University

LIST OF ILLUSTRATIONS

ABBREVIATIONS

BGCC British Guiana Cricket Club
BGEIA British Guiana East Indian Association
BGEICC (EICC) British Guiana East Indian Cricket Club
DCC Demerara Cricket Club
GCC Georgetown Cricket Club (Bourda, British Guiana)
PNC People's National Congress
PPP People's Progressive Party

What was in the minds and hearts of the people of Victorian England which made them see W.G. [Grace] as they did I cannot say for certain. But the passion and forces which are embodied in great popular heroes – and W.G. was one of the greatest of popular heroes – these passions and forces do not yield their secrets to the antiquated instruments which the historians still cling to. Wilton St. Hill and Learie Constantine were more than makers of runs and takers of wickets to the people of Trinidad and Tobago. Who will write a biography of Sir Donald Bradman must be able to write a history of Australia in the same period.

C.L.R. James (1963)

CHAPTER ONE

The Foundation of Indo-Guyanese Identity, with Special Reference to Cricket and Prince Ranjitsinhji's Example – the 1890s

Where a great man has led, many can go afterwards but the honour is his who found and cut the path.
Ranjitsinhji on W.G. Grace (1897)

And when his 'century' goes up,
The people scream and yell,
While caps come off and wave on high,
And handkerchiefs as well.

And see them when he makes a 'duck',
Or caught for 'nine' or 'ten'
Or 'run out' ere he's long been in,
What disappointment then.

The hope of many thousands soon
Are shattered to the ground,
And as the Prince walks slowly out,
A silence reigns around.
'Century' (pseud), 'To Ranji'

The cricket of Ranji [Prince Ranjitsinhji]…was not to be measured in statistics; he was inventive, elegant, exciting to watch…Gilbert Jessop, a man always cool enough about others' merits…described Ranji as 'indisputably the greatest genius who ever stepped on to a cricket field, the most brilliant figure in what, I believe, was cricket's most brilliant period ["the golden age": late 1890s to 1914]'. A year after his death [1934], the Ranji Trophy – the major championship of Indian domestic cricket – was named after him.
John Arlott (1986)

> Rohan Kanhai, as a batsman, has provided a quite remarkable blend of brilliant improvisation and consistency. Almost anyone who ever watched him will recall the remarkable stroke by which he would pick up a full-length ball and swing it to leg with a violent lunge which swung him off his feet and the ball out of the ground [Neville Cardus called it the 'triumphant fall']. He is only 5 feet 7 inches tall but wirily strong, with whippy wrists [like many Indian batsmen] and an immense striking power. His grandparents came from India to Berbice…[a county] in Guyana (then British Guiana) with a strong cricketing tradition.
> *John Arlott (1986)*

Between 1838 and 1917 238,909 people from India were taken to British Guiana (Guyana since 1966) as 'bound coolies' or indentured labourers to work on the sugar plantations. After 1838, freed Africans, traumatised by enslavement for over two centuries by the Dutch then the English, tended to work strategically or withhold their labour altogether from these plantations. Of the Indian labourers who went to British Guiana, the only British colony in South America, 193,154 or 81% arrived between 1851 and 1900; 75,808 or 31.7% were repatriated between 1843 and 1955, under a state-aided system. Only 9,668 or 12.7% of the repatriated went after 1917, when the last indentured labourers arrived in the colony from India. The 1890s, therefore, may be considered a watershed in Indo-Guyanese affairs, for it was just over 50 years since the first batch of 'bound coolies' had arrived, with the termination of slavery. Moreover, a generation of creole or local-born Indians had emerged; a minority of these were now Christians possessed already of the idioms of the ruling British race; they were punctilious about their right to belong to colonial society, being loyal British subjects. The African middle class, allied with their Coloured (mixed race) and Portuguese (of Madeiran origin) compatriots, had been the pathfinders on the road to 'muscular learning', demonstrating ample facility with two major instruments of the civilising mission of the imperial rulers: education and the game of cricket. In a lecture at Queen's College (in Georgetown, British Guiana), in June 1958, C.L.R. James noted the imperial foundations of the democratic impulse in some colonies: 'In the days of their power these European states undoubtedly laid the basis for and helped to develop democratic political institutions. By the end of the 19th century, democracy was at least an ideal, and on a world scale nations were judged by the extent to which they had achieved it or were in process of doing so. Not only in social thought but in art, literature and other important phases of civilisation, the imperialist powers undoubtedly made some splendid achievements'.[1]

This was the foundation of a creole sensibility and the initiative towards liberal democracy from the late 1880s, manifested in a campaign to change the ancient Dutch constitution of British Guiana. They had earned a concession in 1891, when the representative principle, though circumscribed by residual, but reduced, property and income criteria, received a modicum of official affirmation against the inherently elitist and prejudicial nominated mode. Indo-Guyanese participation in this seminal assertion of democratic rights was minuscule, if at all discernible; yet that minor constitutional advance of 1891 inspired a handful of them to endeavour to shape a creole identity.

The decade of the 1890s, plagued by acute depression in the sugar industry, engendered a spate of self-affirmation by the subordinate sections of colonial society. The creole middle class were already imbued with the idea of 'muscular learning': the pursuit of education patterned after English public schools – the classics and cricket – and perceived in the British West Indies as an essential constituent of the refined mind. Cricket in particular, as Jack Williams argues, epitomised in Victorian and Edwardian England a pastoral ideal: order, continuity and moral irreproachability. Consequently, it was possible to invest the game with the means of taming the savagery of the fecund, but disorderly, Tropics. In slave plantation societies in the West Indies, among her oldest colonies, cricket was elevated, as early as the late eighteenth century, as the embodiment of the best in Englishness, with powers to temper the crudity and untamed primordialism – the barbarism – of these colonies from which even the planters had a predilection for escape. Absenteeism, paradoxically, was the index of 'arrival' for the slaveholder who had made it. However, for the Barbadian sugar planters, who were more inclined to settle there, cricket, with its virtues enshrined, lessened the guilt of being slave-owners; but it also helped to rehabilitate their claims of consanguinity with pastoral Albion, the moral and ethical superiority of the civilised motherland. One could extrapolate from Williams to comprehend why cricket was adopted in the British West Indies with such avidity:

> They saw cricket as an expression of their moral worth. Cricket was thought to have higher standards of sportsmanship than other sports. Cricket discourse emphasised that playing cricket encouraged moral qualities such as selflessness, putting the interest of the team before one's enjoyment, accepting the decision of the umpires and captains without complaint, observing the spirit rather than the letter of its laws, all qualities that were seen as resonating with Christian ethics. The interest in cricket of so many clerics reinforced assumptions that the sportsmanship of cricket expressed Christian morality...[2]

At the elite schools throughout the British West Indies and through the churches, Oxbridge masters and clergymen fostered a reverence for cricket; and although they did not initially play with black or coloured (mixed race) men, they conveyed to them its supremacy in the soul of the Englishman. But because white men were a small minority in all the British West Indian islands, even Barbados, they could never dispense with the labour of black and coloured men as groundsmen and, later on, as net bowlers at practice sessions for white batsmen. Indeed, these marginal black men were presented with an extraordinary challenge even within the context of slavery in the early 19th century: in a limited way, they could seek to demonstrate their mastery of the skills of this difficult game, even their superiority – as fast bowlers – to their English owners.

Mastery of the game therefore connoted engagement with the essence of English civilisation – authenticity – the right to belong, indispensable to the construction of identity in this polyglot colonial environment where everybody was an immigrant (the handful of Amerindians in Dominica and those in the interior of British Guiana notwithstanding). Education and cricket would become the premier instruments for establishing one's place in the diverse creole universe, that one was no longer an immigrant. Anchored in the seminal institutions of colonial society in the late 19th century – the elite schools, the bureaucracy and the churches – cricket penetrated even the remotest of villages with rudimentary grasp of the received civilising idioms of the English. Therefore no ethnic group could really be recognised as belonging to the British West Indies if they failed to manifest appreciable competence in cricket. That explains why, as C.L.R. James recalls, even the taciturn Chinese in the Trinidad of his boyhood, in the early 20th century, felt it imperative to demonstrate identity with this irrepressible game:

> A Chinese would land in the island from China unable to speak a word of English. He would begin as a clerk in a grocery store in some remote country district. He and others like him would pool their monthly salaries and turn by turn set up a small business in some strategic spot, usually in the midst of some village populated by Negro agriculturalists...He...lived at the back of his shop, saved his money and in time sold not only foodstuffs but shoes and clothes and gadgets of all sorts. This often made for bad blood between the Chinese and his [black] creditors. But this man, after about fifteen years, would be seized with a passion for cricket. He did not play himself but he sponsored the local cricket team. He would buy a matting for them and supply them with bats and balls. On the Sunday when the match was to be played he provided a feast. He helped out players who could not afford cricket gear. He godfathered very poor boys who could play. On the day of the match you could see him surrounded by the locals, following every ball with a passionate intensity that he gave only to his business. All night and day his shop was filled with people arguing about the match that had passed and the match that was to come. When the team had to travel he supplied transport. The usual taciturnity of the local Chinese remained with him, except in cricket, where he would be as excited and voluble as the rest. You could find people like him scattered all over the island...I don't believe that, apart from his business and his family life, he had any contact whatever with the life around him except his sponsorship of the local cricket club.[3]

After 15 years the Chinese minority were seeking to belong by identifying with that cardinal instrument of creole sensibility:

cricket. However, James seemed to have overlooked the fact that this process had begun much earlier, with the previous generation of Sino-West Indians, sons of those who migrated from China to British Guiana and Trinidad as indentured labourers. They were thoroughly creolised by the early 20th century. Between 1853 and 1866 about 2,500 Chinese were taken to Trinidad, whereas nearly 13,000 went to British Guiana between 1853 and 1879.[4] By the end of the century they were virtually all converts to Christianity and assiduous in their pursuit of 'muscular learning', imbibed through the colonial education system. Henry Kirke has written of cricket among the Chinese of British Guiana from as early as the 1870s. A Chinese journalist visiting the West Indies in 1929 observed also: 'There are few Chinese in the West Indies who have not had the advantage of a high school education, and an increasing number attend Oxford, London and Edinburgh'.[5]

By January 1932, on the eve of C.L.R. James's departure for England, a versatile leg-spinner of mixed Chinese and African ancestry, Ellis 'Puss' Achong (1904-86), made his debut for Trinidad in the inter-colonial tournament. Trinidad defeated both Barbados and British Guiana. This was largely a consequence of Achong's guile on impaired pitches in an age when they were never covered – ever mercurial because of exposure to the vagaries of the elements. In the match against British Guiana, in Barbados, he got 10 wickets, with 7 for 73 in the second innings, as he dexterously made hay of a worn pitch. Indeed, James and Achong had played for Maple, 'the club of the brown-skinned middle class…[c]lass did not matter so much to them as colour',[6] in the late 1920s-early 1930s. Achong represented the West Indies in six Tests, touring England in 1933, when, allegedly, he was the source of the delivery now known as 'chinaman'. But it was another Sino-Trinidadian, R.P. Tang Choon (not mixed), an all-rounder, who was probably the most well known Chinese cricketer in the West Indies. He represented Trinidad in every inter-colonial match between 1934 and 1955. These two notwithstanding, it is incontrovertible that although Chinese in the West Indies had made admirable strides in business and the professions between the Wars, they knew that playing cricket, with some competence, was imperative if they were to be recognised as authentically West Indian. In early 1939, for instance, British Guiana Chinese toured

Trinidad, playing two matches against Trinidad Chinese. The former were dominant, with three Guyanese batsmen scoring centuries: E.S. Gillette, R. Luck and C.V. Too Chung. Gillette later became a Test umpire, as did two other Chinese: E. N. Lee Kow of Trinidad and Douglas Sang Hue of Jamaica.

The Indians in British Guiana and Trinidad, however, comprised over 40% of the population of these colonies, consequently, it was not enough to demonstrate their identity with, or competence in, cricket: it was imperative to prove their skill, if not mastery, at the highest level. The small middle class were the pioneers; but in British Guiana, although many of them were Christians, they looked to Mother India for the example and inspiration in shaping their Indo-Guyanese identity. As Stuart Hall frames it, succinctly and with much power: 'Silencing as well as remembering, identity is always a question of producing in the future an account of the past…it is always about narrative, the stories which cultures tell themselves about who they are and where they come from…[Q]uestions of identity are always questions of representation. They are always questions about the invention, not simply the discovery, of tradition. They are always exercises in selective memory and they almost always involve the silencing of something in order to allow something else to speak'.[8]

Indo-Guyanese creolisation, therefore, was necessarily complex: their received British values were refracted through constructions of emergent Mother India which, by the 1890s, was endowed with a corpus of literature – validating narratives – on its ancient past: a source of self-affirmation. This was unearthed primarily by dedicated European, mainly British, scholars/administrators – Indologists – such as Sir William Jones, Henry Colebrook, Henry Princep, Nathaniel Halhed, Charles Wilkins, H.H. Wilson and others in the Asiatic Society of Bengal since the 1780s, as well as the great 19th century scholar of Vedic or Aryan India, Professor Max Muller (1823-1900) at Oxford. Bernard Cohn sketches the anatomy of Indian historiography:

> The 'discovery' of the relationship between the classical languages of Europe, Latin and Greek, and of Sanskrit, led to refinement of comparative method. This enabled the Europeans to provide India with a macrohistory organised into developmental stages.

> Certain universal features were constructed as markers of progress...India was to be provided with a linear history...Ruins could be dated, inscriptions made to reveal king lists, texts could be converted into sources for the study of the past. Each phase of the European effort to unlock the secret of the Indian past called for more and more collecting, more and more systems of classification, more and more building of repositories for the study of the past and the representation of the European history of India to Indians as well as themselves.[9]

It was a monumental mission fed by pioneering scholarship and resolve – an intellectual achievement that transcended imperial promptings – a credit to these indefatigable men of learning. This creation of knowledge validating the 'idea of India' (as Sunil Khilnani puts it) was the backdrop to the formation of the Indian National Congress in 1885. In British Guiana, the small middle class, comprising people such as Joseph Ruhomon, William Hewley Wharton, Veerasawmy Mudaliar (father of the first Indo-Guyanese first-class cricketer, J.A. Veerasawmy), F.E. Jaundoo, J.R. Wharton, Thomas Flood (one of the founders of the British Guiana East Indian Cricket Club) and the Indian-born, Dr Golab C. Bezbaroa (a graduate of Edinburgh University), could begin to claim the resurgent motherland (often, 'inventions' of it) as the beacon by which to steer. Their endeavour to erase gnawing self-doubt and self-deprecation was driven by indentureship (still extant on the sugar plantations), widespread illiteracy and the tendency in the colony to calumniate all Indians as 'coolies': menial jobbers. It is noteworthy that three of the Indians from Mother India who were central to the process of redefinition of Indo-Guyanese Indianness had all received acclamation in the West, in the 1890s: Dadabhai Naoroji (1825-1917), the first Indian elected to the British House of Commons, in 1892; Swami Vivekananda (1863-1902), whose oratory and learned discourse at the World's Parliament of Religion in Chicago, in 1893, enthralled the West; and the great cricketer, Prince Ranjitsinhji (1872-1933), arguably the best batsman of his generation, who seduced the English imagination with his art, from the mid-1890s to the Great War.[10]

However, it was not Ranji per se who provided the seminal challenge to Indo-Guyanese to achieve cricketing honours. As seen above, it was the will to belong to the colonial polity that rendered this an imperative. In 1891 the Government of India delegated a discerning observer to British Guiana to assess the condition of Indians in the colony; he noticed they had generally attained a measure of economic self-sufficiency that was unimaginable in India. Moreover, he recognised that this was accompanied by a discernibly more self-confident persona in the colony. The latter, arguably, was manifested in the short-lived East Indian Institute in Georgetown in 1892; but vastly more popularly through the game of cricket, on and off the plantations. They were, of course, emulating the passion of African and Coloured boys for the game in spite of the paucity of means. As Ignatius Scoles observed in the mid-1880s, bats and wickets were contrived out of tree-trunks, twigs, branches of the coconut palm or wooden crates; often a ball from balata (the gum of the bullet-tree) was devised. He noted other ingenious improvisations: '…an old paraffin tin, all bruised and battered and just managing to stand, does excellent duty as both bails and wickets. The red leather ball resigns the honour to some old rags tightly twisted and fairly rounded, or at a great push, an oblong mango stone supplies its place'. [11] Nearly sixty years later, Rohan Kanhai (the great Indo-Guyanese batsman) was a boy of five or six learning his cricket in primitive conditions at Plantation Port Mourant, an old sugar estate in the county of Berbice. He recalls the unchanged unpretentious circumstances:

> I learned my cricket in the backstreets and open wasteland around our house using fronds, the dried leaves [branches] of coconut palms shaped into a bat, a piece of cork covered with rags and bound with twine as the ball and twigs snapped from trees as stumps…None of us could afford the luxury of pads and gloves even when we reached the school team at the age of eight. Consequently our arms and legs were always a mass of cuts and bruises. Of course I was daft enough to keep wicket with my bare hands as well as bat, so I got a double helping of trouble…But, however hard and often we were hit, we never ran away from the ball…I'm sure it is because the majority of West Indians are brought up like this that we are such good players off our legs. Who wants to play bat and pad with bare legs?[12]

But there was also a redeeming, elegant side to the game on the plantation, something of beauty amidst the penury, as Ivan Madray (Rohan Kanhai's team-mate for Port Mourant, Berbice, British Guiana and the West Indies) recalled for me in 1987. The time would have been around 1939; Ivan and Rohan were four or five:

> I remember the first time I ever thought about cricket was one day when I went to the Port Mourant Cricket Ground, peeping through a hole in the zinc fence [corrugated sheets], watching the big men in white play. There was something about their clean, white clothes that made the whole thing look like magic. And as I peeped, with no shirt on and my black ass exposed to the public – my pants tried to hide my willy but it would pop out – I felt like I wanted to be like those men. Yes, it was magic to me...It wasn't until many years later I discovered what that big match was all about. It was a final, Flood Cup Final [the symbol of cricket supremacy among Indians in the three counties of British Guiana]. But that day there was a chap playing there who, as if by magic, left a picture of himself in my memory. I was to idolise him in later years. His name was Onkar Naraine, a beautiful batsman and master fieldsman: a tremendous player, a graceful player; he made everything look so pretty.[13]

By the 1880s-90s the sugar planters were actively promoting the game on the plantations, possibly impelled by presumption of its potential for canalising subversive tendencies among their Indian workers. In the same way plots of land for rice growing and communal grazing for cattle and other stock were provided on the plantations as a means of palliating their parents, the sugar planters envisioned cricket for Indian boys as a force for long-term stability and concord on the estates. The civilising propensity of the game had become axiomatic. As I have written elsewhere, it had a beneficial impact beyond the boundary and beyond the plantation:

> Indian boys born in the colony took to cricket with as much enthusiasm as their parents embraced rice and cattle farming. The impact of the game on the community as a whole was profound. On every plantation, in every village, on patches of

> ground between 'logies' [ranges] on the estates, and reefs in the cattle pasture, these boys, whether of Brahmin or Chamar [lowest caste] origin, Hindu or Muslim, played cricket with unbridled enthusiasm. Indeed, it would not be far-fetched to suggest that cricket did much to accelerate the eradication of whatever notion of caste superiority lingered into the early years of...[the 20th century]. It also helped to undermine the wall of incomprehension between African and Indian boys in the primary schools. These cricket matches possessed the coastal landscape of British Guiana.[14]

As D.W.D. Comins remarked in 1891, many Indian children exuded palpable self-confidence on the sugar estates, evident in their relaxed behaviour in the presence of white managers: 'I have been much struck, on my visits to many of the estates...with the trust and affection shown by the coolies, especially the children, to the manager. The ordinary small child in India, at the sight of a sahib [white man] coming into the place, would howl and fly in precipitate dismay; but here they have complete confidence in him, and crowd round delighted and beaming at any small attention they receive...'[15] On 15 August 1891 Comins visited one of the most progressive plantations in the colony, Port Mourant. Situated on the lower Corentyne Coast, in the county of Berbice, this district, which was markedly salubrious and cleansed by the salt wind blowing off the Atlantic to the north, was therefore largely devoid of the malarial scourge of British Guiana. It bred a more vigorous population with a self-assurance that impressed Comins and many other visitors to the area. He narrates a cricketing incident, from July 1891, that illustrates the energy and assertiveness of the people of Port Mourant – their bravura – as well as the immersion of local-born or creole Indians in the cricket 'cult':

> Fifteen or sixteen colony-born coolly [*sic*] youths (Creoles) asked for a three days' pass to plant rice on their own lands. Instead of doing this they went to cricket matches for three days, and then were absent for three more days on their own ground. Mr Murray [the manager of Port Mourant] summoned them, and they were fined $3 or seven days in jail, which latter alternative they all preferred. These were some of his best shovel men, born on the

> estate, and in receipt of high wages, and all took money with them to pay their fines, but when they heard their stay in jail was to be so short, they all decided to go to jail.[16]

Moreover, by 1895 a few middle class Indian men in Georgetown had acquired the skills and the confidence to form a cricket club and challenge teams from ascendant ethnic groups, such as the Madeiran Portuguese. Among these intrepid pioneers were F.E. Jaundoo and Thomas Flood, who had been instrumental in the formation of the short-lived British Guiana East Indian Institute and had forwarded, in October 1892, a congratulatory cable to Dadabhai Naoroji, the first Indian M.P. in the British House of Commons.[17] To play cricket in a formal context, in the capital, Georgetown, against the Portuguese, was tantamount to asserting proficiency in those attributes of civility and civilisation that were presumed to inhere in the imperial game. It was an emphatic claim for inclusion at the highest level of colonial society. It represented a resolve to erase the resilient 'coolie' stain, the taint of barbarism, which clung like barnacles even to successful Indo-Guyanese.

On 26 December 1895 Asiatic Cricket Club played their maiden match against the Lusitania Cricket Club at the Militia Parade Ground, Georgetown. (The greatest Indo-Guyanese cricketer, Rohan Kanhai, was born 40 years later to the day at Plantation Port Mourant.) They defeated the Portuguese team by 38 runs; and the captain, F.E. Jaundoo, was praised for the 'able manner in which he conducted the game throughout'. The Club was described as 'a recently organised club of East Indian members only'. The team comprised Hindus, Muslims and Christians, of north Indian as well as south Indian or Tamil (Madras) stock. The players in this match were: Jaundoo, Soobrian, J. Lazarus, S. Williams, J. Clement, D.W. Sammy, S. Madray, S. Doobay, L.M. Khan, S. Bacchus and J. Nemdharry.[18] This seemingly minor victory was a landmark in Indo-Guyanese cricket. It was achieved against the socially and economically ascendant Portuguese; in the process they enhanced their creole credentials, their right to belong. They were preoccupied with banishing the demeaning 'coolie' stain: cricket and education were therefore instruments of self-liberation. As Joseph Ruhomon (1873-1942), the first Indo-Guyanese intellectual, argued in a seminal lecture in Georgetown on 4 October 1894, it was opportune for them to equip themselves intellectually in order to transcend the 'coolie' universe of limitations. His was a forthright challenge to the small middle class to assume the obligation to set standards:

> Our people have suffered greatly in the past – they have been simply tools in the hands of their employers, and their interests have been sadly overlooked or neglected. But it is high time that they awake to their interests, and put forth their best efforts towards improving themselves in the colony. Our people must be bold, fearless, acquitting themselves as men. Those of you who are influential and powerful in the community, do the very best you can for the advancement of your race in British Guiana…My intelligent and cultured friends, do you know that you can do a great deal in this direction, and that upon you depends the future prosperity and greatness of our race in the colony? The great majority of our people are weak and ignorant. Stretch forth to them a helping hand.[19]

Ruhomon was issuing a challenge to Indo-Guyanese to give priority to education, to emulate Africans in the diaspora and Indians (in Mother India) who were responding to their colonial subjugation by pursuit of core idioms of British civilisation. But he had also imbibed Max Muller's notion of Aryanism – the putative common ancestry of Indians and their British rulers, in the remote past. This imagined ancient 'brotherhood', a fictive commonality of origin, was an example of the 'invention of tradition', creating 'Indias of the mind' (Rushdie), another endeavour to eradicate the 'coolie' stain by conflating India's known ancient achievements with a constructed racial provenance. Ranjitsinhji's (Ranji's) royal pedigree was evocative of the regal persona that permeates Indian history and, even more so for Indo-Guyanese, the folk images which have shaped them, including their legendary heroes of the great Hindu classics, the *Ramayana* and the *Mahabharata*. Moreover, Ranji's rise in England, in the 1890s, coincided with the phase of Aryanism fostered by Professor Max Muller at Oxford; he had even lectured on the subject to the Queen-Empress of India, Queen Victoria, and her family, as early as 1863. In his lecture of October 1892 Joseph Ruhomon embraced Max Muller's thesis, postulating a 'blood relationship' between Indians and the British while anticipating the intellectual supremacy of the former:

> Today I am not only convinced…of the greatness of India as a country, and the greatness of her sons and daughters as a people, but I am joyfully and confidently anticipating the time when in intelligence, in culture, in morals and intellectual attainments, the great East Indian Race [*sic*] shall be second to none in the world…I may add…that we also in British Guiana and all our ancestors in India are closely allied by blood relationship to the British nation, as the following poem by Ben Elvry [an Englishman] entitled 'To India'…will show:-
>
> Brave brothers of the sun-kissed face
> Heirs of the ancient Aryan name;
> Like heritage with you we claim,
> Our tongue betrays our kindred race.[20]

Naoroji and Ranji epitomised the resurgent India: the politician/thinker and the cricketer had demonstrated mastery of two cardinal idioms of the imperial ethos. This, paradoxically, was the foundation for reclaiming their ancestral greatness. To Indo-Guyanese like Joseph Ruhomon, the Wharton brothers and Veerasawmy Mudaliar, in the 1890s, they were a vindication of Aryanism. Naoroji and Ranji, exemplars at the heart of the Empire, compensated for deficiencies and self-doubt in British Guiana while adumbrating their potential for transcending the 'coolie' universe. By appropriating the greatness of Indians, ancient and modern, often unearthed and acknowledged by the West, they were asserting that the 'coolie' taint in the colony was an aberration, a minute interlude in the motherland's ancient grandeur. Moreover, they were claiming their two contemporary heroes, Naoroji and Ranji, for the imagined homeland, 'the East Indian nation'. This was clear from the letter of 1 October 1892, sent by the East Indian Institute of British Guiana to Naoroji, shortly after his election to the House of Commons:

Joseph Ruhomon: the first Indian intellectual in British Guiana, journalist and founder of the British Guiana East Indian Association, in Berbice (1916)

Prince Ranjitsinhji, first Indian to play for England in a Test (1896); the Everest of batsmanship in the 'golden age', before the Great War

> We...deem it not only an honour but a duty of our race in this remote part of Her Majesty's dominions, to render you our unanimous and most hearty congratulations for the distinguished position you have achieved. We are fully conscious of the multifarious difficulties you must necessarily have had to surmount in order to secure your success in this, to our nation, memorable election and that fact alone impels us to doubly prize the honour which the East Indian Nation has, through your meritorious instrumentality, attained – an event unparalleled in the annals of the History of India...[A]lthough we are thousands of miles separated from you, it will be our foremost interest to read of your career...and we further venture to hope that the example which you have so nobly set will be fruitful in actuating others of our ancient race to follow, and thereby rid themselves and countrymen of the political oblivion [into] which they have been presumed hitherto to be sunk.[21]

By the latter half of the 1890s Ranji had become the more potent embodiment of 'the East Indian Nation' to Indo-Guyanese. On 28 October 1896, after that magnificent summer when he made his Test debut, at Manchester, scoring 62 and 154 not out, while also beating W.G. Grace's aggregate in making 2,780 runs, the *Daily Chronicle* in British Guiana carried an article that must have brought pride to Indo-Guyanese and heightened their resolve to master the game. It was inspired by a banquet at Cambridge University, Ranji's *alma mater* from 1890 to 1893; and was suffused with all the potential elements of Indo-Guyanese self-affirmation: recognition at the heart of Empire at the end of the 19th century, through bat and book – cricket and education:

> If happily poor Chester Macnaghten [Ranji's tutor at Rajkumar College, in India], himself an old Cambridge cricketer, had lived long enough to be present in the Guildhall of the great University town tonight, he would have been no true son of Alma Mater if he had not been prouder of the fact that he gave the first lessons on the great pan-Anglican game to Kumar Shri...Prince Ranjitsinhji, than of all the other elements of knowledge instilled by him into the mind of his distinguished pupil...The love of our national pastime thus begotten, has held its sway so strongly

> against all rivals that the young Indian prince who celebrated his twenty-fourth birthday in our midst on the 10th of this month [September 1896], is acknowledged without any disparagement of the great Gloucestershire veteran [Dr W.G. Grace] and others, to be both the finest exponent of the game and the most popular cricketer of the day...[22]

Ranji topped the averages three times: 1896, 1900 and 1904. He was the first batsman to score 3,000 runs in a season and he did so twice: 1899 (3,159 runs) and 1900 (3,065 runs). The newspapers in British Guiana and the British West Indies reproduced articles from the English press, continually, on the mastery of the Prince, particularly his cascading brilliance that illuminated Sussex before the Great War. Between 1893 and 1920, in 500 first class innings (496 played between 1893 and 1912), he scored prolifically: 24,692 runs, at an average of 56.37. Rowland Bowen observes: 'The "silken-shirted Hindu" remained in the country for most of the period, though he had to give more and more of his time to managing his own state's affairs in India. To the English public, he typified the broadmindedness of Empire, as it was supposed, and he gave them a different mode of playing too'.[23] But it was his style – and its power to enthral creole admirers in the West Indies – which must have lifted the spirits of Ranji's Indo-Guyanese devotees and inscribed his name indelibly as a veritable icon in shaping their identity. That precocious disciple of muscular learning, C.L.R. James (1901-89), movingly recalls Ranji's presence among the triumvirate of cricketers who possessed his imagination, on the eve of the Great War – a maker of his colonial universe, 'the things that made a whole':

> [T]here I was, way out in the West Indies, before I was ten, playing games and running races like other little boys, but almost in secret devoting my immense energies to the accumulation of facts and statistics about Grace and Ranjitsinhji, and reading *Vanity Fair* on the average once every three months...Me and my clippings and magazines on W.G. Grace, Victor Trumper and Ranjitsinhji, and my *Vanity Fair* and my puritanical view of the world. I look back at the little eccentric and would liked to have

> listened to him, nod affirmatively and pat him on the shoulder. *A British intellectual long before I was ten*, already an alien in my own environment among my own people, even my own family. Somehow from around me I had selected and fastened on to *the things that made a whole* [emphasis added].[24]

'The things that made a whole': the best of the colonial encounter, things of beauty and the intellect – graceful possessions – that tutored educated British West Indians of the middle class, people like the Jameses, Manleys, Lewises, Adamses, and Ruhomons, possibly more comprehensively than other colonial peoples with internal reverences shaped primarily by their indigenous cultures. Ranji's mastery, nonpareil in the eyes of most of his contemporaries, was among the graceful possessions of empire that James pursued, and absorbed, in his youth.

Ronald Mason writes that Ranji enhanced the game in a manner that brooks no comparison, in the so-called golden age, before the Great War: '[He was]…a very great player by all standards, of an extraordinary lightness and quickness, a figure who had his worthy successor but no true equal, a natural artist who moulded the game to the dictation of his own art…'[25] This speaks of imagination, creativity – a revolutionary in the field. Ranji died in 1933 and the *Dictionary of National Biography* memorialised his unique gift:

> Quite as impressive as the quantity of runs made by Ranjitsinhji was the style in which they were made. At the outset he relied chiefly on back-play, watching the ball closely and being marvellously quick in dealing with the fastest deliveries. His cutting and gliding on the leg side were superb in their certainty. Later he became more orthodox in his methods and scored with plenty of power in front of the wicket. From first to last he remained known to the British public as one of the greatest, perhaps the greatest, cricketer, of his generation.

In 1940, seven years after Ranji's death, Eric Gill, the sculptor, who had watched Ranji at his majestic best, over several years at Sussex, retrieved from his memory a sublime portrait of beauty and delicacy that lit up many a summer afternoon:

> Even now, when I want to have a little quiet wallow in the thought of something wholly delightful and perfect, I think of Ranji on the county ground at Hove...There were many minor stars, each with his special and beloved technique, but nothing on earth could approach the special quality of Ranji's batting or fielding...[S]uch craftsmanship and grace entered into my very soul.[26]

Fiona MacCarthy, Gill's biographer, reflects on the place of Ranji's art in shaping the sculptor's sensibility. It is, indeed, the stuff of greatness: 'The young Eric Gill was...keen on cricket and remembers the impression made on him by the legendary grace of Ranjitsinhji...[This] is particularly interesting in view of Gill's later enthusiasm for the arts of India, in particular the sensual figurative sculpture. His memories of Ranji were not kept as memories of superlative style and body beautiful but became a kind of symbol of discipline and craftsmanship and – the basis of his view of art – of truth to nature, of playing according to the nature of the thing'.[27] This quality of excellence shaped seminally by its peculiar Indian provenance, and transmitted through numerous newspaper articles, would have impressed Indo-Guyanese aspirants to recognition in creole society before the Great War.

Ranji's mastery struck a chord with Indo-Guyanese at a strategic juncture in their endeavour to belong in the West Indies. The fact that his genius was manifest in an idiom that commanded respect from creoles in the region magnified his heroic stature. Therefore his grace, the quiet supremacy of style, could be absorbed as an antidote to the badge of 'coolie' inferiority; besides, his royal pedigree was cherished by Indo-Guyanese. I wish now to explore briefly two narratives which illustrate his transcendent presence in the Indo-Guyanese psyche: one from 1915; the other, a very personal one, which has lodged in my memory and sustains an indissoluble link with cricket as well as Mother India.

In 1914 Indo-Guyanese founded their first organised cricket club, the British Guiana East Indian Cricket Club (EICC), in Queenstown, Georgetown. On 13 December 1915 the Governor, Sir Walter Egerton, opened the new ground and pavilion, as war raged in Europe. He spoke in celebratory terms of their antecedents, their achievements in the colony, as well as India's proficiency at cricket and the unstinting contribution of Prince Ranjitsinhji – Indians as a whole – to the war effort:

> You belong to a race which is of ancient civilisation. You come, most of you or your forefathers, from the great valley of the Ganges and from the Madras Presidency [the Tamil minority]...The presence of East Indians in this colony has been a great factor in its prosperity, and one great thing you have done within recent years is to introduce your own native industry of rice planting...[N]ot only have you benefited the whole population and the colony by doing that, you have also benefited yourselves, and you have made the poorer classes of your race a much more contented lot than they were when the rice began...I will remind you that cricket is a game which took root in India very soon after we English went there, and East Indians have shown themselves proficient in the game in India; and in India one of your chiefs, Ranjitsinhji, was one of the best players of cricket. He is not batting now! He is fighting for the Empire – (Hear! Hear!) – fighting for the Empire like many of your race (prolonged cheers). The East Indians in France and elsewhere in the fighting line have distinguished themselves. They have shown what we all knew, [and] what the Germans didn't believe, that they came of a fighting stock – (Hear! Hear!) – and can always give a good account of themselves (cheers).[28]

This was affirmation from the highest official in British Guiana, an Englishman, that they were no longer aliens or birds of passage – mere 'coolies' on the periphery of colonial affairs. They belonged because they deserved to although many were still inclined to define them as aliens. The Governor underlined several virtues: their greatness as a people from ancient times; their progress through continuity of effort in establishing the rice industry in British Guiana – indeed, 'a great factor in its prosperity' – which benefited the 'whole population' of the colony; the acquired excellence in the premier imperial game of cricket in the motherland epitomised by Ranji's excellence; India's loyalty and generous contribution to the war effort (including Ranji's); the assertion that they 'came of a fighting stock', supposedly a long-held belief at the heart of Empire. In the process he was projecting their cricketing and agricultural initiatives in the colony as a bridge both to India and the West Indies, while imbuing their racial pedigree with martial glamour, embodied by Ranji's magnificence within the boundary and his loyalty to the Empire manifested in his sacrifice in the theatre of war. Ranji, more than any other Indian until Gandhi, engendered in Indo-Guyanese a sense of self-worth that eventually drove their humiliation and self-deprecation beyond the 'coolie' stain. But it was Governor Egerton's underlining of their seminal place in the civilising of mankind that must have provided the most potent antidote to the 'coolie' shame: they are a people with an ancient tradition, including the field of sport. He had commenced his speech by referring to their very ancient civilisation: 'their race was highly civilised before his race [British] had commenced to put on clothes, and they were, and had always been, a race fond of sports and games'.[29]

It is interesting that a few weeks before the opening of the EICC ground, an Indian correspondent from La Penitence (south Georgetown), had remarked on the importance of retaining their link with India. Gulabkhan was suggesting that Hindi should be taught in schools in British Guiana: 'I do not see how a wholesome connection could be kept up between here and India without preserving the Indian literature or language…As an East Indian I must neither abjure nor ignore the Indian language nor its literature. Nothing reduces individuality, manhood and national characteristics as the loss of language. It is my language that helps to create in me genuine patriotism and love. It is my language that introduces me to my ancestry and identifies me with the past histories of my nation'.[30] Gulabkhan's command of English was clearly impressive; and he must have felt at home in the creole world of British Guiana. But he was very apprehensive of losing valid communion with his ancestral legacy. India's power to define is not easily eroded; therefore, although creolised Indo-Guyanese yearned to belong, this would be pursued primarily on their terms.

I grew up, in the early 1960s, with an image of Ranji as a mythical figure, virtually a deity from our great Hindu classic, the *Ramayana*: many eclectic images from it danced in my boyhood imagination. A blurred picture of the Prince executing his delicate, but imperious, leg-glance, had found its way into my bulging book of cuttings on cricket. It was examined minutely, over and over, for some secreted magic; that, too, danced in my imagination. Another impression of him, in regal attire, culled from a 'library' book, had seduced my impressionable mind to lodge him amongst the framed pictures of Hindu deities in our home, the object of my mother's daily *puja*. Ranji was not just a great cricketer; his legendary place in the Indo-Guyanese mind had infused this incomparable game, which possessed us from morning till night, with an element of divinity, despite our primitive gear. Tales of his miraculous feats in England in what seemed like ancient times could mentally transport our people in British Guiana from the cane-field to the heart of England – Lord's. This tended to strengthen a perennial curiosity: to get to England one day. Moreover, it sustained an elemental desire to become somebody – the will to go beyond boundaries. So I was predisposed to wallow in the most fantastic narratives about the Prince, who had seduced the English long ago like no other Indian had or could.

My father's knowledge of the game was rudimentary indeed. He could neither bat nor bowl. A bat looked funny in his hands a couple of times I cajoled him, when I was little, into negotiating my off-breaks. But, occasionally, when he ventured assuredly into the game's rich narrative legacy, I fell for his certainties: miraculously, his renditions became unimpeachable. He would tell often how the 'racialist' Australians had refused to allow Ranji 'to step foot' in their country, when he toured as a Test player for England in what seemed like another age. He would 'pollute' their country. He related with an authority that betrayed no fallibility or fabrication, that Queen Victoria was so exasperated by the humiliation meted out to 'her Prince' that she ordered the ship to return to England forthwith if Prince Ranji could not land. The tour must not go on without him. Shamed by their great Queen, the Australians relented; and Ranji proceeded to score a century in the first Test.

It was many years before I learnt that Ranji did tour Australia in 1897-8 with Stoddart's English team, and that he scored 175 in the first Test at Sydney. However, I was really upset that I could unearth no evidence whatsoever to support dad's tale that the Australians had sought to exclude Ranji on grounds of race. But I could not bring myself to tell him so, and in a strange way, I was

Ranji's regal provenance added magic to his mastery and inspired Indo-West Indians

still claimed by the fantasy: myriad versions of this tale were rendered by Indo-Guyanese. I have pondered much on my father's narrative, but only in recent years have I come to fathom its significance for him and other Indo-Guyanese. Ranji, 'the prince of cricket' in the 'golden age of cricket', was evocative of the royal persona that resonated in the Indo-Guyanese imagination: the archetypal repository of wisdom and goodness in their repertoire of folk images – epitomised by the golden age of Lord Rama's rule (*Ram Raj*) in the *Ramayana*. That filled the vacuum, the cultivated amnesia with regard to the impoverished India whence they came. Moreover, the fantasy that Victoria, the Queen-Empress of India, had intervened to protect the dignity of 'her Prince' from the 'racialist' Australians, was suggestive of invented ancient royal links between Britain and Mother India, a vindication of their 'Aryan pedigree'. They were not mere 'coolies'; and cricket, particularly the regal bat of Prince Ranjitsinhji – the glamour of his play, acknowledged in England, Australia and the West Indies – was clearing the way for rehabilitation of the ancient glory of the motherland.

This was the foundation and the wider context of Indo-Guyanese cricket between the wars. His Highness, the Maharajah Jam Sahib of Nawanagar, Ranjitsinhji (1872-1933), was the beacon; he was peerless. H.S. Altham has assessed the legacy of this gifted, intrepid and imaginative artist:

> [H]e was blessed with supreme natural gifts, and an alert and receptive mind, physique that was at once strong, supple and perfectly co-ordinated, and, as a result, a lightning quickness of conception and execution that no man, not even Victor Trumper [Australia's greatest batsman before 1914], has ever quite equalled. But it was by unremitting application that he trained himself to make the utmost of these innate advantages...In method, Ranji was a law unto himself. His extraordinary quickness of eye and mind allowed him to do things utterly impracticable for others. He would play back to the fastest bowlers on the fastest wicket, and never had to hurry his stroke; his cutting was marvellous; his leg-side play has never been approached, and he broke the hearts of the bowlers by the way he deflected their fastest breakbacks to the [fine-leg] boundary. It

> was not a glance, as we now understand the term: the ball was met with the full face of the bat, and at the psychological moment those wrists of steel pivoted, and the ball sped away to leg. But it is less commonly realised that he was always a wonderful driver, and, indeed, in his later years discarded defence more and more for attack, and often played the innings of pure hitter, only that it was backed throughout by his marvellously resourceful back-play.[31]

For Indo-Guyanese, the resilient 'coolie' image was exacerbated by creole assumption that they were weak and ungainly: effeminate. Often broken prematurely by hard labour on the sugar plantations and in the rice fields, they readily embraced the sublime images of grace, beauty and regal infallibility evoked by their Prince, emanating from the heart of the Empire. The acknowledged stamina and legendary flair of Ranji offered atonement for the demeaning physical image, encapsulated by their supposed docility on the sugar plantations. The reverence for the game and the self-belief Ranji stimulated in many Indo-Guyanese would have been fortified by the following excerpt from a book, edited by C.B. Fry (his close friend and fellow batsman for Sussex and England), which was reproduced in the *Argosy* of British Guiana on 5 August 1899, when he was 26 years old and at the peak of his powers:

> The distinctive trait of Ranjitsinhji's cricket is an eclectic quickness both in the conception and execution of his strokes. Thereby he is able to do such things as a slower eye and wrist dare not attempt. In making the ordinary strokes he differs from the run of batsmen in that he judges the flight of the ball about half as soon again, and can therefore shape for his strokes more readily and with more certainty. At the same time he need not, owing to his marvellous rapidity of movement, allow himself as much margin for errors as others find necessary. And it is this quickness which enables him to take, even upon the fastest wickets, the most unheard-of liberties without fatal results...He has a miraculous knack of turning the ball accurately from the pitch, and flicks it round to the on-side with subtle, yet terrific power...There never has been a greater master of cutting and leg-play.

But Ranji was more than a great cricketer. As Sir Neville Cardus, who watched him in his youth, observed, he brought to England, during the 'golden age' of cricket, a distinctive quality. His abundant gifts, some unique, enriched the game, giving it something peculiarly Indian – the 'genius of his race':

> Ranji was the most remarkable instance in all cricket history of a man expressing through the game not only his individual genius but the genius of his race. No Englishman could have batted like Ranji: ' Ranji', said Ted Wainwright once [he toured Australia with him in 1897-8] , ''e never made a Christian stroke in his life'. The light that shone on our cricket fields when Ranji batted was a light out of his own land, a dusky, inscrutable light...When Ranji came to cricket it was a thoroughly English game...It was the age of the straight bat and the honest length ball. And at that time, English and Victorian through and through, this miracle of Ranji happened in our land. The ancient ways of doing things were subverted. The cricket, born of old Hambledon...was changed into something rich and strange whenever Ranji batted....When Ranji passed out of cricket a wonder and a glory departed from the game for ever. It is not in nature that there should be another Ranji. We who have had the good luck to see Ranji, let us be grateful.[32]

It is often pointed out that Ranji was very loyal to the British Empire and that he was no devotee of Gandhi. Ashis Nandy notes that he opposed even 'the most moderate anti-colonial movements' led by the liberals in the first and second decades of the 20th century; and that as late as 1931 he told British MPs that he was 'absolutely opposed...to all this talk of independence'. Yet, Nandy observes, 'most Indian nationalists...clutching at any straw which might redeem their self-esteem as Indians, ignored Ranji's politics and tried to make a nationalist hero of him. What mattered to them was that Ranji had beaten the English at their own game and he had, as [Neville] Cardus puts it, "played the game as no Englishman ever played it, or could play it"'. [33] Indo-Guyanese, too, imagined him as belonging to 'the East Indian Nation' – a beacon of illimitable possibilities: a window on the world. He was a symbol vindicating that they could all aspire to, and achieve, a fuller life. His politics, if they knew anything about it, was immaterial. He spoke of possibilities.

Ranji lives on – an irrepressible legend in the Indian imagination! In the English imagination, too! In a somewhat fictional biography of him, Ian Buruma portrays the legend of Ranji as an aspect of English folklore: 'I am not quite sure when the legend of Ranji impressed itself on my mind. Perhaps it was round…[the age of] ten…I remember what it was that first struck my fancy; nothing more than a fleeting image, really; of Ranji coming in to bat, wearing a silk shirt buttoned up to the wrists – 'to hide his dark skin', so they said. It is no exaggeration to say that Ranji's silk shirt was one of the icons of my youthful imagination…Ranji's shirt was…akin to the wristy flicks of his bat, the silky strokes off his leg. As a contemporary British enthusiast [Ted Wainwright] observed, admiringly one presumes: "He never played a Christian stroke in his life"…But Ranji, the Indian from Gujarat, was an English folk hero, not simply the greatest cricketer of his time. He was a fairy-tale prince in an age of steam engines, steel bridges and the first motorcars. He was so famous that children sang songs about him, and grown men wept when they saw him play'.[34]

John Major (in his recent book) is more mundane, but magnanimous, in his celebration of him, 'the living embodiment' of the encounter between East and West: in him 'the twain' did meet. The former Prime Minister has sketched an indelible portrait of the first Indian to play Test cricket for England, in 1896:

> Ranji was a revelation to English crowds, who had seen nothing like him before. He was the personification of the silky skills that would become the emblem of Indian batting. He was all style – in appearance as well as at the wicket. His slicked-down hair, and flowing silk shirt buttoned at the wrist, enchanted spectators as he unfolded dazzling cut strokes and introduced the leg-glance – which brought him a torrent of runs from a formerly barren part of the cricket ground. Moreover, Ranji had the added mystique of being a royal prince. The whole package was box-office magic, and the crowds flocked to see him…Between 1895 and 1920 he scored seventy-two centuries in a career that grossed nearly 25,000 runs at an average of 56.37. It was phenomenal run-scoring, and yet it was

> not the quantity of runs, but Ranji's manner of scoring them that built his reputation…English cricket enfolded Ranji to its bosom, and he rewarded it with an unbeaten century on his Test debut against Australia [at Manchester] in 1896.[35]

However conservative Ranji's politics, his skills, his grace, the deftness – the seductive touch and universal acclaim at the fount of imperial endeavour – elevated all Indians, at home and abroad. And like Rohan Kanhai, over 60 years later in the colonial backwater of British Guiana, it mattered not what he thought of his compatriots, it was solely how they saw him that was at the heart of the matter. Their perception, of course, was validated by the fact that it mirrored how the English saw him. In the 'golden age' before the Great War, Ranji was seen as the successor to the immortal William Gilbert Grace, as the following poem by 'Century' depicts him:

ODE TO RANJI IN INDIA

No pen can write, no tongue can tell
The praise that is your due,
You made your name beside the Cam
When you first got your 'blue' [for Cambridge].

Grace was Champion of the World
Before your Highness came,
But now it seems to me that you
Have robbed him of his name.

You play the bowlers all alike,
You make the fields forlorn,
You fear not Hearne's deliveries,
And Richardson you scorn.
You hit the balls both right and left,
You fear not Bland or Butt,
You place the leather through the 'slips',
You make that fine 'last [late?] cut'.
With 'century'on 'century',
You gladden British hearts,

And marvellous enthusiasm,
Your wondrous play imparts.

And when you have not made a score,
They cheer you none the less,
When you appear, 'tis whispered round
'Here comes the great K.S.'.

They call you Ranji just for short,
And other nicknames too;
You are the 'Wonder of the Age',
A cricket marvel you.

In your three years of English-life,
You've pleased a mighty nation,
When you return I hope that you'll
Keep up your reputation.
And when I visit cricket grounds,
This year, my heart will yearn
To see you on the field again,
And know your safe return.[36]

When Ranji died of a heart attack, aged 61, in April 1933, the *Daily Chronicle* of British Guiana gave copious coverage to 'one of the greatest cricketers who ever lived'. It also commented on his reputation as the Maharajah of Nawanagar: 'He was an enlightened ruler, who in his twenty six years' reign introduced many reforms into his state and considerably developed its resources'. The sudden passing of the Prince must have upset his Indo-Guyanese admirers, but they would have got some consolation that 'his nephew, Prince Duleepsinhji, has inherited his cricketing ability'. Indeed, he was already playing for England.[37] A few weeks later the same paper carried a page one tribute to Ranji. It memorialised his marvellous gifts planted in the hearts of many Indo-Guyanese:

> In his active cricketing days, Kumar Shri Ranjitsinhji was one of the most versatile and brilliant batsman ever seen. Individual and distinctive in style, and possessed of exceptional keenness of eye,

> and great power and flexibility of wrist, he could, on a fast wicket, do anything in the way of scoring; indeed, if the word genius might be used in connection with cricket, it surely applied to him. He could take the good length ball off the middle stump with a measure of certainty no one has ever approached. He was no model for a player of average skill. For any endeavour to imitate his strokes was fatal to most people. Originally he appeared to lack the strength necessary for driving, and made all his runs behind or square of the wicket, and mainly on the leg side. Later in his career he employed the drive and invested that stroke with plenty of power, but he is remembered chiefly for the wonderful skill with which he glanced the ball to leg.[38]

It is noteworthy that in 1933, the year of Ranji's death, J.A. Veerasawmy, the first Indo-Guyanese first-class cricketer and a disciple of Ranji – to whom he was 'presented', at the Oval, in 1911 – had inaugurated a series of lectures on cricket at his *alma mater*, Queen's College. His first lecture, titled 'How to hold the bat and ways of bowling breaks with the forward spin', was illustrated with images of batting and bowling. The spirit of Ranji was irrepressible in British Guiana.[39]

In June 1933 Peter Ruhomon reproduced in his weekly column ('Indian Intelligence by the Pandit'), in the *Daily Chronicle*, a tribute to Ranji, in poetic prose, by 'A.G.G'. A.G. Gardiner (the English essayist and journalist) must have moved Ruhomon immensely. His ode resonated with Ranji's many Indo-Guyanese devotees, at a time when they were already doing well in first division cricket in Georgetown and Berbice, the Parker and Davson Cups respectively:

> The last ball has been bowled, the bats have been oiled and put away, and around Lord's the grand stands deserted and forlorn. We have said farewell to cricket; we have said farewell too to cricket's being. The game will come again with the spring and the new grass and the burgeoning trees. But the king will come no more. No more shall we see him tripping down the pavilion steps, his face wreathed with chubby smiles; no more shall we sit in the jolly sunshine through the livelong day and watch his incomparable art till the evening shadows fall athwart the greensward and send us home content. The well-grace actor

> leaves the stage and becomes only a memory in a world of happy memories. And so 'hats off' to the Jam Sahib – the prince of a little state, but the king of a great game![40]

I often like to give the final word on the place of cricket in societies such as India and the West Indies, even England, to C.L.R. James. This is his observation from 1960, shortly after the England tour of the West Indies: '...no one will ever shake my opinion that the 1950 [West Indies] cricket team in England, the three W's, Ram and Val, did more for West Indian public relations in England than any other single event I know of. Before the War, Constantine did similarly. A.G. Gardiner, the famous editor, has said that Ranjitsinhji's cricketing powers first made the British public aware of Indians as a people, and not as a colonial abstraction'.[41] That was why when Indo-West Indians embraced the art of Ranji, harnessing it to undermine the 'coolie' image thus lifting their self-esteem, it was not seen as pretentious, a spurious claim. West Indians yearned for the day when they could engage their own masters of the game to advance their social and political aspirations. Learie Constantine was their first representative man. Like Ranji, his acclamation was bolstered by his 'magic', his peculiar gifts, allied to recognition in England.

And as James argued often, and underlined in a lecture in Georgetown in April 1965, West Indians were peculiarly adept at mastering most facets of the received civilisation. They had very little of their own on which to go:

> [A]t the writing of fiction, at handling the English language, at cricket, at all branches of medical attention, transport, etc., people of the Caribbean have proved themselves easily the most advanced of all the formerly colonial coloured peoples. We have showed an extraordinary capacity to master and practise all the techniques of modern civilisation...We have the energy and the capacity to master what is foreign because historically we have nothing of our own, no national identity. We are all expatriates.[42]

NOTES

1. C.L.R. James, 'On Federation', in his *At the Rendezvous of Victory* (London: Allison and Busby, 1984), p. 93.
2. Quoted in Clem Seecharan, *Muscular Learning: Cricket and Education in the Making of the British West Indies to the End of the 19th Century* (Kingston, Jamaica: Ian Randle Publishers, 2006), pp. 14-5.
3. C.L.R. James, *Beyond a Boundary* (London: Serpent's Tail, 1994 [1963]), pp. 63-4.
4. Walton Look Lai, *Indentured Labour, Caribbean Sugar* (Baltimore: The Johns Hopkins University Press, 1993), pp. 189-90; Brian L. Moore, *Race, Power and Social Segmentation in Colonial Society: Guyana after Slavery, 1838-91* (New York: Gordon and Breach Science Publishers, 1987), p. 161.
5. *Ibid.* [Look Lai], quoted on p. 214.
6. James, *op. cit.* [1994], p. 50.
7. See the *Daily Chronicle*, 18, 23, 24 February 1939.
8. Stuart Hall, *Myths of Caribbean Identity* [The Walter Rodney Memorial Lecture, October 1991], (Coventry: Centre for Caribbean Studies, University of Warwick, 1991), pp. 2-3.
9. Bernard S. Cohn, *Colonialism and its Forms of Knowledge: The British in India* (Princeton: Princeton University Press, 1996), pp. 79-80.
10. See my *India and the Shaping of the Indo-Guyanese Imagination, 1890s-1920s* (Leeds: Peepal Tree Press, 1993); and my *Joseph Ruhomon's India: The Progress of her People at Home and Abroad and how those in British Guiana may Improve Themselves* (Kingston, Jamaica: The University of the West Indies Press, 2001).
11. Ignatius Scoles, *Sketches of African and Indian Life in British Guiana* (Georgetown: 'The Argosy' Press, 1885), pp. 33-4.
12. Rohan Kanhai, *Blasting for Runs* (London: Souvenir Press, 1966), pp. 12-3.
13. Frank Birbalsingh and Clem Seecharan, *Indo-Westindian Cricket* (London: Hansib, 1988), pp. 94, 96.
14. *'Tiger in the Stars': The Anatomy of Indian Achievement in British Guiana, 1919-29* (London: Macmillan, 1997), p. 311.
15. D.W.D. Comins, *Note on Emigration from India to British Guiana* (Diary) (Calcutta: Bengal Secretariat Press, 1893), p. 15.
16. *Ibid.*, p. 31.
17. See my *India and the Shaping of the Indo-Guyanese Imagination*, [*op. cit.*, 1993], Appendix V.
18. See the *Argosy*, 21, 28 December 1895.
19. See my *Joseph Ruhomon's India*, [*op. cit.*, 2001], pp. 67-8.

20. *Ibid.*, p. 63
21. The *Daily Chronicle*, 7 October 1892.
22. The *Daily Chronicle*, 28 October 1896, reproduced an article, 'The Prince of Cricketers', from the *Daily Telegraph* (London).
23. Rowland Bowen, *Cricket: A History of its Growth and Development throughout the World* (London: Eyre and Spottiswoode, 1970), p. 141.
24. James, *op. cit.* [1994], pp. 17-8.
25. Ronald Mason, 'W.G. Grace and his Times, 1899-1999', in E.W. Swanton (ed.), *Barclays World of Cricket* [3 rd. ed.], (London: Willow Books, 1986), pp. 17-8.
26. Quoted in Alan Ross, 'The Presence of Ranji', in Michael Davie and Simon Davie (eds.), *The Faber Book of Cricket* (London: Faber and Faber, 1987), p.345.
27. Fiona MacCarthy, *Eric Gill* (London: Faber and Faber, 1989), p. 15.
28. The *Daily Chronicle*, 14 December 1915.
29. The *Daily Argosy*, 14 December 1915.
30. *The Daily Argosy*, 11 November 1915.
31. H.S. Altham, 'Ranji, Fry and Jessop: the Golden Age of Batting', in Alan Ross (ed.), *The Penguin Cricketer's Companion* (Harmondsworth: Penguin Books, 1981 [1960]), pp. 231-2.
32. Neville Cardus, 'Ranji, Fry and Sussex', in his *Play Resumed with Cardus* (London: Queen Anne Press, 1990 [1979]), pp. 79-80.
33. Ashis Nandy, *The Tao of Cricket: On Games of Destiny and the Destiny of Games* (New Delhi: Oxford University Press, 2000), pp. 70-1.
34. Ian Buruma, *Playing the Game* (London: Vintage, 1992 [1991]), pp. 1-2.
35. John Major, *More than a Game: The Story of Cricket's Early Years* (London: Harper Perennial, 2007), pp. 368-9.
36. Leslie Frewin, *The Poetry of Cricket: An Anthology* (London: Macdonald, 1964), pp. 271-2.
37. The *Daily Chronicle*, 4 April 1933.
38. The *Daily Chronicle*, 20 May 1933.
39. The *Daily Chronicle*, 19 September 1933.
40. The *Daily Chronicle*, 25 June 1933.
41. The *Nation*, 17 June 1960.
42. *Guiana Graphic*, 15 April 1965.

CHAPTER TWO

J.A. Veerasawmy, 'Doosha' Persaud, the British Guiana East Indian Cricket Club (EICC) and the Quest to Belong between the Wars

Professor Edward Shils states that intellectuals in India told him often that two of the decisive events in the 'establishment of India's national self-esteem' were Ranji's accomplishments as an international cricketer before the Great War, and the award of the Nobel Prize in Literature to Rabindranath Tagore in 1913. He points out that in both cases the West was 'forced to acknowledge the merits of India'.[1] Richard Cashman has observed:

> Although Ranji and his celebrated nephew, Duleepsinhji (1905-59), built up their cricket reputations and played most of their cricket in England, and described themselves as English cricketers, Ranji's impact on India was great because he was an Indian who achieved remarkable success in England, overshadowing many of the great English players of the late-Victorian Golden Age of cricket. Ranji achieved this distinction because he caused a revolution in the game through the introduction of highly original and daring strokes, notably the leg-glance, and by stamping his own personal genius on the game. 'When he batted', wrote Neville Cardus, 'a strange light was seen for the first time on English fields, a light from the east...[it] was lovely magic and not prepared for by anything that had happened in cricket before Ranji came to us'.[2]

In British Guiana, too, Indians were proud of Ranji and Tagore; but the influence of the Prince was more deeply felt. His ennobling play before white crowds in England and Australia bred self-esteem, while enhancing their identity with an assertive Mother India, framed by her ancient grandeur and her contemporary resurgence. Ranji was therefore at the core of the pursuit of Indo-Guyanese identity and their quest to belong in the British West Indies.

This was the context in which Indian boys in British Guiana embraced cricket before the First World War. The most notable beneficiary of Ranji's consuming example was John Aloyisius (J.A.) Veerasawmy (born 1891), the first Indo-Guyanese to represent the colony in an inter-colonial match, in 1910. He was born on 12 May 1891; his father, Veerasawmy Mudaliar, a Christian of Tamil stock, was chief interpreter of the Immigration Department and a founder, in 1892, of the short-lived British Guiana East Indian Institute. So he was located within the embryonic Indo-Guyanese middle class that craved recognition in creole society and yearned to belong; but they wished to do so on their own terms. Their endeavour to be creolised was refracted through Mother India's resurgence from the 1880s, with the formation of the Indian National Congress in 1885.[3] Like J.A.Veerasawmy, Joseph Alexander (J.A.) Luckhoo (1887-1949), a young cricketer from New Amsterdam, came from a Christian Indian family, yet that did not diminish their communion with the motherland and her aspirations for greater autonomy within the Empire. It also quickened their resolve to master basic colonial idioms: cricket and education – muscular learning.

In 1909 J.A. Luckhoo had scored a century in a 'representative match' at the Parade Ground, Queenstown, New Amsterdam; he was seen as a batsman of considerable promise. In 1910 Veerasawmy, a medium-pace bowler, represented British Guiana in the inter-colonial match against Trinidad, at the Queen's Park Oval, on 19-21 January; they were overwhelmed by Trinidad, by an innings and 180 runs, with Lebrun Constantine (father of Learie), scoring 116. Veerasawmy, the first Indian to play first-class cricket for British Guiana, bowled 8 overs for 37 runs and did not take a wicket. It was not an auspicious beginning, neither was it for P. Gajadhar, a slow left-arm bowler, the first Indian in the West Indies to play inter-colonial cricket. In January 1909 he represented Trinidad against Barbados, at Kensington Oval; Barbados defeated their guests by 5 wickets. Gajadhar was economical in both innings but he got only one wicket; in the first his figures were: 22 overs, 6 maidens, 43 runs, 0 wicket; in the second: 7 overs, 1 maiden, 21 runs, 1 wicket. He never played in another first-class match. J.A. Veerasawmy did not do so again until September 1921; in fact, no other Indo-West Indian played

J.A. Luckhoo: pioneer Indo-Guyanese cricketer and captain of the British Guiana East Indian Cricket Club; eminent lawyer (King's Counsel) and the first Indo-Guyanese legislator (1916)

in an inter-colonial match between his previous one in 1910 and his next for British Guiana 11 years later.[4] The First World War disrupted inter-colonial cricket severely: after the completion of the triangular tournament between Barbados, British Guiana and Trinidad in January 1912, it was not resumed until February 1920.

Veerasawmy, a very effective medium-pacer who bowled a consistent line augmented by a potent in-swinger, left British Guiana for London in mid-1910, to study law; Luckhoo had preceded him there for the same purpose, in 1909. However, Veerasawmy continued to play cricket in England, appearing regularly for the Clapham Ramblers Cricket Club in London, and on several occasions for the Gentlemen of Surrey. In 1911 his greatest boyhood dream was realised: he was 'presented' to his hero, Prince Ranjitsinhji, at the Oval. Luckhoo graduated in law in 1912, Veerasawmy in 1913; and they both returned to British Guiana and distinguished themselves by playing, organising, promoting and lifting the quality of Indo-Guyanese cricket, irrespective of caste, class or religion, from 1915 to the end of the 1920s.[5] These two men were among the chief architects who fostered club cricket through a prolonged and frequently disheartening apprenticeship. Throughout the 1920s only two Indian players represented the colony in inter-colonial matches: Veerasawmy, who played against Trinidad in 1921, at the Queen's Park Oval, and against the same team, at Bourda in Georgetown, in 1922; and Charlie Pooran, a right-handed batsman, who played one match against Trinidad in February 1929. Eleven years after Veerasawmy made his first-class debut, he played his second game: Trinidad won again by an innings, but he was outstanding in the one innings in which he bowled: 37 overs, 13 maidens, 67 runs, 5 wickets. In Veerasawmy's third and last inter-colonial match, a low-scoring one when the Trinidadian left-arm orthodox spinner, Victor Pascall (Learie Constantine's mother's brother), got 11 for 62 and British Guiana lost by 29 runs, he bowled only 9 overs, 1 maiden, 42 runs, 1 wicket.[6]

Charlie Pooran, allegedly from Plantation Port Mourant (I am unable to verify this), was possibly the first player from that extraordinary sugar estate to represent British Guiana. But his sole match for the colony, against Trinidad at the Queen's Park Oval, from 31 January to 4 February 1929, was not a memorable personal experience. Trinidad was endowed with several of the players immortalised by C.L.R. James in *Beyond a Boundary*: Clifford Roach (Maple), Joe Small (Stingo), Wilton St. Hill, Edwin St. Hill, Cyril Fraser, Ben Sealey and Learie Constantine (all of Shannon). British Guiana made 90 in the first innings and 153 in the second. Trinidad won by 223 runs. Pooran was out lbw Small 0, in the first innings; in the second he was bowled Constantine 0. During the 1920s Indo-Trinidadians did not fare better: A. Hamid, a middle order batsman, who played against British Guiana in 1922 (the last of Veerasawmy's three inter-colonial matches), and made scores of 6 and 4; and A. Razack, against British Guiana, in Barbados, in February 1924. Razack batted at nine, made 7 and 1, and bowled one over.[7] It was not an illustrious initiation into first-class cricket for Indo-West Indians; but they were learning the ropes by sustaining a vibrant club structure to compete effectively in their respective colonies. Indo-Guyanese and Indo-Trinidadians also played each other regularly, in the 1920s, thus fostering a solid sense of their Indo-West Indian identity.

Before the First World War Indians were playing the game throughout British Guiana with immense passion, but it lacked cohesion and organisation. However, the emergence of an Indian middle class, with a compulsion for recognition at the highest level of colonial society, was a stimulus to their commitment to competitive cricket. For this, a cricket club with a good ground, facilities for ongoing practice and a modicum of social space were indispensable. Veerasawmy's work in British Guiana, towards this end, was exemplary: in 1914, with the support of several prominent Indo-Guyanese, he founded the British Guiana East Indian Cricket Club (EICC). In 1915 he leased his property in Queenstown to the Club, and later that year, as noted earlier, the ground was laid out and a pavilion constructed. When the Club was opened on 13 December 1915 the *Daily Chronicle* lauded 'the indefatigable efforts' of the secretary-treasurer, Veerasawmy, who 'in season and out of season, has always striven for the interests of his cricketing protégé'. They also gave credit to the captain of EICC, J.A. Luckhoo, 'a tower of strength...[whose] determined spirit will assuredly in the future make for the success of the Club'. The piece concluded with recognition of Alladat Khan (a bookkeeper from Plantation Providence, East Bank, Berbice, 'no mean cricketer') who travelled to Georgetown for the opening ceremonies: 'His presence served to prove how united is the sturdy East Indian stock to which he has the honour to belong'.[8] Khan was a Muslim. The paper was making a subtle, but astute, observation that would become axiomatic: the EICC was an instrument for shaping Indo-Guyanese identity across regional and caste, as well as religious, boundaries. It also helped to minimise discord between Indians and other groups in this multi-racial society, held together tenuously by the imperial power.

The first match played on the EICC ground at Queenstown took place on 18 December 1915, five days after the opening ceremonies. Governor Egerton was again in attendance, 'in the presence of a large gathering'. One team was captained by J.A. Luckhoo, the other by M. Ally. It is noteworthy that Luckhoo opened the batting with that other pillar of the Club, J.A. Veerasawmy; moreover, they were also the opening bowlers for their team. Luckhoo's XI reached 125, with R. Bacchus making the top score of 43; Azeez Rohoman got 3 for 13. Ally's XI responded with 83 (only A.S. Rohoman with 44 reached double figures). Luckhoo did not get a wicket, but Veerasawmy, demonstrating that he had lost none of the guile because of his studies in the UK (1910-13), was very impressive: 12 overs, 4 maidens, 28 runs, 7 wickets. Five of these were bowled.[9]

As Thomas Flood, a popular Indian businessman and President of the EICC from its inception to his death in 1920, observed at the opening function in 1915, this was the first time in the history of British Guiana that 'Christians, Hindus and Muhammedans' had founded such an organisation. He anticipated that it would redound to the benefit of the youths of the colony: 'It will tend to bring about not only better feelings amongst themselves, but also amongst the other members of the community with whom they will, during their games, be bound to come into contact'. From the beginning the Club was truly representative of Indians of diverse religious persuasions – Christians, Hindus and Muslims – as well as north Indians and south Indians (Tamils). This was reflected in the composition of its first executive, in 1915-6: Thomas Flood (president); R.R. Kerry (vice-president); J.A. Veerasawmy (secretary/treasurer); J. Subryan, R., J., and A.

Rohoman, Francis Kawall, J.S. Pariag, E. Bacchus, P. Sawh, R.B. Gajraj (committee members), and J.A. Luckhoo (captain).[10]

Flood did not state that the formation of the EICC was indicative of Indo-Guyanese quest to belong; neither did he mention their earnestness for recognition by creole society nor their anxiety to eradicate the lingering 'coolie' stain. However, it is significant that five Indians contested the general elections in 1916 (including Flood, J.A. Luckhoo and J.A. Veerasawmy); and for the first time one was elected to the colonial legislature: the captain of the EICC, Luckhoo. Later that year, Joseph Ruhomon, the first Indo-Guyanese intellectual, along with his cousin, E. A. Luckhoo (brother of J.A.), and a few others in the town of New Amsterdam, in Berbice, founded the British Guiana East Indian Association, which would become, in the 1920s-30s, the premier Indian political organisation. The birth of the EICC, therefore, reflected the rise and cohering of an Indian middle class across religious lines, and their resolve to be accepted as a legitimate component of British Guiana and the British West Indies.[11] The Club accelerated the pace of Indo-Guyanese cricketing apprenticeship; because its performances were covered in the daily newspapers, since its inception in 1915, its impact was felt by most Indo-Guyanese.

The EICC was admitted to the second division Garnett Cup competition in 1915. Their best player was, of course, J.A. Veerasawmy. In a match against the Guiana Cricket Club (GCC), in September 1916, he made 148 in a score of 365 for 5 declared. EICC demolished GCC for 39: Veerasawmy got 7 wickets for 10 runs. His batting in the match was superb: 'He treated the bowling with supreme contempt...with a wealth of strokes played all around the wicket'. But his abundant talent was being squandered in second division cricket, so in 1917 he joined the British Guiana Cricket Club (BGCC) in order to play in the Parker Cup, the symbol of cricket supremacy in the colony. Veerasawmy thrived in first division cricket. His bowling in a BGCC v. GCC match, in October 1920, exemplified his skills, mental dexterity and stamina: 'He is regarded as our most destructive bowler on impaired wickets, but on Saturday last he showed that he can command respect even on perfect pitches which the Bourda Club produce...He bowled throughout with great judgment and skill, and required as much circumspection in his 28th over as in his first. The balls that beat and bowled C.V. Hunter and [John] Parker [both first-class cricketers; Hunter toured England in 1923] would have puzzled better batsmen'.[12] In May 1922 a respected commentator observed: 'C.R. Browne and Veerasawmy are the only two bowlers amongst our local cricketers who could have any chance of being selected in a West Indies team for their bowling alone'.[13] Cyril Rutherford Browne ['Snuffie'] (1890-1964), born in Barbados, toured England with the West Indies team in 1923 and in 1928, when they were accorded Test status. He played in four Tests, taking 6 wickets at 48.00: two in England in 1928 and two in the West Indies in 1930. Browne had settled in British Guiana in 1916. Veerasawmy, it will be recalled, played in three inter-colonial matches, in 1910, 1921 and 1922. But, with inter-colonial cricket in abeyance during the First World War, he was deprived of the ultimate challenge that could have brought his considerable gifts as a fast-medium bowler to fruition. Besides, his demanding legal practice in British Guiana aggravated the problem, although he continued to play club cricket. His capacity for leadership was of a high order: he captained BGCC in 1917 and 1918.

Moreover, Veerasawmy maintained a fruitful engagement with the Club of his heart, the British Guiana East Indian Cricket Club (EICC), of which he remained the leading light. EICC won the second division Garnett Cup in 1919, and were one of the four teams that tied in 1919. The Club was victorious in 1925, 1926 and 1927, the first to win it on three consecutive occasions. Their consistently high performance reflected the application of the players and the proficiency of its administrators, all of whom were either accomplished businessmen, such as Thomas Flood, H.B. Gajraj and Azeez Rohoman, or esteemed professionals, like Veerasawmy and J.A. Luckhoo. They knew they represented all Indians in the colony; that alone was incentive to do well.

By 1927 EICC had obviously transcended the level of play of their designation, so they sought elevation to the prestigious first division Parker Cup. The request was rejected because their ground at Queenstown was deemed too small. However, following the intervention of Kunwar Maharaj Singh, the delegate from India who visited the colony in 1925 in connection with the proposed Colonisation Scheme, EICC acquired a lease on a

J.A. Veerasawmy: versatile fast-medium bowler; first Indo-Guyanese to play inter-colonial cricket (1910); lawyer/magistrate and founder of the British Guiana East Indian Cricket Club (1914)

substantial block of land on Camp Road, Thomas Lands, in Georgetown. The Governor, Sir Cecil Rodwell, had expedited the process, and this 'veritable swamp', in the vicinity of the iconic sea wall, was transformed quickly into a beautiful ground with a spacious pavilion. He opened it on 30 April 1928, and in 1929 EICC was admitted to the Parker Cup.

At the heart of Indo-Guyanese cricket, between the wars, was J.A. Veerasawmy. I have written elsewhere of his sterling effort: 'Veerasawmy's contribution to the development of cricket among the Indians of British Guiana was an epic achievement…an aspect of their social history. He was their best cricketer, but his work as an organiser, promoter and administrator, coupled with his impeccable sportsmanship and civilised conduct at the highest levels of colonial society, made him an epitome of the purest ideals of this great game'.[14] He was the best manifestation to the Indo-Guyanese of the power of muscular learning. He was their 'Ranji' of the 1920s however pale the comparison. Governor Collet had acknowledged his virtues in a dispatch to the Colonial Office in April 1922: 'Mr Veerasawmy is a young man of very pleasing manners. He is well educated and appears to have the instincts of a gentleman. There are persons to whose opinion I attach great value who say…that he undoubtedly has the instincts of a gentleman, and, therefore, is more fully accepted as an associate with Europeans than would most Indians and some Europeans'.[15] Yet this did not make him an 'Uncle Tom', for he was resolute in his pursuit of whatever he considered paramount to the advancement of Indo-Guyanese.

On 25 January 1920 the *Daily Chronicle* noted that he 'takes a keen interest in the welfare and development of his race…[and] has been instrumental in arranging inter-colonial cricket fixtures between East Indians of the colony and Trinidad, and also inter-county fixtures [the Flood Cup between Indians in the three counties: Essequibo, Demerara and Berbice]'. Indeed, in 1914, the year after he returned to British Guiana following his legal studies in London, he was instrumental in arranging the first match between Indo-Trinidadians and Indo-Guyanese, which was won by the former, in British Guiana. In May 1919 British Guiana Indians, on a tour of the island, defeated Trinidad Indians in the 'test' match at San Fernando. On their return to British Guiana, the

EICC presented a gift to the captain on tour, Mohamed Insanally, who would captain the Club from 1919 to 1927. The architect of Trinidad's defeat, Veerasawmy, was the recipient of a ball on which was mounted an embossed silver plate. The insignia read:

Demerara [British Guiana] v. Trinidad, May 1919
J.A. Veerasawmy – 2nd innings

O	M	R	W
11	0	23	9

In a moving speech in Trinidad at the conclusion of the tour, Veerasawmy observed that it represented 'an important step in the progress of East Indians in the West Indies…showing their worth in spheres of life other than business, to command the respect of other sections of the community in which they live…' He exhorted Indians to uphold 'the honour of the noble race to which they belong', and he implored them 'never to stop striving for the advancement of the name of India and never to forget, wherever you roam, however wealthy you may be, however trained and accomplished you may become, you will always be considered as sons of India'.[16] He implied that their mounting proficiency in the game was a demonstration of their credentials as West Indians: a people could not feel that they belonged until their competence at cricket had gained the recognition of other groups. But he was unambiguous that their creolisation must not result in the erosion of their Indianness. It is noteworthy that the tour was taking place just a few weeks after 379 unarmed Indians were killed and 1,200 wounded (on 13 April 1919) by British troops at Amritsar in Punjab. It was the catalyst for the meteoric rise of Gandhi, the embodiment of India's moral ascendancy in pursuit of freedom from colonial rule. Veerasawmy's sentiments must have been triggered by the patriotic surge precipitated by Amritsar.

In January 1920 it was reported that Veerasawmy would soon be seeking assistance from the government of British Guiana to take an Indian team from the West Indies to India. The idea apparently originated from a meeting he had with some 'gentlemen' from India, in London, in 1919. The objective was to forge closer links between Indo-West Indians and their ancestral home, and the tour was projected for 1922 or 1923. Nothing came of it as the end of indentureship, in 1917, and the collapse of the proposed Colonisation Scheme to renew immigration from India in the 1920s, with provision for a steamer service to India, precipitated an accelerated physical disengagement with the motherland. This must have disillusioned Veerasawmy, whose father went to British Guiana, indentured from Madras, and worked his way into the colonial civil service and prominence in the Indian community. He himself had travelled widely in India in 1914, after his graduation as a lawyer, visiting Madras, Bombay, Calcutta, Benares, Lucknow, Agra, Delhi, etc, north and south India. Though a Christian and at ease with British culture, he was demonstrably proud of his Indian heritage. In 1922 he proposed the teaching of 'a complete course of Indian history' in the schools of British Guiana. Nothing came of this too.[17]

Throughout the 1920s Veerasawmy was not remiss in his resolve to foster cricket contests between Indians in British Guiana and Trinidad. In 1924 Trinidad Indians visited the colony again; in 1925 and 1929 Indo-Guyanese reciprocated. But he was no less assiduous in fostering the game locally, in Georgetown as well as the rural areas, in the counties of Demerara and Berbice, through the annual Flood Cup tournament. The latter was the nursery of the Indo-Guyanese cricket tradition that would begin to bear fruit by the late 1930s. It was the foundation of their monumental achievements of the 1950s-60s. As noted earlier, a liberal spirit, augmented by pride in Mother India – her ancient legacy in diverse spheres of learning as well as Gandhian India in revolt against colonial rule – made the EICC more than a cricket club. It was a crucial instrument in forging Indo-Guyanese identity across religious, regional, as well as political, lines. It is necessary to repeat that from its birth Hindu, Muslim and Christian Indians worked harmoniously in the team and in the administration of the Club. Cricket made an astounding contribution (largely unacknowledged) to the forging and sustaining of unprecedented tolerance among Indians of all persuasions in British Guiana. It is arguable that Hindu-Muslim relations have been the best in any country to which Indians have migrated since the 1830s; and this owes much to the dominance of the plantation in the colony and the consequential fostering of solidarity among Hindus and Muslims; but the role of cricket in the process should not be underestimated.

Cricket among Indians in the counties of Demerara and Berbice was permeated by an eloquent cordiality and commonality of purpose by people of all religious persuasions. A few examples illustrate the depth of this proclivity for tolerance. Mohamed Insanally, a Muslim, born in 1885, was captain of the EICC for nine years, from 1919 to 1927, having succeeded J.A. Luckhoo. He led British Guiana Indians on their successful tour of Trinidad in 1919 (as noted earlier); and did so again in 1924 when they defeated the Indo-Trinidadians, by one run, at Bourda in Georgetown. He also led EICC on numerous occasions in the Garnett Cup and the Flood Cup competitions. Insanally was a prime force in the development of their new ground in 1927-8. When he relinquished the captaincy in 1927, he was succeeded by another Muslim, A.S. Rohoman, as was the President of the EICC, businessman H.B. Gajraj. In 1929 seven of the 14 Indo-Guyanese cricketers who toured Trinidad were Muslims, although they constituted only 15 percent of the Indian community: A.S. Rohoman (captain), M. Rohoman, K. Rohoman, B. Saddick, M. Deen, Assad Khan and Alladat Khan, the stalwart from Berbice.[18] The Rohoman family (unrelated to Joseph and Peter Ruhomon) were immersed in the game as they were in commerce, owners of the oldest Indian store on Water Street, the hub of commercial life in Georgetown. In fact, they were the virtual sponsors of Bechu, the 'bound coolie' radical, who tormented the Goliaths of privilege by his uncompromising letters to the *Daily Chronicle*, in the late 1890s. The three Rohoman brothers were among the principal shapers of the EICC's success in the 1920s.

On 5 May 1938 the *Daily Chronicle*, in its Indian Centenary issue, observed that 'the British Guiana East Indian Cricket Club (EICC) stands as a monument to the East Indians for their enterprise in sports.' It proceeded to underline the work of Thomas Flood, its first president, and the indefatigable J.A.Veerasawmy (both Christians), in the advancement of the game in their community. Flood had donated the Flood Cup in 1917. This became the symbol of cricket supremacy among Indians in the counties of Essequibo, Demerara and Berbice, and the competition, sportsmanship and general ethos, the camaraderie thus nurtured, did 'much to create a harmonious relationship' among Indo-Guyanese. At the inauguration of the Flood Cup, twenty years earlier, the *Chronicle* had commented prophetically: 'Since the establishment of the EICC [in 1914], a large number of East Indians have take a keen interest in cricket and some, as a result of constant attention to the game, have shown marked improvement. It is felt that this competition will have the effect of bringing together those East Indians residing in the two counties of Berbice and Essequibo, and that in the future, there will come from their midst men who will make a name for themselves in the cricketing world'.[19]

Indo-Guyanese cricketers were a long way from the summit then; and even by the end of the 1930s, were still only in the foothills; but they were learning the ropes slowly, patiently coming to terms with the terrain. In the county of Berbice, far removed from the limelight of Georgetown (its remoteness exaggerated by a poor, often impassable, single road-link), that passion was already evident in abundance, in the 1920s. Berbice had won the first Flood Cup, in 1917; Demerara did in 1918; the competition was suspended in 1919 because of the Trinidad tour. By 1920 a pattern was set in Berbice – the team was drawn primarily from sugar plantations: Alladat Khan (their premier player) and P.R. Barran (Providence), G.H. Khan (Blairmont), Somar, Wailoo, A. Shabid (Bath), Balkarran (Albion), James Kempadoo, Nanan and Samaroo (Port Mourant).[20] As noted earlier, estate managers had been promoting the game at least since the 1890s, and several Indian cricketers on the estates had, by their exemplary play, stimulated interest on and off the plantations. In fact, as early as 1895-6, the game was being played with apparent avidity by the patients at the Berbice Asylum (Mental Hospital), at the confluence of the Berbice River and the Canje Creek. The Superintendent noted: 'Cricket has been played for the amusement of the patients on numerous occasions…' They had created a beautiful ground in the compound, and as the Report of the Surgeon General for 1895-6 states: 'The grounds have been kept regularly weeded, and a large cricket field has been laid down in the central square, which has provided a much needed means of out-door recreation for both patients and staff'.[21] The game had, indeed, reached every sector of the county. The Mental Hospital team would become a formidable one in the Davson Cup, in the 1950s-60s, with several staff-members representing Berbice and British Guiana: Leslie

Amsterdam, Indal Persaud, Victor Harnanan, Charles Paul, Randolph Ramnarace and Hamil Murray.

By the early 1920s, so versatile was the play of several of the Indian backwoodsmen from Berbice that they regained the Flood Cup in 1921, overcoming Demerara whose players were primarily Georgetown-based, from the EICC. The progressive manager of Plantation Port Mourant, J.C. Gibson, a partisan of the cricketing obsession, presented the best player in that match, A.B. Dukhan, with a bat. Success at cricket released tangible benefits on the sugar estates: the best players were allocated time for practice, and invariably elevated to more remunerative and prestigious jobs, away from the sugar-cane fields. In a society still in the shadow of slavery and indentureship (the latter did not cease until 1917, with the last indentures cancelled in 1920), cricket conferred status on the player endowed with demonstrably finer skills. They received the adulation and respect of Guyanese whatever their racial background or prejudices in other spheres.

As the *Daily Argosy* observed in October 1920, the plantations had created several fine grounds with good pitches; this engendered the passion for the game: the skills could be honed through assiduous practice. They also noted that Flood Cup cricket was a vindication that 'East Indians are not one whit behind the rest of the community in their enthusiasm for the game'.[22] Indeed, by 1925, many of them were competing in the Davson Cup, the symbol of cricket supremacy in Berbice, donated by the progressive owners of three sugar plantations in Berbice: Providence, Bath and Blairmont. The Davson family were pioneer reformers in the sugar industry, especially their progressive manager at Blairmont, Guy Eccles. Jock Campbell, later the reforming head of Booker, the largest sugar company in British Guiana, recalled the seminal impact of the culture of reform he witnessed at Blairmont in the mid-1930s. Eccles had demolished the abominable 'logies' or 'nigger yard', the ranges that went back to slavery; built cottages for his workers and installed glass windows in them, contrary to the condescending presupposition of his fellow sugar planters, that 'they'll break the glass in no time'. He had also taken a monumental step towards eradicating the scourge of malaria by employing the great Italian malariologist, Dr George Giglioli. Campbell has reflected on his legacy: 'Now it was Guy Eccles at only 33 who, with the support of the Davson family against all the odds, against all advice, had wrought this transformation. And, of course, he hadn't only opened windows in sugar workers' cottages – he opened windows in men's minds, including my own'.[23]

Another young man whose mind also was opened by Guy Eccles was Alladat Khan, the pillar in the establishment of Indo-Guyanese cricket in Berbice. Born in 1888, he graduated from the Imperial College of Tropical Agriculture in Trinidad, where he studied sugar technology and management. Between 1908 and 1925 Khan was an accountant and sugar chemist at Plantation Providence, East Bank, Berbice; between 1925 and 1932 he was an accountant with Davson's Estates and Factories at Plantation Blairmont. He had earned the respect of Guy Eccles, consequently he could rely on his unfailing approbation in promoting the game among his Indian compatriots. Alladat Khan also played a major role in the inauguration, management and propagation of the Davson Cup. His leadership must have been of a high order, for he was routinely elected captain of the Berbice EICC, between 1915 and 1936, when he was aged 48. In 1919 and 1929 he toured Trinidad with the British Guiana East Indian Cricket Club.[24]

The halo the Davson Cup had acquired by the mid-1920s was an impetus to cricket in many Indo-Guyanese villages, on the periphery of the sugar plantations. Consequently, several of those representing Berbice in the Flood Cup in 1925 were non-estate cricketers: E. Emambaccus (Sheet Anchor), J. Etwaroo (Cumberland), A.B. Boodhoo and M. Mootoo (Rose Hall, Corentyne), A. Emambaccus (Adelphi) and Johnny De Groot (No. 2). They all played regularly in the Davson Cup. The structure to facilitate and sustain a high level of club cricket was in place; it fed the passion in the villages although the facilities available there were transparently poorer than on the plantations. In March 1925 Harold Moore, a naturalist, remarked on the rampant abandon of Indian boys on the Corentyne Coast, in Berbice, possessed by the cricket 'cult'. Not even a monsoonal deluge could sap the ardour of these 'embryonic cricketers', playing 'bat-and-ball', an allusion to soft-ball or sponge-ball cricket, characterised by under-arm bowling. But the intensity of application was not diminished:

> I was greatly amused by the action of a number of Indian lads who were playing on the neighbouring pasture a game of bat-and-ball, which though but a caricature of cricket, none the less laid the foundations for the subsequent glorious performances of some of the colony's best cricketers of the past...Ordinary cricketers would have run for shelter from such a downpour. Not one of the country boys thought of doing such a thing...The bowler continued to bowl in the teeth of the driving rain, the batsman to bat, the fielders to chase the ball. Three of the players seized favourable opportunities during the progress of the game to strip themselves hurriedly of all clothing except their lap cloth. They would not have their movement curbed by heavy, wet cloth. I may say that the rural districts abound with embryonic cricketers, both Black and Indian, of similar unquenchable enthusiasm and physical stamina...[25]

On 24 June 1929 Rev. C.F. Andrews, Gandhi's personal friend and principal adviser on Indians overseas, on an extended sojourn in British Guiana, addressed members of the East Indian Cricket Club, appropriately, on the question of Indian unity. He referred to the bedevilling bane of India – untouchability and chronic Hindu-Muslim bigotry. However, he expressed his heartfelt pride in the social changes evident wherever he travelled in British Guiana: '[Indians had] completely obliterated that old, wrong, deep-seated division [between Hindus and Muslims]'. It was deeply satisfying, he underlined, to observe that Hindu, Muslim and Christian Indians 'sat at the same table...shared the same meals...[and] shared friendship in harmony and love...' He was most gratified to see Brahmins 'with great love and affection welcoming and embracing their brothers, who in India might be regarded as outcastes'. He considered these marvellous changes, in so short a time in the colony, 'a great and noble victory'. And he counselled them to continue to support the EICC because 'through cricket and by playing good cricket they would achieve unity more quickly'.[26] The prominent Indians present at Andrews's address to the Club did not deviate from the path of intra-communal tolerance. While they remained in their discrete religious organisations, they were also invariably members of the British Guiana East Indian Association (BGEIA) – potential religious dissonance was invariably sublimated by their perceived common political interest. Among them were several members of the EICC executive in 1929, a genuine microcosm of the community: H.B. Gajraj (president), a Muslim; Francis Kawall (vice-president), a Christian; Ramprashad (junior vice-president), a Hindu; David Iloo (secretary), a Christian; and Ranjit Singh, captain between 1930 and 1941, a Hindu.

Throughout the 1930s Indo-Guyanese continued to master the game in the counties of Demerara and Berbice. But in Essequibo, appropriately dubbed 'the Cinderella County', where all the sugar plantations had collapsed (save Hampton Court which closed in 1935), the chronically weak economy and the absence of club cricket retarded the game: often they could not muster a team for the annual Flood Cup tournament. Meanwhile, Demerara and Berbice, though ascendant, did not succeed in producing Indian cricketers for the colony's inter-colonial team in the 1920s. It was a prolonged apprenticeship, indeed, and must have engendered private agony in the community. By 1929, as noted earlier, only two Indo-Guyanese players had represented British Guiana: Veerasawmy and Charlie Pooran; the latter played in one match, against Trinidad, in early 1929. It may be recalled that he did not give Indo-Guyanese cause for celebration, having made nought in both innings. He never played another first-class match.

Two Indo-Guyanese cricketers played in the intercolonial tournament in the 1930s: R.B. Rohoman (1910-53), a right-arm off-break bowler from BGCC, and Chatterpaul Persaud, a right-handed batsman. Richard Rohoman, from the prolific cricketing family of the EICC, was a fine slow bowler, whose bowling analysis against Barbados (in Trinidad) in January 1934, was the best hitherto recorded by an Indo-West Indian: 56.4 overs, 6 maidens, 194 runs, 11 wickets; yet Barbados won by 143 runs. When he played for the colony again later that year, against Trinidad at home at Bourda, he bowled only 9 overs in the whole match and took no wicket for 46 runs.[27] Like Charlie Pooran, Richard Rohoman is invisible in the Indo-Guyanese cricket narrative. The quest to belong remained largely elusive.

Chatterpaul 'Doosha' Persaud was born in Kitty, near to Georgetown, on 6 December 1906 (not 15 June 1912 as is cited on reputable web sources such as 'Cricket Archive' and

Chatterpaul 'Doosha' Persaud in 1937: the first Indo-West Indian to score a century in inter-colonial cricket

'Cricinfo'). Therefore, he as nearly 31 when he made his debut for his colony in 1937: no youth! His father, Orilall (*sic*), went to British Guiana from India as an indentured labourer and was sent to Plantation Lusignan, East Coast Demerara. It is not certain where his mother, Lutchmin, was born. Both had died by the time 'Doosha' became a fine cricketer in the 1930s. After his astounding performance in his first first-class match for British Guiana, in October 1937, the *Daily Argosy* named him 'Man of the Week' and wrote a brief portrait of him. They noted that he still lived at Kitty, where he had become something of an 'idol'.[28] His age notwithstanding, the paper concurred that he 'has been rightly acclaimed as one of British Guiana's cricket stars of the future'. They explained the basis for optimism: 'He is not a sudden find but has only now secured an opportunity of giving of his best, and gives every promise of going far in the cricketing world. He is possessed of most of the attributes necessary for a great batsman. He has a quick brain, good eyesight, wrists and footwork, is exceedingly keen on the game, and above all he is modest and level-headed...He had a great love for cricket from his very early days and would travel long distances to take part in a game'.

At the age of 14, in 1920, he made his debut in the second division Garnett Cup, for the Botanical Gardens Cricket Club. Inexplicably, he subsequently went down to third-class cricket, the Wren Cup, representing the Kitty Sports Club, which he led from 1924 to 1927. He then played for La Penitence Cricket Club, at the same level, in 1928-9. It is clear then that several of his seminal years were squandered. At a crucial stage he was not getting the challenge a man with his gifts required to enhance the quality of his play. However, he joined the British Guiana East Indian Cricket Club (EICC) in 1930. After playing three Garnett Cup matches, he was promoted to the first division Parker Cup team, led by A.S. Rohoman, brother of Richard Rohoman, the British Guiana off-break bowler. It was a step that confirmed his stature as a batsman.

'Doosha' recorded his first Parker Cup century in 1931; he made over 500 runs in 1933, with a score of 118 against BGCC 'B'. In 1935, apart from playing in this competition, he also featured in six Garnett Cup matches for the EICC, scoring 620 runs in nine innings, with three centuries. He made 122 not out against the Chinese Sports Club. He also took 32 wickets for a mere 104 runs. In 1934 he had taken 15 wickets in the Parker Cup, bowling his medium pace deftly on pitches that were mercurial because they were not covered. Therefore, his batting must be assessed similarly: it required excellent defence, mobility in footwork and considerable all-round technical skills to prosper in such volatile circumstances. Many more flamboyant batsmen perished ignominiously because of the movement and uneven bounce extracted from ill-prepared, uncovered pitches. 'Doosha' was a meticulous practitioner of the basics of good defence, judgement of length and line and placing the ball. He was a skilful on-driver and a deft cutter of the delivery that was fractionally short. It was believed, however, that his play could have been enhanced by exploiting opportunities to drive more frequently on the off.

'Doosha' represented Demerara Indians in several matches in the Flood Cup. His best score was 73, against Berbice in 1934. He also played against a Trinidad Indian team that visited the colony in 1932, and was a member of the EICC team that went to Surinam in 1935. He was a beneficiary of fine coaching at the Georgetown Cricket Club by an English professional, A.J. Richardson. Before 'Doosha' appeared in the intercolonial tournament in 1937, he had participated in the trials that preceded it, organised each year since 1933. The *Argosy* was generous in their verdict on Persaud's debut season, 1937:

> That he has more than fulfilled the expectations of a few far-seeing judges of the game is now a matter of history. Persaud crowned himself with glory in the [1937] Tournament...His batting was one of the highlights...and his all-round performance was most meritorious. He played not like a newcomer to that class of cricket, but like an old stager and came out second in the batting averages with 100.6, scoring 302 runs [in three innings], the best aggregate...Persaud also took six wickets at a cost of 179 runs, an average that hardly gives an accurate idea of the excellent service he rendered his team in this department of the game. He was not up to his usual standard as a fieldsman, this being seriously affected by his long stays at the wicket.[29]

He was a batsman of class – not flamboyant, but impeccable in defence while possessing an admirable range of strokes. He was imbued with abundant powers of concentration that convinced many that he should have been selected for the West Indies tour of England in 1939. Persaud was the most successful Indo-Guyanese cricketer to represent the colony before the greatest of them all, Rohan Kanhai (born 1935), emerged in the mid-1950s. However, the structure of West Indies cricket could not enable club cricketers of recognised talent to demonstrate their skills or develop them in a decisive manner towards Test standards. So 'Doosha' Persaud was another casualty of the rudimentary state of first-class cricket in the region. He had that exemplary debut season in 1937; but there was no inter-colonial tournament in 1938 because of the labour unrest that enveloped the region, and he had a disappointing one in 1939; he was not selected to tour England that year. He played only eight first-class matches and scored 644 runs at an average of 49.53. His highest score of 174, in a partnership of 381 with Peter Bayley (268), against Barbados at Bourda, in 1937, was the first century by an Indo-West Indian in inter-colonial cricket. British Guiana won by an innings and 229 runs.[30] In the next match, against Trinidad at Bourda, he made 96 and 32 and took 6 wickets for 126, in a very close contest that gave British Guiana victory by 2 wickets. They regained the Intercolonial Cup, and the *Daily Chronicle* recognised the decisively steady hand of Chatterpaul Persaud, 'the most vertebrate batsman' in the colony, who in three innings made 302 runs at an average of 100.6:

> Persaud deserves all the acclamation he is receiving. He has been destined...to contribute substantially to the stiffening of the team's batting. He was the safety-first partner in the record fourth-wicket stand of 381 [v. Barbados]. He was again the cautiously plodding partner yesterday in the record 5th wicket stand...[of 179 v. Trinidad]...Persaud was the hero...of the tournament. In each of British Guiana's three innings his was a steadying influence...[a] great series of innings, by a man who has demonstrated that he is the safest batsman in the southern West Indies...This tournament is already being called Persaud's tournament, the most remarkable tribute that can be made to his consistency and reliability'.[31]

This view was popularly held. Persaud received an autographed bat from Wm Fogarty Ltd in Georgetown; another from Messrs Ferriera and Gomes Ltd; a watch from Mr E. Schreier from the Swiss House; a clock from Pestano's Outfit Stores, among many others.[32] But this could not be merely a tribute to 'Doosha' Persaud, coming as it did on the eve of the centenary of the Indian presence in British Guiana (5 May 1938). It was necessarily claimed as an achievement of all Indo-Guyanese, going a good way to validating their quest to belong in the British West Indies. The fact that the tributes to Persaud's excellence in 1937 as 'all-rounder' (he got 4 for 90 in Trinidad's second innings, at a crucial stage of the match), emanated from diverse sources, many non-Indian, magnified his performance. His mastery of the basics as well as his cautious play and prodigious patience were the foundation of his reliability. It is arguable therefore that 'Doosha's' legacy was inherited by two remarkable Indo-Guyanese batsmen of different generations: Joe Solomon (born 1930) and Shivnarine Chanderpaul (born 1974).

J.I Ramphal [Lala Lajpat] spoke for all Indo-Guyanese in his celebration of 'Doosha's' 174 on debut against Barbados, in his weekly column, 'Indian News and Views', in the *Daily Chronicle*. They yearned for him to play Test cricket for the West Indies. This would signal unequivocally that they were no longer sojourners in the new land; they belonged:

> When the first match of the present Intercolonial Cricket Tournament began at Bourda on Monday, September 27 [1937], the good wishes of every Indian in the country went to the B.G. East Indian Cricket Club's all-rounder, who was making his debut in intercolonial cricket. High as our hopes were, however, little did we dream that this young man would have accomplished the distinguished feat of scoring 174 runs…and so make history in intercolonial cricket. Born of humble parents, Chatterpaul, or Doosha as he is commonly called, began his cricketing career at an early age. When quite a young man, he was admitted to the ranks of the B.G.E.I.C.C, where he received his first training as a cricketer at the hands of that veteran, Mr R.J. Singh. Persaud was not a born cricketer. His steady application – born of an ambition to play for his country – earned him a place in the Parker Cup

> team. Since then he has played cricket continuously and has shone in every department of the game. His innings [of 174] was indeed a glorious one. As we sat there looking on at this slim, but fearless, young man who was playing so determinedly, we could not help but be impressed with his variety of shots. Magnificent hooks, late-cuts and sound defensive play…[which made] his innings one of the most outstanding ever played at Bourda….We [therefore] desire to record the congratulations of our entire Indian community to this young man and trust he will acquit himself so creditably during the remainder of the tournament that he will gain for himself the chance of being selected to represent the West Indies…[33]

In December 1937 the *Indian Opinion*, organ of the main Indian organisation in the colony, the British Guiana East Indian Association (BGEIA), carried the following poem equating 'Doosha' Persaud with the stylish batsman from India, Duleepsinhji (1905-59), the nephew of Ranji, who also played for Cambridge, Sussex and England. In his first Test against Australia, at Lord's in 1929, Duleep scored 173. His 'effortless ease and brilliance' had brought another shaft of delight to Indo-West Indians. Persaud's young admirer was celebrating his local hero in the image of another hero from the motherland, Duleep, the successor to Ranji:

C.S. PERSAUD

Conquering hero of a conquering band.
Stalwart six-hitter to the Ladies' stand [at Bourda]!
Powerful wielder of the willow polished.
Everlasting memory of a partnership
established.
Records you have broken and records
made,
Sterling foundation for a certain victory
laid.
Able assistance by Bayley, our local
'Bradman', given.
Under thunderous applause, your score
had risen.

'**D**oosha, Guiana's Duleep' – is in cricket's
history written.
Ramjas Tiwari

The previous month, November 1937, in the *Indian Opinion*, another young admirer of 'Doosha' Persaud, 15 year old Harold Persaud from Berbice, was imagining his hero as a 'boy from Hindustan [India]', suggestive of his inheriting the gifts of Ranji, Duleep, and the Nawab of Pataudi, those regal heroes from Mother India. That the young poet could still see 30-year old 'Doosha' Persaud as 'the boy from Hindustan', was more evocative of the portrait of Duleep, in *Wisden*, painted by the cricket writer and later president of the MCC, H.S. Altham, who had observed the young prince as a schoolboy in England: 'In natural gifts of eye, wrist and footwork he is certainly blessed far above the ordinary measure…[T]here is no doubt about the judgment and certainty with which he takes toll of straight balls of anything but the most immaculate length. His late-cutting is quite beautiful and there is a certain ease and maturity about his batting'.[34] 'Doosha's' style did not mirror the opulence of stroke-play of the Princes from the motherland. But, as Trevor Marshall observes: 'In the 1930s the exploits of Duleepsinhji and the Nawab of Pataudi, the growth of continental Indian nationalism and their own emergence as a community in Trinidad [and British Guiana] provided greater confidence for…Hindus and Muslims in Trinidad to participate in creole pastimes'.[35]

ON HEARING OF C.PERSAUD'S STRIKING CENTURY AGAINST BARBADOS

Once as I sat composedly by
Engrossed in a crossword puzzle,
I heard beside me a joyful cry,
And an unusual amount of bustle.
I wheeled in time to see
A pack of boys come in,
Who danced about in ecstasy,
Like a madden'd highland clan.

'What's all the row about?' asked I,
As I pocketed the puzzle unsolved;
Like a crack of the pistol came the
reply –
'The century of C. Persaud'.

And thus I came to learn
Of Chatterpaul's fine display,
Of his co-operation with Peter Bayley,
Of the Barbadians' great dismay.

I whistled softly and bent my head,
And thought of the skill of man,
To defend three sticks from morn till
night;
The deeds of the boy from Hindustan.
Harold Persaud

However, there was another, possibly unconscious, prompting behind the young poet's characterisation of Chatterpaul Persaud's cricketing glory as the 'the deeds of the boy from Hindustan'. It was rooted in the immigrants' yearning for recognition by the host society: of the mastery by one from their own community of a defining idiom of that society. Cricket was the Everest of achievement on the social landscape of the British West Indies: it was cathartic. As usual, C.L.R. James has immortalised this for us, drawing on black Trinidadian adulation of their elegant batsman from the 1920s, Wilton St. Hill (1893-1957), although he played only three Tests for the West Indies, without success, while his first-class performances for Trinidad and the West Indies were mercurial (five centuries in 43 matches with an average of 27.15):

> I know that to tens of thousands of coloured [black] Trinidadians the unquestioned glory of St. Hill's batting [primarily in domestic cricket] conveyed the sensation that here was one of us, performing *in excelsis* in a sphere where competition was open. It was a demonstration that atoned for a pervading humiliation, and nourished pride and hope. Jimmy

> Durante, the famous American comedian, has popularised a phrase in the United States: 'That's my boy'. I am told that its popularity originates in the heart of the immigrant, struggling with the new language, baffled by the new customs. All his pains were transcended by the sight of [a] young hopeful reciting *The Village Blacksmith* or Lincoln's Gettysburg oration, *civis americanus*, on the way from his log cabin to a house, if not white, would at any rate be large.[36]

The *Indian Opinion* of Christmas 1937 had apprehended the real place of Chatterpaul 'Doosha' Persaud in the Indo-Guyanese mind. 'That's my boy', they were saying. He was transporting them from 'coolies' into men who were no longer 'immigrants'. The ease with which he had adapted to first-class cricket was an unchallengeable validating index. They may soon be seen to belong. Such was the burden with which non-white West Indians had long saddled their cricketers! When they failed it was a kind of collective death. Cricket could not just be a game among diverse peoples with inchoate, vulnerable identities – the absence of nationhood:

> 'Doosha' Persaud has created new records. He has had the proud distinction of being the first Indian to score a century in inter-colonial cricket. His score of 174 against Barbados is the highest made by any cricketer in his first appearance in inter-colonial cricket. His partnership with Bayley [of 381] is the highest recorded in the history of these tournaments...Thus we see that Persaud has been justly acclaimed the hero of the inter-colonial tournament. He has all the necessary characteristics that go to form a great cricketer. Above all, he is very modest, and far from being proud. *We share his success from the point of view that he is a pure-blooded member of our race. We feel proud of his achievements in a field in which we are poorly represented. He has raised our prestige and brought honour and glory not only to himself and us, but also to his country.* His performance has been one of the highlights of sport in this country, and we sincerely hope that this success will urge him to perform greater feats not only in inter-colonial but also in West Indian cricket, to which he no doubt aspires, and for which he is certainly qualifying himself [emphasis added].[37]

But 'Doosha' would lift his Indo-Guyanese devotees to the heavens only to be reclaimed by the anonymity whence he came. His name means nothing to most Indo-Caribbean people today. The lack of an adequate competitive framework for enhancing his demonstrated skills quickly took its toll. As noted earlier, no intercolonial cricket was played in 1938 because of violent labour protests throughout the British West Indies. But in April of that year Persaud did play for Trinidad and British Guiana Indians v. Trinidad (the colony side), which the latter won by 10 wickets. He made 7 and 73 in that match dominated by the leg-break and googlies of Tang Choon, who took 8 for 68. And in August 1938 R.S. Grant, the Cambridge blue (who would captain the West Indies in England in 1939), led a team from Trinidad in British Guiana. Persaud, representing the latter, displayed his form of 1937 in the first match, with a score of 116 not out. In the second one he disappointed his many local followers, who had become habituated to his unfaltering consistency: his scores were 2 and 41. But the solitary failure could not diminish their certainty that he merited selection to the West Indies team. Indians in the region, prematurely, were somewhat euphoric, anticipating 'Doosha' as their first Test cricketer, bearing the torch lit by Ranji and Duleep.

However, the following year, 1939, Persaud's batting was a disaster. It was crucial for him to leave a decisive impression with the selectors that he could score away from home, on the eve of the tour of England that summer. But against Trinidad (in Barbados), in the intercolonial tournament, he made 0 in the first innings and 36 in the second; in the match against Barbados (also in Barbados), his scores were 18 and 21. It is true that he did get 4 wickets for 49 in Trinidad's first innings and 6 for 92 in both innings of the match against Barbados, but it was primarily as a batsman that he was expected to advance his credentials for Test selection. He did not fare better in the crucial trial match between a Combined XI v. Jamaica, designed specifically to facilitate selection of the team for England. His scores were 0 and 5 not out. He was not chosen.[38] In fact, the only Guyanese selected was Peter Bayley (1916-96), with whom he had broken the record partnership for all wickets in West Indies cricket: 381. Bayley was a white Guyanese and deserved his place; but Indo-Guyanese were gravely pained by 'Doosha's' omission. No Indo-West Indian had come as remotely close to making the West Indies team as him. Bayley toured England in 1939 but did not play in a Test match. He never played in a Test.

After the match against Barbados, his low scores notwithstanding, the *Daily Chronicle* was still sanguine that Persaud was a 'strong favourite' to tour England, although they conceded that he was 'not too hot on the field'. They also noted that he was taking up an appointment with the firm of T. Geddes Grant Ltd., of which Rolph Grant, the Trinidad and West Indies captain, was a principal. Rolph was the brother of the previous West Indies captain, G.C. (Jack) Grant.[39] 'Doosha' must have felt that at the age of 32 the time available for him to stake his claim to Test cricket was limited; and Trinidad offered far better possibilities for him to do so. British Guiana was still a backwater. Moreover, the Grants had substantial influence in West Indies cricket through their club, the prestigious Queen's Park Oval; and they must also have given him a financial incentive he could not get at home. His moving to Trinidad, however, did not compensate for his weak performances of early 1939; and his age must have sealed the case against him and enhanced that of two Trinidadian teenagers, Jeff Stollmeyer and Gerry Gomez.

The *Daily Argosy* alluded to the source of 'Doosha's' difficulties in reaching the summit of West Indies cricket, noting that although he had been called to practise regularly for several years, he had failed to gain the selectors' eyes when he was still in his twenties.[40] As noted above, Persaud was not selected to tour England in 1939. Yet the *Daily Chronicle*, an unwavering campaigner for his selection, attributed the obduracy of the selectors to the absence of a representative from British Guiana on the Selection Committee of the West Indies Cricket Board of Control. But they did concede that 'Doosha's' recent performances 'were very disappointing'.[41] In March 1939 it was announced that Leslie Hylton, the Jamaican fast-bowler, was being drafted in to the touring party; no similar silver lining presented itself to Persaud. The *Chronicle* proffered the consolation that 'Doosha' Persaud's 'ability with the bat is unquestioned, except perhaps in Trinidad. His medium-pace bowling, with its own peculiar style, may be useful in England'.[42] The paper was alluding to the fact that the two Trinidadian teenage batsmen, Jeff Stollmeyer (born 1921) and Gerry Gomez (born 1919), were given preference over Persaud. Stollmeyer's score in the intercolonial match against Barbados was 11; he did not play against British Guiana; he made 12 and 28 against Jamaica. Gomez made 0 against Barbados, 1 against British Guiana and 2 and 161 not out against Jamaica. Neither of them played in the trial match against Jamaica.

After Hylton was added to the team, the Georgetown Cricket Club, the premier club in British Guiana based at the historic Bourda ground, made a desperate effort to get 'Doosha', too, on the ship to England. They cabled the West Indies Cricket Board of Control offering to send him to England 'on privately subscribed funds': 'Will selectors and Board agree Persaud's inclusion West Indies side if expenses paid privately?' The response was: 'Board regret unable to agree the inclusion of Persaud'.[43] Unbearable though his non-selection to his admirers, it was not a singular misfortune. As Dindial Singh, an Indo-Guyanese correspondent from Georgetown, observed at the time:

> In 1937 Persaud made the highest aggregate in the whole Intercolonial Cricket Tournament and took the most wickets in the second innings against Trinidad. In 1938 he made 116 in the Goodwill Tour [against a visiting Trinidad XI, captained by Rolph Grant]. This year [1939] he was second in the batting and bowling averages for British Guiana v. Trinidad [he made 0 in a score of 56 and 36 out of 171; his latter score was second only to Victor Stollmeyer's 83. Trinidad won by 10 wickets.] In these circumstances, it is amazing that Persaud has been excluded from the West Indies cricket team. It is also astounding that Jeff Stollmeyer, with nothing spectacular to his credit, should be chosen before [Cyril] Merry, an improved player who represented West Indies on the last occasion [1933].[44]

Rupert Tang Choon, the Chinese all-rounder from Trinidad, also missed the boat. He was reportedly 'the best slow bowler in the West Indies, with…phenomenal hitting power'.[45] Forty-four years later, in 1983, Jeff Stollmeyer was reflecting on the omission of Merry and Tang Choon from the West Indies team to England in 1939. He was magnanimous to both; but, like most, including Indo-West Indians today, he seemed to have forgotten Chatterpaul 'Doosha' Persaud – not a word on him! But then, C.L.R. James did not make a single reference in *Beyond a Boundary* to that indomitable servant of Trinidadian cricket, Rupert Tang Choon, the best Sino-West Indian cricketer ever.

> Looking back at the selection of the team, there no doubt was a certain amount of hit and miss...Of the Trinidadians who missed out the most unfortunate were Cyril A. Merry [1911-64] and R.P. Tang Choon [1914-85]. The former, blooded in 1933 [in England, where he played his only two Tests and made 34 runs], when he probably did not deserve selection, was now without doubt the best batsman in Trinidad. Experienced, mature and with a resounding cover-drive, I can only conclude that if he had been selected I would have been omitted. Cyril never showed any animosity towards me, however, and continued, as always, to be my mentor [he was ten years older]...[T]here was another omission which called for comment, and that was the Chinese cricketer, Rupert Tang Choon. Before the tournament and trials in 1939, this dashing cricketer must have been considered a certainty, but poor form at the wrong time spoiled his chances. Several times while on tour I could not help thinking what an attraction this dynamic cricketer would have been to the cricketing public of England. Rupert was an explosive player batting, bowling or fielding and no better team man ever graced the cricket grounds.[46]

The inter-colonial tournament was not held in 1940 because of the War; it was resumed in 1941, but British Guiana did not participate that year, neither did it in 1942 and 1943. Persaud did make one appearance for Trinidad, in 1941, at the Queen's Park Oval: he had scores of 58 and 18. This was his last first-class match; he was 35 years old. Of course, no Test cricket was played during the Second World War, none involving the West Indies between 1940 and 1947, so Persaud, approaching his late 30s, must have concluded that he was cheated by the vagaries of form compounded by forces too big to comprehend. He seemed to have disappeared precipitously from all forms of the game, another of the numerous cricketing casualties of the War. He stayed on in Trinidad – lost even to Indo-Guyanese folk memory.

For Indians in British Guiana, growing in self-belief because of their success with rice, cattle and commerce since the Great War, and by the 1930s, buoyed by the Mahatma's nationalist crusade in India and their own ascendancy in the professions, the only void in their identity formation was the eloquent absence of one of their own in the West Indies cricket team. Having never produced one, fleetingly in 1937-8, they were guardedly optimistic that with Chatterpaul 'Doosha' Persaud's performance in the intercolonial tournament of 1937 and his steady progress in 1938, they were on the threshold of the crowning achievement that would seal their recognition as a West Indian people, however resilient their attachment to Mother India.

After Persaud's and Bayley's record of 381 for the fourth wicket, in September 1937, the special correspondent of the *Daily Chronicle* had left Indo-Guyanese with the vision that their new hero would take them to the pinnacle. He wrote:

> We shall hear a great deal more about Persaud, this slim Indian batsman, whose entrance into the intercolonial field can only be described as romantic. Like the Nawab of Pataudi [1910-52], who signalled his appearance against the West Indies at Worcester with a score of 162 [not out; in 1933, when Worcestershire won by 1 wicket], Persaud has made a dramatic debut in intercolonial cricket. The feats of Ranjitsinhji, of revered memory, have left among cricket writers the tradition that whenever an Indian performs remarkable feats of batsmanship, you should use the word 'wizard' or 'magic' or 'uncanny' in describing them. There was nothing of the wizard about Persaud. His was a straightforward innings of 174 runs made honestly, by the employment of much thrift and industry.

He adds:

> At the same time, there is no knowing to what heights Persaud's naturally good leg-side play may attain if he concentrates on its development. He is quite definitely the superior of Bayley on this side of the wicket. At an early stage of his innings he had demonstrated that the cut was foremost among the shots in his repertoire. It is a pity that, after he had passed at least 120, he did not permit himself free rein in exploiting his cover drive. His defence is so good (and he was on view for a sufficiently long period

> to enable critics to make an accurate assessment) that he has only to make two or three considerable scores between now and the close of the 1938 season, in order to ask the West Indies selectors some pointed questions.[47]

Throughout the 1930s the Flood Cup continued to stimulate rivalry between the cricketers of the EICC and their compatriots in Berbice; it also facilitated a credible standard of play that fostered pride and self-belief among Indo-Guyanese cricketers and their fans. The Cup was won by Berbice in 1930; it was not contested in 1931 and 1933; 1932 witnessed a tie; while EICC won in 1934, 1935 and 1936, with the match in 1937 abandoned because of bad weather.[48] The power of the game to possess the Indo-Guyanese imagination is evident in the following report by 'Akbar Shah' (J.I. Ramphal) of the tied final between Demerara (EICC) and Berbice, in Georgetown, in 1932:

> [M]y hopes for the success of the Flood Cup have been fully realised. The game was closely and keenly contested. Rivalry existed, but it was healthy and becoming and never before was the BGEICC pavilion…so crowded with men *and women*, who throughout displayed keen interest. All were stirred, and during my long association with my people I have no recollection of any other instance where great and poor, old and young, all gathered with absolutely no distinction and enjoyed themselves. It was indeed a happy occasion, and it would have delighted the founders to see their efforts bear fruit. May this be only the start in a better feeling amongst all Indians [emphasis added].[49]

It is noteworthy that J.A. Veerasawmy, aged 41 and a senior magistrate in Berbice, represented the county of Berbice in the low-scoring tied final of the Flood Cup in 1932. It was played in July and persistent rain had rendered the pitch potentially perilous. Berbice (captained by Alladat Khan) won the toss and, as expected, inserted Demerara (captained by R.J. Singh); they were dismissed for 41: M. Rohoman top scored with 10; Chatterpaul 'Doosha' Persaud made 7. The veteran Veerasawmy, still brilliant at exploiting impaired pitches, was unplayable: 9.2 overs, 1 maiden, 17 runs, 6 wickets. Berbice feared worse: they made 36; only J.R.

Persaud reached double figures. But the *Argosy* focused on Veerasawmy's 'fine bowling': '[His] ability with the ball on impaired wickets needs no comment...[He] opened the bowling for the Berbice team and his first four overs would have proved a severe test for the best British Guiana and West Indies batsmen today. He kept a good length, flighted the ball beautifully and his leg-turn [leg-cutter] was sharp and very dangerous. That the Demerara team's total reached 41 was due to much good fortune, for time and again Veerasawmy beat the wicket by the slightest possible margin'.[50] The next day Demerara were all out for 50 in their second innings, Chunilall making 15, the highest score; 'Doosha' Persaud made 4. Veerasawmy was again dominant: 14 overs, 5 maidens, 19 runs, 6 wickets. His match analysis reads: 23.2 overs, 6 maidens, 36 runs, 12 wickets. Set 56 for victory, Berbice failed by one – the first tie in the Flood Cup was recorded. M. Rohoman got 5 for 22, thus completing the match with 7 for 34.

At the presentation ceremony, Veerasawmy explained that several years ago he had approached one of the founders of the British Guiana East Indian Cricket Club, Thomas Flood, to provide a cup for inter-county cricket among Indians in the colony. He obliged willingly. It had been competed for nine times: Demerara was victorious on four occasions, Berbice three, while one was drawn and the just concluded one an unprecedented tie. The acting President of EICC, Francis Kawall, complimented both the late Thomas Flood and J.A.Veerasawmy for their monumental contribution to Indo-Guyanese cricket; however, he deeply regretted that Essequibo had again failed to participate. He appealed to Indian businessmen in that economically depressed county to endeavour to 'stimulate interest in the noble game among the young men of Essequibo, so that future tournaments would be triangular in nature, as the donor of the Cup intended'. As noted earlier, the closure of all sugar plantations save one that struggled on briefly into 1935, meant that the great nursery of Indo-Guyanese cricket, the source of its oxygen, had evaporated. Seeking to inspire Indian youths all over the colony to play the game, Kawall found inspiration from Mother India, as was the custom. He reportedly concluded thus: 'He could not but make reference to the performance of the Indian team on tour in England [their inaugural Test series in 1932, four years after that of the West Indies], and he was sure that they all felt proud to read the results of the matches and also the brilliant batting performances of the two young Indians, Duleepsinhji and the Nawab of Pataudi, who were making history in English cricket'. As with Ranji, Indo-Guyanese kept their eyes on how their Indian compatriots were progressing in the 'noble game'. It was a key star by which to steer.[51]

By virtue of the tie in 1932, Berbice, the current holder, retained the Flood Cup, which was presented to their captain, Alladat Khan, by Mrs J.E.R. Ramdeholl, daughter of the late Thomas Flood. Mrs Ramdeholl said that it was the first Flood Cup match she had seen, but she enjoyed it because it provided the tightest possible finish. Khan then called on Indians throughout the colony to play the game 'in the true spirit win or lose'. Both J.R. Persaud (of Berbice) and Chunilall (Demerara), the top scorers with 15, received bats, while Veerasawmy received the ball with a silver shield from J.A. Luckhoo, K.C., for his brilliant bowling in the match.

Therefore, it is no coincidence that J.I. Ramphal was simultaneously acclaiming Indo-Guyanese cricketing triumph while asserting that they disapproved of being called 'East Indian'. By the 1930s the pejorative term, 'coolie', was no longer used publicly; it was replaced by the more complimentary 'East Indian'. But it was a measure of their growing self-belief, and their desire to be considered West Indian, that Ramphal rejected the continual use of the term 'East Indian', in the newspapers, when identifying the perpetrators of various acts of infamy. He cited the following captions by way of illustration: 'East Indian lad convicted for theft'; 'Young East Indian slayer'; 'Five East Indians bond over'; 'East Indian gamblers rounded'. He concluded: 'Everything bad seems to be associated with the East Indian. Nothing complimentary seems to find connection with that term'.[52] Three weeks later Ramphal underlined Indo-Guyanese claim to belong by advocating the eschewing of 'East' from the term. They are of the region; they are 'Indians'; and he was proud to be identified thus in future. He was categorical, in his didactic manner:

> [I]n the December issue of the now defunct organ, *Forward Guiana*...[a] writer...advocated the abolition of the prefix, 'East', to the name of our race. It is now ninety years since we have thus

> been styled, yet I see no great difficulty in changing it. All we Indians need to do is to avoid studiously to characterise ourselves 'East Indians'. Let us speak in terms of Indians. We are the children of Indian fathers and mothers, and we are Indians. Let us set the fashion and other races will follow suit. Let us see that the [East Indian Cricket] Club and the [British Guiana East Indian] Association drop out the 'East' from their designation and all will smooth itself in a short time...I am an Indian. What are you *bhai* [brother]? Put this question today to each of the friends you meet. Put it to your little ones. Drill it into their ears – we are Indians. I am an Indian, and I am proud of it. What are you?[53]

Indo-Berbician cricketers continued to play the game at a high standard. As the *Indian Opinion* observed in May 1938, club cricket in Berbice had already yielded a crop of fine players, who had all appeared in the Davson, Ferreira and Kennard Cups, over several years: 'Numerous Indian cricket clubs have been formed in the various estates and villages...[boasting] a few names well-known in cricket circles – Alladat Khan, J. De Groot, J. Kempadoo, Dhanraj, Etwaroo, A.B. Dookhan, G. Sooknandan, Seelall, C. Patrick, J. Naipaul and Latcha – all of whom have performed mighty feats with either bat or ball, or gloves'. Several of these were from Port Mourant. However, the British Guiana selectors rarely ventured out of Georgetown, so the 'mighty feats' of these backwoodsmen remained for a long time under a bushel. But two Indo-Guyanese, John Bahadur and Johnny Naipaul, did represent the colony before the end of the Second World War: each played one first-class match. A leg-break/googly bowler, Bahadur (1917-81), from the county of Essequibo, played his one match against Trinidad in March 1944 at the Queen's Park Oval. He bowled in one innings only (8 overs, 0 maiden, 49 runs, 1 wicket), as Trinidad won by an innings and 217 runs. Bahadur's sole wicket was that of Wilfred Ferguson, the leg-break bowler; but that was hardly a consolation as Ferguson made 60 runs in a decisive partnership with Elias Constantine (brother of Learie), who scored 139. Meanwhile the Guyanese batsmen failed to master the leg-spin of Ferguson: 9 for 83 in the match.[54]

Johnny Naipaul (1927-83), another leg-break/googly bowler from Plantation Skeldon, in the county of Berbice, made the

British Guiana team in the intercolonial match against Barbados in October 1944, at Bourda, and like Pooran and Bahadur, he did not exceed the legendary one-match consolation. In the first innings his figures were: 25 overs, 2 maidens, 87 runs, 3 wickets; in the second: 15 overs, 0 maiden, 52 runs, 0 wicket. Clyde Walcott and Frank Worrell represented Barbados; Clyde's score of 125 in the second innings was decisive in their victory by 72 runs. None of Naipaul's three wickets was that of these two brilliant young batsmen.[55]

By the end of the Second World War a vibrant cricket culture had taken shape, but it would be another ten years, 1955, before the first great Indo-Guyanese cricketer emerged as a player for British Guiana: Rohan Kanhai. To comprehend this fact it is necessary to assess the diverse forces, domestic and external, that were instrumental in his emergence. It is also essential to explore the character of the environment that made Kanhai: the peculiarities of Plantation Port Mourant, a sugar estate on the lower Corentyne Coast, in the county of Berbice.

NOTES

1. Edward Shils, *The Intellectual between Tradition and Modernity: the Indian Situation* (The Hague: Mouton, 1961), p. 78.
2. Richard Cashman, *Patrons, Players and the Crowd: The Phenomenon of Indian Cricket* (New Delhi: Orient Longman, 1980), p. 35.
3. The biographical information on J.A. Veerasawmy is taken from: C.O. 111/643, Collet to Churchill, no. 161, 27 April 1922, encl.: memorandum by J.A. Veerasawmy; *Who is Who in British Guiana, 1945-8* (Georgetown: The Daily Chronicle Ltd., 1948), pp. 537-8.
4. The statistical details on Gajadhar and Veerasawmy are taken from *cricketarchive.com*. I have also relied heavily on Jimmy Richards and Mervyn Wong, *Statistics of West Indies Cricket, 1865-1989* (Kingston, Jamaica: Heinemann, 1990), for statistical material.
5. See note 3.
6. See note 4.
7. *Ibid.*
8.. The *Daily Chronicle*, 15 December 1915.
9. The *Daily Argosy*, 19 December 1915
10. The *Daily Chronicle*, 14 December 1915.
11. See my *'Tiger in the Stars': The Anatomy of Indian Achievement in British Guiana, 1919-*

29 (London: Macmillan, 1997), Part IV: 'The Rise of an Indian Middle Class in British Guiana'.
12. *Ibid.*, see Chapter 20: 'Indians at Play: Cricket and Indian Unity', p. 316.
13. The *Daily Argosy*, 20 May 1922.
14. See note 11, pp. 316-7.
15. See note 3.
16. See note 11, p. 317.
17. See note 3.
18. See note 11, pp. 318-9.
19. The *Daily Chronicle*, 25 January 1917.
20. The *Daily Argosy*, 20 May 1920.
21. I am grateful to Letizia Gramaglia of the University of Warwick for this (personal communication, 29 June 2008).
22. The *Daily Argosy*, 16 October 1920.
23. See my *Sweetening 'Bitter Sugar': Jock Campbell, the Booker Reformer in British Guiana, 1934-66* (Kingston, Jamaica: Ian Randle Publishers, 2005), pp., 55-9.
24. *Who is Who in British Guiana, 1945-8* (The Daily Chronicle Ltd., 1948), p. 291.
25. The *Daily Argosy*, 25 March 1925.
26. The *Daily Argosy*, 25 June 1929.
27. See *cricketarchive.com* for statistical details on Richard Rohoman.
28. The *Daily Argosy*, 23 October 1937.
29. *Ibid.*
30. The *Daily Chronicle*, 1, 2 October 1937.
31. The *Daily Chronicle*, 7, 10 October 1937
32. The *Daily Chronicle*, 10 October 1937.
33. The *Daily Chronicle*, 3 October 1937.
34. Quoted in the *Wikipedia* entry for Kumar Shri Ranjitsinhji.
35. Trevor Marshall, 'Ethnicity, Class and the Democratisation of West Indies Cricket', in Hilary Beckles (ed.), *An Area of Conquest: Popular Democracy and West Indies Cricket Supremacy* (Kingston, Jamaica: Ian Randle Publishers, 1994), p. 28.
36. C.L.R. James, *op. cit.* [1994], p. 93
37. 'The Birth of a New Star in the Cricketing Firmament', the *Indian Opinion*, (Christmas Number, 1937).
38. The statistical details on Chatterpaul Persaud are taken from *cricketarchive.com*
39. The *Daily Chronicle*, 22 January 1939
40. The *Daily Argosy*, 23 October 1937.
41. Leader, the *Daily Chronicle*, 8 February 1939.
42. The *Daily Chronicle*, 7 March 1939.

43. The *Daily Chronicle*, 18 March 1939.
44. The *Daily Chronicle*, 20 March 1939.
45. The *Daily Chronicle*, 25 March 1939.
46. Jeff Stollmeyer, *Everything under the Sun: My Life in West Indies Cricket* (London: Stanley Paul, 1983), p. 34.
47. The *Daily Chronicle*, 1 October 1937.
48. The *Indian Opinion*, May 1938.
49. 'News and Views of Indian Interest', the *New Daily Chronicle*, 31 July 1932.
50. The *Daily Argosy*, 23 July 1932.
51. The *Daily Argosy*, 24 July 1932.
52. The *New Daily Chronicle*, 17 July 1932.
53. The *New Daily Chronicle*, 7 August 1932.
54. See *cricketarchive.com* for statistical details.
55. *Ibid.*

CHAPTER THREE

Port Mourant and the Revolution in Indo-Guyanese Cricket after the War: Waiting for Rohan – the Precursors, 1944-54

> [G]reat cricketers and their style must be seen in relation to the social environment which produces them.
> *C.L.R. James (1963)*

> There must be something special in the Berbice air, some special mixture in the soil of Port Mourant, to have grown such a crop of cricketing genius.
> *Ian McDonald (1983)*

Hilary Beckles has written on the labour rebellion throughout the British West Indies in the latter half of the 1930s, noting that West Indies cricket could not elude the tempestuous political reality beyond the boundary:

> The Garvey movement, insisting on black political and economic enfranchisement, had integrated the masses…Black nationalism became the cutting-edge ideological force throughout the West Indies, and by 1938 the masses had confronted local whites and the imperial state in a series of rebellion during which they demanded the political franchise, social reform, and access to economic resources. It was a revolutionary decade for the West Indies, and cricket, the people's primary cultural form, became infused by this ideological temperature.[1]

Indo-Guyanese, too, inspired by the rebellious spirit, became immersed in the fight for trade union rights, manifested in the founding of Ayube Edun's *Guiana Review* in 1935 and his formation of the Manpower Citizens' Association (MPCA), in 1937, to represent workers in the sugar industry. Many Indians still resided on sugar estates; on some the housing was deplorable and child-labour common. They also sought broader civil and political rights,

Cricket in the cattle pasture, early 1955: playing at No. 11 Village, in Berbice, seven miles from Plantation Port Mourant. The batsman is Walter Timmers, the wicket-keeper is Patrick Dwarka (Kit)

such as universal adult suffrage, articulated by the British Guiana East Indian Association. But they were still caught in an in-between state – on one hand, craving to be accepted as belonging to the colony and the region; on the other, insisting on forging stronger links with Mother India. They wished, therefore, to belong on their own terms. Inspired by the nationalist struggle for freedom from colonial rule in India, their own political endeavour was refracted through Mahatma Gandhi's transcendental rebellion: the moral irreproachability of a cause. As late as their centenary celebrations, in May 1938, Indo-Guyanese were requesting an agent-general from India as their principal representative, although there were four Indians elected to the colonial legislature and several professional and business people had already emerged from the community. Moreover, Indians had made an outstanding contribution to the development of the rice and cattle industries, so they were discernibly ascendant by the late 1930s-40s. But a tendency to look over their shoulders for guidance from the ancestral homeland tended to inhibit their political advance in British Guiana.

A major psychological hurdle prolonging the sense of 'otherness', the angst over belonging, was occasioned by their failure to produce a cricketer of genuine class, good enough to play in Tests for the West Indies. And the aborted career of 'Doosha' Persaud, their best player up to the end of the 1930s, exacerbated the anxieties about belonging, the economic and professional achievements notwithstanding. It would take the Independence of India in 1947 for them to begin to escape the shadow of the motherland. It is arguable, however, that aspects of their Indian legacy (attitudes to race and colour, for instance) are not susceptible to easy modification.

This was the context in which their charismatic leader, Cheddi Jagan (1918-97), from Plantation Port Mourant, emerged at the end of the 1940s; his radical politics and the accompanying self-assertion were the backdrop to the rise of the greatest Indo-West Indian cricketer: Rohan Bholalall Kanhai, born on 26 December 1935, on the same plantation. A Marxist, Jagan took on the sugar planters in a veritable crusade, attributing all the ills of colonial society to the extraordinary dominance of 'King Sugar' – one company in particular, Booker, which owned over 80 per cent of the plantations by the late 1940s. But Cheddi Jagan's politics of rebellion was not some idiosyncratic aberration, a mercurial interlude of youth. As I have argued elsewhere, his socialisation at Port Mourant, in the 1920s and early 1930s, had deeper foundations:

> The Corentyne Coast in Berbice was the 'coolie' heartland. It comprised a string of flat, fertile, villages extending for miles along the coast, interspersed among sugar plantations, bathed uninterruptedly by the fresh Atlantic breeze...From the 1920s through the 1940s Indians made small, but firm, strides in rice...cattle...market gardening and the retail trade [commerce]. Each step constituted a gnawing away at the fetters, material and psychological, that bound them to the plantations. And here, on the Corentyne, greater economic progress spawned a sturdier spirit of independence. Some became quite prosperous: education acquired a special meaning as the economic foundations solidified. And the Canadian Mission schools in the villages, and the Berbice High School [and the Corentyne High]...were the nurser[ies] for Indian school teachers, doctors, lawyers and other professionals. The economic landscape was changing, and with this came a more strident, robust vision of illimitable possibilities. But an historical sense of hurt, fed by continuing deprivation on many plantations, was never far from the surface...[I]t had a recidivist quality...This was what made the rebel in Cheddi. And [the] greater educational opportunities, with widening intellectual attitudes, released the iconoclast in a small, but influential, minority of Indo-Guyanese in the late 1940s. These were young Rohan Kanhai's most impressionable years.[2]

Jagan's and Kanhai's rebellious instincts were shaped by features of plantation life peculiar to Port Mourant, from the 1890s to the 1940s, possibly before. It will be recalled that in 1891 'bound coolies' from this plantation had gone to jail for a week for absconding to cricket matches for three days, instead of working on their rice fields for which they had obtained the approval of the manager. I have not been able to ascertain when Port Mourant was brought under cultivation, but this was certainly under slavery. Indeed, the names of various sections of the plantation are signposts to its labour force and its heterogeneous composition: 'nigger yard' (African); 'potagee quarter' (Madeiran Portuguese); 'bung [bound] yard' (Indian). In 1820 Stephen Mourant owned Port Mourant; in 1852 it was bought by John Kingston; his family owned it for the rest of the century. Even in the early years Port Mourant was a well-run estate. In 1880 the owners procured a Crown Land licence to dig a canal to the Canje Creek (a tributary of the Berbice River), to the south: irrigation water was obtained; a large stretch of land, 'considered the very finest cane land in British Guiana', became accessible, and better shipping facilities were constructed on the Canje. In 1883 a perceptive observer wrote of Port Mourant: 'A noble canal, 13 miles in length, connects the sugar works...with the Canje Creek...The sugar manufactory has been kept up with the spirit of the times...The very fine mixed soils of sandy loam and shells which crop out on the coast in front of Port Mourant help to make it one of the most salubrious places in which to reside in the three counties'.[3]

Besides, this was a sugar plantation in a relatively malaria-free zone, so the people here were discernibly more energetic and industrious; imaginative and assertive – rebellious, too – going against the grain of the docile 'coolie'. Moreover, the fact that they had a progressive manager from 1908 to 1938, J.C. Gibson, magnified those instincts and gave the people of Port Mourant a predilection for innovation. A spirit of self-confidence flourished; it was manifested in a palpable flair, a panache that was recognised and envied by outsiders. Gibson's contribution to this process, however unintended, cannot be underestimated.

Gibson knew the county of Berbice as well as anyone; it had become home. He went there in 1890, and worked his way up from overseer to manager, at Plantation Rose Hall, in the East Canje district. In 1908 he moved to Port Mourant as manager. That year the estate produced 4,165 tons of cane; when he left in 1938 it produced 15,938 tons. Increased acreage, good husbandry and new factory equipment had contributed to this; but Gibson's skills as an administrator, his gift for fostering good labour relations with his predominantly Indian work force of nearly 12,000 (6,513 of whom resided on the estate), was a crucial factor in Port Mourant's reputation for prosperity. He was a strict man, but a fair one. He provided land for his workers to rear their cattle and well-watered plots for them to cultivate rice. Gibson had also facilitated the building of their own cottages on the estate, to replace the derelict ranges, the infamous 'logies', called the 'nigger yard', because some of them were there since slavery and had been patched up ever since. He constructed a narrow-gauge railway to transport his workers to the fields several miles inland.[4]

In mid-1929 Rev. C.F. Andrews, Gandhi's friend, confidant and adviser on Indians overseas, visited Port Mourant. He was lifted by 'the remarkable healthiness of the people', their energetic and lively appearance. Andrews reached this verdict despite going there 'under the very worst weather conditions'; it was a testimony to J.C. Gibson's leadership. He pointed to the 'progressive character' of the plantation, their concern for the social conditions of the Indian labourers. He considered Gibson's 'efficiency, ability and knowledge of good labour condition' peerless among managers in British Guiana. Compared with his visits to other sugar estates, Andrews left Port Mourant very satisfied indeed: '[H]ere at last I saw what could be done with people living in their own separate houses and owning their own land for rice cultivation…this is one of the best mornings I have had since I came to the colony'.[5] In late 1929 the British Guiana East Indian Association (BGEIA) corroborated this, in their memorandum to the Olivier Commission: 'In our long experience with our people we have not found many born or living at Port Mourant desiring to leave the estate. This is due not only to the greater freedom which they enjoy, but to the opportunity given them for permanent settlement'.[6]

In March 1933 Gibson was recovering from a serious illness, so one of the local papers took the opportunity to reflect upon the stewardship of the veteran Manager: '[He] is one of the colony's most capable and experienced planters and enjoys the utmost confidence and regard of his employers…Mr Gibson is [also] very much liked by his staff at Port Mourant; and the labourers on the estate have come to regard him as one genuinely interested in their welfare. It is due to his wise and paternal management that the estate has attained to its present stable and prosperous position'.[7] Ivy Jailall was born at Port Mourant in 1924 and grew up there in the 1930s; her grandparents were indentured labourers from India. She remembers J.C. Gibson as the colossus of the plantation. But she states that he always allowed workers to fish, collect firewood, gather wild vegetables (such as *ban karaila* and *karmi bhagee*), gave them water for their rice-field and allowed them to graze their cattle on estate land. But he was very cross and would reprimand them if they abandoned unwanted small fish on the dam, instead of returning them to the canals. She considers him a 'just man' who helped the people of Port Mourant.[8]

In 1936 John Dodds, who had had 18 years of experience on sugar estates as an administrator, told the Labour Dispute Commission of the exemplary achievement at Port Mourant in 'augmenting auxiliary sources of income' for the workers: '[They] had thrown open large areas of rice lands for cultivation. In every walk of life at that estate, there was consequently a definitely higher standard of living than on any other sugar estate in the country. There seems to be a personal contact between the estate authorities and the people, and the general *tout ensemble* gave a general feeling of prosperity and joy of living'.[9] Jock Campbell, whose family owned the neighbouring sugar plantation, Albion, knew Gibson well, having visited him often in 1935-6. He has assessed the character of the people of Port Mourant: '[It] was a very well-run estate. The people were big and they were healthy in that area because of the salt air. There was no doubt about it, they were particularly healthy and the malaria was less serious…[So] when we started peasant cane farming in my day [1950s], the Port Mourant canc farmers were way ahead of any other workers in the industry – they were marvellous people'. Campbell adds: '[Gibson]…was a tough manager but a just man…He was feared but he was respected…I was very impressed with the physique and ability, the resolution and a sort of independence of the front-line workers'.[10]

Gibson was a keen cricketer and an avid promoter of the game at Port Mourant. In 1916 he was instrumental in the formation of the Port Mourant Sports Club, 'to foster the playing of cricket'. Although he was closely involved in its affairs, its predominantly Indian members, including several prominent ones from the Port Mourant-Rose Hall (Corentyne) area, played the leading role in its administration. Gibson was the president, but the sports committee of the Club comprised J.W. Permaul, a successful businessman, J. Kattick, its secretary, and M. Sewdin, a landed proprietor. Later, from 1919, Sherlock Sabsook did valuable work as administrator of the Club. Gibson was unstinting in his support for cricket; for many years the captain of Port Mourant was James Kempadoo, his chauffeur.[11] The team had become a formidable one, and by 1936, two years before Gibson retired after nearly 30 years at the plantation, Port Mourant consistently won the Davson Cup, the symbol of cricket supremacy in Berbice.

In presenting the Davson Cup to Port Mourant, winners in 1936, C.E. Tulloch of Davson Estates remarked on the towering stature of that plantation in the competition. The Cup was initiated by the Davson Sugar Estates for teams from their own plantations (Blairmont, Bath and Providence) in 1921, but it had been opened to all clubs in Berbice, plantation and village, since 1925. It provided the framework and the challenge that lifted the quality of play markedly, creating a credible parallel competitive environment in the county to the Parker Cup in Georgetown. By 1936 Port Mourant had won the Davson Cup on five occasions, nearly 50 per cent of the time. This was a true measure of the quality of organisation and the social atmosphere prevailing under Gibson's imaginative leadership on the plantation. Providence had won the Cup twice, Rose Hall (Corentyne) twice, Voorburg (a village in East Canje) twice; the Berbice Cricket Club, Bath and Albion once each. Tulloch elaborated on the transformation engendered by the competition:

> The idea…[Colonel Ivan Davson] had in mind when he offered the Cup was the bringing together of sportsmen in the true spirit of the game and recently I have noticed a great improvement in this respect. There were formerly cases of dissatisfaction and protest, very often justified, arising from bad umpiring, and the questioning of umpiring decisions…But I am glad to see that the standard of umpiring is on the improve, and I hope that it will continue so and that umpires will be strictly honest and impartial as then there will be a great future ahead for Berbice cricket. As is noticed we are getting more and more recognition from the selection committee in Georgetown. I would therefore advise cricketers to stick to the game, and through the Board of Control which is functioning here at present they will get their chances when deserving.[12]

On the latter point, Tulloch was being overly optimistic: it would be another two decades before the czars of Georgetown recognised the plenitude of talent in the backwoods of the county of Berbice – they had to be forced to the well of recognition. The young Cheddi Jagan, aged 18, left Port Mourant in 1936, the year of the plantation's fifth victory in the Davson Cup, to study in the United States. It is arguable that the rebellious temperament he manifested after the Second World War and the single-minded challenge he posed to the sugar planters were forged in the context of Port Mourant's temper of self-assertion. If that plantation were less vibrant, lacking the manifest progressive spirit, it is possible that Cheddi's ardour for revolutionary rhetoric would have been substantially less vigorous. The rebel temperament was shaped by hope and quickened by the challenges opened up to Indians under J.C. Gibson's stewardship, in the more salubrious environment on the Corentyne Coast of British Guiana. This was also the world that made Rohan Kanhai, Basil Butcher, Joe Solomon, Ivan Madray and several other professionals of distinction.

But it was a measure of the self-assurance bred at Port Mourant that the relationship between Hindu and Muslim Indians was perceptibly harmonious; Africans constituted a very small minority. In January 1936, for instance, over 200 people, including women from both religions, attended a seven-day recital from the *Quran*, conducted by Moulvi Fazal Kareem Abdool. In his introductory remarks, outlining the object of the function, he expressed gratitude for 'the hearty support given by the management of the estate', under J.C. Gibson; and he also thanked the Hindus at Port Mourant for their 'close co-operation and assistance'. It was an environment that had already built the foundation for ambition and a sturdier Indo-Guyanese identity.[13] A week after this event, it is noteworthy that in a prize-winning essay, 'Suggestions for Improving the Status of the Indian community', a young Indo-Guyanese, P.R. Jailall, had advocated the provision of more land on sugar estates in order to lift more of their compatriots above the poverty line: 'Poverty-stricken Indians who work and live on sugar estates should be lent sections of... [unused] lands to work up, for although the trade in sugar may be a lucrative one from a colonial point of view, it is scarcely of any benefit to Indian peasants who toil hard to exist, and who live and die as a creature of the lower animal kingdom clothed in ignorance and illiteracy. Glorifying the mind has its advantages, but decrying the importance of physical development is an evil...Indian clubs catering to physical advancement should be supported'.[14] At Port Mourant such enlightened measures had long been implemented, with the consequential general prosperity, including discernibly better health and a higher level of community consciousness among the Indians of that progressive plantation. It was the foundation of its astounding cricket culture by the 1930s, when four future West Indian Test cricketers were born at Port Mourant, the same decade when another of her great sons left to study in the United States: Cheddi Jagan.

Ivan Madray (born 1934), the leg-spinner, who, along with Rohan Kanhai (born 1935), Basil Butcher (born 1933) and Joe Solomon (born 1930) – all Port Mourant men – had represented British Guiana and the West Indies by 1958, recalls that several formidable cricketers had emerged on the plantation by the 1930s-40s; but the selectors in Georgetown remained oblivious of them. These included Johnny Teekasingh, the best, 'a superb leg-break bowler…one of the best bowlers in my time, even when I played Test cricket'. Indeed, he continued to play well into the 1950s for Port Mourant, an unsung hero and mentor to several young players in Berbice. It must have give him abundant pride when, in early February 1957, Rohan Kanhai was selected to tour England with the West Indies team that summer. A few days later the *Daily Argosy* carried the following caption on its sports page:

JOHNNY TEEKASINGH ACCEPTS CONTRACT IN SURINAME
POPULAR SPORTSMAN TO COACH DUTCH CRICKETERS FOR ONE YEAR

'Uncle Jannie' was widely revered. He had represented British Guiana Indians in the Kawall Cup, the symbol of cricket supremacy between Indians in British Guiana, Suriname and Trinidad. He played in that tournament in Trinidad in 1938 and 1946, in British Guiana in 1941 and in Suriname in 1948. He had also represented the British Guiana East Indian Cricket Club in first division Parker Cup and its successor, the Case Cup, in Georgetown. The tradition of Berbice cricketers seeking recognition by playing in the capital is rooted in his example. He last played for Berbice in 1950 against a British Guiana XI. He had an illustrious record in the Flood Cup, the symbol of cricket supremacy among Indians in the counties of British Guiana: Berbice, Demerara and Essequibo. Teekasingh captained the Berbice team on three occasions and he retained his place in that tournament for 20 consecutive years.

He had the 'welfare of young players on the Corentyne at heart', adding that he had had several young players 'under his wings'. He was alluding to Butcher, Kanhai, Madray and Solomon, among others. He regretted that, because of 'unemployment', he had taken a job in Georgetown thus relinquishing his 'coaching programme'. In early 1957 he was embarking on a one-year coaching assignment with the Suriname team, in preparation for the Kawall Cup. It is possible to comprehend why so many people adored Johnny Teekasingh: not only was he a superb leg-spinner (perceived as a difficult craft in the West Indies), but he imparted much of his knowledge, garnered over several decades, to young cricketers on the Corentyne, in Berbice. But, beyond the boundary, too, he exhibited a generosity of spirit that suggested good breeding. On the eve of his departure for Suriname he thought of his benefactors in Georgetown: 'It would be most unfair of me if I did not say a word of thanks to those persons who have been most kind to me during my short but pleasant stay in Georgetown. I deeply appreciate everything they have done for me and would always remember same'.[15] It is therefore deplorable that virtually nothing is known of this pillar of cricket in Berbice: a foundation stone, arguably, of Butcher, Kanhai, Madray, Solomon, Kallicharran, and many others. The game has illustrious antecedents on Berbice sugar plantations, but that history remains submerged.

Ivan Madray's tribute to 'Uncle Jannie', testifies to his seminal role, from the 1930s to the 1950s, in moulding the character of cricket on the Corentyne Coast of Berbice:

> I admired Johnny Teekasingh; 'Uncle Jannie', we called him. He was a superb leg-break bowler. And people at these big games [in the Davson Cup], used to shout: 'Jannie! Jannie! Jannie! Fielda [Kempadoo, captain of Port Mourant] put on Jannie'. And whenever he came on to bowl, it was like a miracle. This old man, to me, was one of the greatest bowlers in my time, even when I played Test cricket. Port Mourant Cricket Club heard of my bowling…and Uncle Jannie came to our house and asked my

> father for me to join Port Mourant. He said: 'Dis bai a bowl good. If he can bowl like me, dis bai ga play cricket, big cricket [Test cricket]...So I started to play for Port Mourant, where Uncle Jannie had taken over the captaincy from Fielda Kempadoo. I was very happy about that. You see, Uncle Jannie was the first person responsible for me building the confidence that led me to first-class cricket...[H]e was a vital force in shaping my life as it developed over the years. And I remember my first match for Port Mourant as a youth: he brought me on to bowl; I was very frightened, but I didn't want to let him down. He said: 'I want you to bowl just like me [leg-breaks]'. I said: 'Nuh Uncle, me ga bowl off-break'. He said: 'Yu a bowl leg-break. Yu see dis belt ya!' That was the word (seriously, but really in jest): 'Yu see dis belt. If yu na bowl leg-break, me ga tek dis belt and beat yu'...I can't remember who we played against, it could have been Plantation Albion or Plantation Skeldon, but I went on to bowl leg-breaks; and I soon established myself as a top player alongside Uncle Jannie and others.[16]

Nearly twenty-one years after I interviewed Madray, in London, about 'Uncle Jannie', I went back to him and asked whether he had a final recollection on his mentor. Ivan responded: 'As a boy when I watched him, he always seemed to be the person who bowled out the other side. He was a first-rate leg-spinner: he was never afraid to toss it up, to tease you into coming down to hit him over the top. But he imparted a good deal of spin and he had fine control of length, so you were always courting death when you took him on. After the faster bowlers had done their bit, the people would demand: "Jannie, Jannie, time fu Jannie!" Then the magic would begin. He made leg-spin bowling an art, something to behold'. Yet, like so many gifted cricketers of the time, their last days were not crowned with glory. Ivan tells the painful tale: 'I was very sad when I went home one year and found that Uncle Jannie had had a stroke. I wished I had the power or the means to do something for him. I saw this man whom I adored struggling – shuffling with great difficulty. I spoke to his family and told them how sorry I was, for he had done so much for me'.[17]

Prominent among the 'others' were 'Black' Etwaroo, Lutch Jaggernath and Fielda Kempadoo: stalwarts from Port Mourant, equally unsung. They, too, sustained the passion for the game and kept the aspiration of representing the colony alive in their proteges. Joe Solomon and Basil Butcher have told me that they learnt their cricket in a very competitive environment, fostered by the tradition of hard play long enshrined at Port Mourant. Teekasingh, Kempadoo, Etwaroo and others epitomised that tradition. Meanwhile, three other players had shown that it could be done, the chronic neglect notwithstanding: John Trim (1915-60), a black Guyanese fast bowler from Port Mourant; Sonny Baijnauth, a left-arm medium pacer/orthodox left-arm spinner from the neighbouring plantation, Albion; and Ganesh Persaud, an EICC batsman, who represented British Guiana regularly between 1947 and 1952. But Trim was the exemplar for the young cricketers from Port Mourant: he played for British Guiana and toured India in 1948-9 and Australia in 1951-2, appearing in 4 Tests. Trim made his debut for the colony in March 1944, against Trinidad, at the Queen's Park Oval, and he continued to do so regularly until the early 1950s. He was already 29 when he first played for British Guiana; and 33 in his first Test match, against England at Bourda, in March 1948. However, in those four intermittent Tests his bowling was impressive: 18 wickets for 291 runs at an average of 16.16. And in two of them he played a major part in the outcome. In 1948-9, on the tour of India, when West Indies won 1-0, his bowling in the decisive Madras Test was crucial to their victory by an innings and 193 runs. Trim's analysis for the match was: 43 overs, 12 maidens, 76 runs, 7 wickets. On the Australian tour of 1951-2, he played in the Melbourne Test only, but he got 5 for 34 in the first innings and Australia barely passed the target of 260, to win by 1 wicket.[18]

Basil Butcher said he only met Trim once; he had moved to Georgetown when they were kids, but the fast bowler told him that he was in the same class in school as his mother. However, his reputation was a part of the folklore: it enriched the cricketing tradition at Port Mourant.[19] Ivan Madray, too, recalls that Trim had long left Port Mourant, when he was growing up in the 1940s, but his stature as a pathfinder was inviolable:

> I had heard of John Trim, we all heard of John Trim, but I had never seen the gentleman. I found out later that he was from

> No.11, Port Mourant. He lived near my *moasie's* [mother's sister's] house. So his little house was like a shrine to us, because he had played Test cricket for the West Indies, in India…[H]e was a legend to us little boys: he was the first man to leave Port Mourant to play for British Guiana and the West Indies. So, in some little way, he cleared the path for us. Although John Trim was black, we saw him as our own. That was before politics and race made a mess of our way of thinking.[20]

But the wider environment, too, in sports and politics, fed a sustaining vision to the cricketers of Port Mourant. In 1950 the first Indo-West Indian player, Sonny Ramadhin (born 1929), a spinner from Trinidad, represented West Indies in a Test. The landmark is also memorable because his second, in June 1950, was at Lord's, and it was won by the West Indies, by 326 runs – their first victory in England. Ramadhin, who had only two first-class matches to his credit before he toured England, made a massive contribution to that victory. He and Alf Valentine (1930-2004), the Jamaican left-arm spinner, were so dominant that they accounted for 59 English wickets in the four-Test series; all the other bowlers combined got 18. Ramadhin took 26 wickets at 23.23 each, including 11 for 152 in the historic Test at Lord's that immortalised 'those two little pals of mine'.[21] Learie Constantine explores the technical underpinning of his mastery – and mystery – as many great batsmen could not distinguish his off-break from his leg-break, which he bowled with no discernible change of action: 'The mystery about Ramadhin is that he is different from all other off-break bowlers. He does not cut the ball down with palm facing his body, but rather the palm appears to be thrown at the batsman to whom he is bowling. This opens up an avenue for deception with his leg-break which he mostly rolls, and batsmen have been unable to detect which is which. On top of that he pushes one at you the speed of which leaves you vulnerable if at the time you are concentrating on discovering the difference between his off-break and the leg-break [the flipper]. So immediately after arriving [in England] he began to puzzle the best batsmen in the country'.[22]

Ramadhin, just 21 years of age, was pivotal to the first West Indies victory. Although Valentine got seven more wickets than him in the Tests, 33 at 20.42, John Arlott considered Ramadhin the 'finer' of the two: 'His spin proved extremely difficult to detect and, even by the end of the tour, only Parkhouse and Hutton among English batsmen could be said to recognise with any certainty his leg-break ...[H]e bowled on the move and with a lively turn of the wrist, so that frequently the ball, delivered from his low, slight height and coming through on a worryingly low arc, kept low and came quickly off the pitch, to force good batsmen into extremely undignified strokes. He bowled always in his cap and with shirt sleeves buttoned to the wrists...Three quick steps up to the crease and his arm swung over quickly on his delivery skip and, then, immediately, he was eager to bowl again'.[23]

Arlott was mesmerised by Ramadhin's variety, control and the rapidity with which he executed his craft. It was taxing even for the learned spectator to discern the complexity of the exercise; how much more demanding it was of the energy of the English batsmen that glorious summer of 1950! He observes: 'He was always a diligent and persistent bowler who varied his bowling from ball to ball, the arc, the point of delivery, the degree and direction of spin all being altered in turn, so that the batsman facing him was given no mental rest. Although he was extremely quiet, he had a needle brain which missed nothing of the reactions of his opponents and little in any one else'.[24] This was compliment of a very high order; it underlined the mental resilience behind the mastery. To Indo-Guyanese this was an enormous psychological stride: their claim to belong could begin now to rest on a foundation of merit that resonated with all peoples in the West Indies.

Robert Christiani, the Guyanese batsman, played in all four Tests in England in the summer of 1950. He was able to observe Ramadhin's 'mysterious' bowling at close range, before it was 'mastered' by the infamous pad-play of several English batsmen, in 1957. This is Christiani's recollection; it is from an interview with Frank Birbalsingh, in Toronto in 1992:

> Ramadhin used the same anti-clockwise for both his off-break and leg-break. Whether it was the dark colour of his hand, or the speed of his movement, English batsmen could not tell which way the ball would turn. Even West Indian batsmen at first had trouble

The 'mystery' spinner: Sonny Ramadhin from Trinidad, the first Indo-West Indian Test cricketer (1950)

> spotting Ramadhin in the nets. There is an apocryphal story about Ramadhin and his mastery over English batsmen in 1950. Once, the wife of Norman Yardley, the English captain, phoned the pavilion asking to speak to him. When she was told he had just gone out to bat, she asked who the bowler was. On hearing it was Ramadhin, she said: 'In that case, I will hold the line'.[25]

It is doubtful whether many of his Indo-Guyanese admirers grasped the complexity of Ramadhin's craft; none of them would have seen him. He had never played in British Guiana. They would, however, have heard of his reputation from his two only first-class matches, against Jamaica in January-February 1950, in Port of Spain. In the first match, which Trinidad won by an innings and 196 runs (Trinidad batted once for 581-2, with Ganteaume 147, Stollmeyer 261, and Trestrail 161 not out), Ramadhin's analysis was: 49.5 overs, 15 maidens, 106 runs, 8 wickets. The second match was drawn, but in the first innings Ramadhin bowled 29 overs, 7 maidens, 76 runs, 4 wickets.[26] So that something of the mystery of this 'coolie' from some village in Trinidad had stirred a portentous fascination in many in British Guiana. For those on the plantations and in the villages, it was as if the Hindu Gods had delivered him perfect to redeem their gnawing physical inadequacy. It was as if their prayers were being answered without the rigour and discipline that are imperatives in the mastery of a craft.

It is noteworthy that the gifted Ramadhin apart, possibly the Indo-West Indian cricketer they pinned their greatest hope in for Test honours after the War was Ganesh Persaud (1925-81). He represented British Guiana in nine first-class matches, making his debut at Bourda on 13 October 1947, against Jamaica, when both George Headley and Frank Worrell played for the latter. His last first-class match was against Jamaica at Bourda in October 1952. A right-handed batsman, who played first-division cricket for many years for the British Guiana East Indian Cricket Club, with some distinction, he scored 512 runs in his nine first-class matches, with an average of 34.13; his highest score was 96, against Barbados at Bourda in September-October 1951. He scored three half-centuries, and in his three matches against Barbados, he had an average of 49.40. His scores in the nine matches were: 35 not out and 58; 2 and 76; 44 and 29; 1 and 5; 33 and 28; 96; 21 and 25; 1 and 6; 46.[27] Ganesh Persaud's inconsistency, following on the unheralded departure from the game of Chatterpaul Persaud, must have been the source of much pain for Indo-Guyanese, yearning for an Indian batsman to command a place in the West Indies Test team.

It is difficult to ascertain why Ganesh did not perform more creditably, but it is important to note that British Guiana did not win any of the matches in which he played: they drew five and lost four by a substantial margin.[28] It was a period of prolonged mediocrity in Guyanese cricket. There was only one Guyanese player who made the West Indies team regularly: Robert Christiani (1920-2005) with 22 Tests. An elegant batsman, he had enthralled all with the beauty of his stroke-play in inter-colonial matches, between 1939 and his retirement in 1954. As Frank Birbalsingh describes him: '…the number of runs he scored was less important than how he scored them…He combined instinctive improvisation and acrobatic skill with the precision and delicacy of a ballet dancer'.[29] But he was unable to reproduce the scores or the style at the highest level: in his 22 Tests he scored only 896 runs at an average of 26.35. It could therefore be argued that Ganesh Persaud's potential, uninspired by resolve or standards of excellence in Guyanese cricket, remained embryonic. But Ivan Madray recalls touring Trinidad with Ganesh as captain of British Guiana Indians, in April 1954, to play Kawall Cup cricket against Trinidad Indians. He said that after the tournament a combined Indian team from the two colonies played an all-Trinidad team, led by Jeff Stollmeyer, the West Indies captain. He will never forget the stroke-play of Ganesh, who made 92, an innings of elegance punctuated with beautiful cover-drives. Ivan adds that he shared a good partnership with Sonny Moonsammy, whose innings also was marked by several daring strokes. He considers Ganesh Persaud one of the best batsmen he ever saw in British Guiana: his style was easy on the eye. However, he had come to the end of his first-class career, another richly endowed batsman who has disappeared from the Indo-Guyanese narrative. Chatterpaul 'Doosha' Persaud is not alone.[30]

It is interesting that only one Indian represented British Guiana in their match against the touring Test team from India, in March

1953: Ganim Khan, from Skeldon, a left-arm spinner who got a solitary wicket in this his only first-class game. It was not a time of cricketing glory for Indo-Guyanese. Ganesh Persaud had already played what would be his last first-class match, and Ramadhin notwithstanding, Indo-Guyanese did not have much to show the motherland by way of cricketers at the highest level. In fact, it was the visitors from Mother India, on their first tour of the West Indies, who ignited the spirit of Indo-Guyanese cricket in the early 1950s. There were still many India-born former 'bound coolies' alive in the colony; they saw or followed the Test match in Georgetown in March 1953 closely. Elahi Baksh, an Indian from Berbice, observes that that Indian team is entrenched in the social history of Indo-Guyanese: 'Indo-Guyanese who had never seen a proper cricket match in their lives made the long journey to the city of Georgetown simply to catch a glimpse of these cricketers who, if they were not film stars, were at least true Indians, original models of which we Indo-Guyanese felt ourselves to be mere debased replicas'.[31]

The Indians were a marvellous fielding side, as Mihir Bose relates: 'Even more than their batting the Indians' fielding surprised the West Indians…[who] with their long history of brilliant fieldsmen, are not easily impressed by visiting fielders, but even today, in the Caribbean, this Indian team is talked about as the best fielding side to tour the area. The catching could still be suspect…but it was the ground fielding that took the eye…This was a young man's tour and Gadkari, Ghorpade, Gaekwad, Apte and Umrigar formed a wonderful quintet of fielders, quickly covering the ground, and making flat, hard, accurate returns to the wicket-keeper. Such fielding can never be conveyed in terms of figures but the abiding memory of that tour was of Weekes, Worrell and Walcott hitting the Indian spinners murderously hard into the covers. "Four!", shouted the crowd as the ball left the bat, only to find an Umrigar or a Gadkari or Apte or Ghorpade or Gaekwad cutting it off'.[32] In fact, the 'quintet' never materialised in any Test, but during the fourth Test in Georgetown, witnessed by 18-year old Ivan Madray, the fielding evoked deep, personal resonance:

> It was a fantastic fielding side: people like Manjrekar, Polly Umrigar, Apte were like lightning in the field. They chased the ball

> to the boundary as if their lives depended on it; picked it up and hurled it, in one motion, right above the bails. Effortlessly. Cleanly. All day. It was a feast to me; it was like eating a bowl of rice. My stomach was filled; I was filled with joy watching the Indians play. I was filled with sadness leaving that scene of the Test match and returning home [to Port Mourant]. But I became more dedicated to my cricket; I played with a new courage. And I made the pledge to play first-class cricket on that ground [Bourda].[33]

Moreover, in a four-match series India lost only one Test to a team that included Weekes, Worrell, Walcott, Ramadhin and Valentine. And in the decisive Test, in Barbados, the sole Indo-West Indian player, Ramadhin, was magnificent as India were dismissed for only 129, giving West Indies victory by 142 runs: 24.5 overs, 11 maidens, 26 runs, 5 wickets. The little Indo-Trinidadian 'mystery spinner' sustained Indo-Guyanese hopes of producing a great West Indies batsman one day – the true measure of a community's arrival, the foundation of its right to belong: a person who still commands more reverence from West Indians than any Nobel laureate. (They have produced three of the latter [Arthur Lewis, the economist; Derek Walcott, the poet; and V.S. Naipaul, the novelist], but beyond the elite, they are largely unread.)

In March 1953, in British Guiana, Vinoo Mankad, India's all-rounder, had scored 66 in the first innings, and, in the West Indies sole innings in which they made 364, he bowled a marathon 68 overs, 23 maidens, 155 runs, 3 wickets. Worrell, Weekes and Walcott batted well, with scores of 56, 86 and 125 respectively, but the West Indies runs were made at under 2.4 runs per over. This was a consequence of the nagging accuracy of Mankad and the technical versatility of India's only world-class bowler, the leg-spinner, Subhash Gupte, whose figures were: 56.2 overs, 19 maidens, 122 runs, 4 wickets. Madray attributes his resolve to become a better leg-spinner and to play first-class cricket at Bourda to Gupte's magnificent example: 'He was my idea of what a leg-spinner should be...his stamina, his intelligence, and his ability to control his emotions. On a number of occasions when he was hit, he would stroll back slowly, thoughtfully, to his bowling mark, as if nothing had happened'.[34]

Madray recalls what the presence of the Indian touring team in British Guiana, in 1953, meant to him. He had gone to Bourda primarily to see the Indian cricketers. It was his first trip to Georgetown; he was still in high school; and although it was a drawn Test, the Indians made a profound impression on him: 'I saw Gupte and Mankad. And when I returned to Port Mourant after the Test, I said to my family: "One day I will play cricket on that ground". I said it to my friends also: "One day I will play cricket on that ground". It was a year later, in 1954, that I played in the trials at Bourda'.[35]

The trial match that took Madray to Bourda in November 1954 was curtailed severely by incessant rains; it had been postponed twice: 'the elements are against us', the *Daily Argosy* bemoaned.[36] It was eventually played on 26 November 1954, and was considered 'a pointer in connection with the proposed visit [of British Guiana] to Barbados' in early 1955:[37] the inter-colonial tournament. The trial match attracted undue interest because Clyde Walcott, the great West Indies batsman, now the cricket organiser on the sugar plantations (including Port Mourant), was scheduled to play for the 'Rest' v. a combined Georgetown Cricket Club (GCC)/Demerara Cricket Club (DCC) XI. GCC were the first division Case Cup champion in 1954. Bruce Pairaudeau, the West Indies opening batsman, captained the combined team; it included Lance Gibbs, the talented young off-spinner.

The trial was promoted as something of a watershed for British Guiana: perennially at the foot of regional cricket, it seemed now on the verge of striking a rich vein. There was Lance Gibbs, of course, and an apparently unfathomed range of young talent from the county of Berbice, particularly from that enigmatic plantation, Port Mourant. The Berbicians were anticipated thus: 'The appearance of these players in the city should give not only an idea of their potentialities, but also provide good arguments for fans'.[38] The young backwoodsmen had clearly generated widespread curiosity among Georgetown's many discerning cricket fans: 'Three promising young Berbicians who performed creditably in Essequibo, during the recent inter-county tournament, will be seen in action at Bourda. They are "Cobra" Ramdat, a "find", who was instrumental in routing both Essequibo and Demerara, with his left-arm spinners, [Ivan] Madray [a leg-spinner] and [Basil] Butcher'.[39] It is interesting that

Rohan Kanhai was not scheduled to play in the trial match. But on the day when the match finally got some reprieve from the monsoonal deluge, the following terse note appeared in the *Daily Argosy* of 26 November 1954: 'It is now known that Ramdat of Berbice, who was included in the "Rest" side, is suffering from an injured ankle and will not be available. His place will be taken by Kanhai, another Berbician'.

Kanhai, a wicket-keeper and opening batsman, was replacing a left-arm spinner! The bizarre circumstances are imprinted indelibly in Rohan Kanhai's mind. And he considers 'Cobra' Ramdat's misfortune the toehold that enabled him to do just enough, in the trial in Georgetown, to be selected in the British Guiana side against Barbados, in early 1955. This is Kanhai's version of events:

> Evidently there were three vacancies in one of the sides [the 'Rest'] and the British Guiana Cricket Board asked Berbice, our county, to fill them. 'Cobra' Ramdat, a left-arm spinner who struck with the swiftness of his namesake, was an obvious choice. The other two spots were allocated to Port Mourant…The club reckoned that three players – Basil Butcher, Ivan Madray and myself – all had equal claims. The haggling went on and on without ever getting nearer to a solution, until eventually someone came up with a bright idea of drawing names out of a hat. You can guess who lost. That Thursday night I was nearly in tears. To a boy of 18 a break like that takes on enormous proportions. It was like the end of the world to me…Next morning Mr Duncan Stewart, the Berbice President, knocked on our door to tell me that 'Cobra' had twisted an ankle. 'Would I go to Georgetown?', he wanted to know. Would I go? I would have walked the whole 90 miles if he had asked me to…[40]

It is likely that Kanhai, born and bred on the sugar plantation in Berbice, had never been to Georgetown. He said that names like Clyde Walcott and Bruce Pairaudeau, who played in that trial match, 'belonged to the newspapers and radio, not real everyday life on the sugar plantation'.[41] He had probably never eaten with knife and fork, never made a speech; he would have been intimidated by the social etiquette of creole middle class life, shaped by local whites, Portuguese and the coloured and black middle class. Consequently, he was probably ill at ease, burdened by apprehension that he would commit an error betraying his rural 'coolie' roots. He did not have the redeeming benefit of the Georgetown upbringing of several of the cricketers from the British Guiana East Indian Cricket Club (EICC), such as his Indo-Guyanese team-mate for British Guiana, the medium-pacer and batsman, Wilfred Edun (1930-90). Even the sing-song dialect of Port Mourant, enriched by its folk allusions and raw wit, spoke of the rustic 'coolie' universe. That Georgetown journey on the morning of Friday, 26 November 1954 must have been a terrifying experience indeed: the fear of failure within the boundary compounded by the social limitations beyond it. Kanhai recalls: '[A]fter the first excitement, the rot set in. I began to feel nervous and couldn't sleep. By the time I caught the bus with Basil and Ivan at 4 o'clock in the morning my heart was pounding like a tom-tom. What a journey that was – 15 miles by bus to New Amsterdam [the main town in Berbice], across the ferry [on the Berbice River], then a long, hot ride by train into Georgetown all the time clutching my old tattered cricket bag to me and trying to look outwardly calm...but beneath all the nonchalant expression...[I was]...dead scared'.[42] It is probably true that Rohan has never overcome the social inhibitions, his fame, international reputation over many decades and his virtual deification by many Indo-West Indians notwithstanding. This may well be the source of his intractability, his legendary reputation for being mercurial: 'difficult'

Apart from being scared, Kanhai must have been exhausted by the time his train arrived in Georgetown, with no more that an hour to spare before he had to open the batting at Bourda. His partner was Glendon Gibbs (1925-79), the seasoned opener for British Guiana, from Georgetown, a black civil servant who would have been totally at ease within and beyond the boundary. Moreover, it had been unremittingly monsoonal for weeks: he would have had no significant practice. Kanhai remembers most of what took place on this his maiden trip to the famous cricket ground, once the weather had relented to allow the excited crowd a bit of cricket: 'The heavens had opened...and the outfield was saturated. I remembered thinking that fours would be hard to hit through it, but I need not have worried. I opened and left quickly, caught in the slips [by Pat Legall] off Richard Hector for a blob'.[43] He did get some consolation but that could not minimise his sense of failure: 'That day people told me that I shouldn't worry – hadn't Hector once bowled the great Len Hutton? They were trying to be kind, but a failure is a failure…' (In February 1954, in the match between British Guiana and England [MCC], Hector had Hutton caught in the slips by Glendon Gibbs for 0.) That fear of failure would never leave him completely; indeed, it is arguable that his audacious, sometimes self-destructive, play was his peculiar way of dealing with the insecurities that were essential ingredients in his make-up.

In fact, Kanhai's memory of that seminal trial match, in Georgetown, was not totally accurate, but the sense of being a failure must have so clouded his recollection that he felt ever afterwards as if he had made nought in that match. He did not. Very little play was possible on the first day; none on the second day; the drawn game saw a full day's play on the final day. This is the *Daily Argosy's* version of the abbreviated first day's play in which the 'Rest' made 50 for 3. It is noteworthy that the paper struggled to get the names of the novices from Berbice right:

> The outfield was most treacherous and the wicket [pitch] itself slow. Bruce Pairaudeau, who won the toss, decided to put in the opposition team. Glendon Gibbs and R. Kahai [*sic*] opened up but the Berbician was dismissed early being caught by Legall for 3 off Hector. Wilfred Edun came and went after scoring 4 with the total at 19. Walcott made his appearance and saw the total reach 32 when [Glendon] Gibbs made his exit after scoring 18. Walcott was 19 not out. C. Butcher [Basil] [*sic*] of Berbice was 2 not out when play ended. Lance Gibbs was the most successful bowler claiming 2 for 11…[44]

Kanhai was not rated as a top-class wicket-keeper, and he probably knew that; but it did provide him with a compensatory string to his bow. He might not have been selected as early as he was for British Guiana without this supplementary asset. He recalled the last day of that trial match. His team had collapsed for 113; his Port Mourant team-mate, Butcher, top-scored with 35 while Walcott made 30 run out. Lance Gibbs was the most impressive bowler: 4 for 34. The GCC/DCC combined team responded with 137 for 9: the other Port Mourant man, leg-spinner Ivan Madray, bowled 12 overs, 4 maidens, 48 runs, 3 wickets. Wilfred Edun had 3 wickets for 17 runs. It is interesting to note that two of Madray's wickets were achieved with the aid of wicket-keeper Kanhai: stumped. Madray maintains that Kanhai was one of the few wicket-keepers who could unfailingly read his bowling. This was a consequence of many years of mutual understanding at Port Mourant. In that trial match Kanhai got four dismissals: two catches off Edun's bowling and the two stumpings off Madray's. His recollection that he had five dismissals in that match is faulty; but he had made an impression: '[I] surprisingly won myself a place in the British Guiana trials to be held on the same ground the following week'.[45]

After the two trial matches, 25 players were called to practise in preparation for the impending inter-colonial tournament in Barbados in early 1955. Six of these were Indo-Guyanese: Kanhai, Madray, 'Cobra' Ramdat, Sonny Moonsammy (Berbice), Ganesh Persaud and Wilfred Edun (EICC/Georgetown). Basil Butcher, the Port Mourant batsman of African descent was also called. The two other Berbice players named were from sugar plantations as well: Ramdat (Providence, East Bank Berbice) and Moonsammy (Skeldon). Ganesh Persaud, as seen above, was the principal Indo-Guyanese batsman since 'Doosha' Persaud, but his career was coming to an end (he had not represented the colony since 1952). Wilfred Edun, the medium-pacer and batsman, would tour New Zealand with the West Indies team in early 1956, but he did not play in any of the Tests. The *Daily Argosy* welcomed the virtual revolution in local cricket: the selection of five Berbice players (Kanhai, Butcher, Madray, Ramdat and Moonsammy) for the three trial matches scheduled for December 1954-January 1955. They expressed the hope that their respective employers would give them leave to participate. It was a patently amateurish framework: the root of the squandering of the abundant gifts of players such as 'Cobra' Ramdat and his subsequent anonymity. Had it not been for Kanhai's passing reference to his impressive fledgling talent, I would not have become aware of him.

The monsoonal weather of 1954 claimed January of 1955: only one of the three trial matches could be played. The *Daily Argosy* (12 December 1954) captioned its report on that match thus:

BUTCHER STAKES EARLY CLAIM TO COLONY SELECTION
SCORES SOUND 74 OUT OF TEAM'S 185 ALL OUT

The paper had got it right even if they could not get B.F. Butcher's name right: they persisted in referring to him as 'C. Butcher'. His innings was obviously of a high standard; it was achieved in spite of a sodden, heavy outfield, amidst rain Kanhai later deemed 'true Manchester style'. In this context, Butcher's performance deserved the lavish praise it received: 'C. Butcher of Berbice made an early bid for selection on the British Guiana team to tour Barbados next month, when, in an innings noted for its facility in handsome stroke-play, he contributed 74 out of Glendon Gibbs's side total of 185. Coming as it did after top-scoring in the recent feature match [he made 35], his innings was more than one of promise to a side which, at the moment, seems to be woefully deficient in first class batsmen'. Five wickets had fallen for 37 runs before Butcher restored a degree of respectability to the team's batting: Glendon Gibbs 0; Ganesh Persaud 0; Clyde Walcott 0; Sonny Moonsammy (stpd Kanhai b Lance Gibbs) 2. Butcher was bowled for 74 by 'Cobra' Ramdat whose figures were 7.1 overs, 0 maiden, 22 runs, 1 wicket. Lance Gibbs's were: 13 overs, 3 maidens, 50 runs, 4 wickets; while Ivan Madray bowled 6 overs, 2 maidens, 13 runs, 3 wickets. The *Argosy* concluded its acclamation of Butcher's batting, noting that he had impressed the spectators, many of whom were knowledgeable on the finer points of the game: '... with a revealingly fine defence, [he] proceeded to delight the large crowd with a chanceless knock. His driving was fluent and he pull the ball off the wicket [pitch] with uncanny ease, while a late-cut which pierced the slips brought rounds of applause'.[46]

Bruce Pairaudeau's team responded with 233 for 7. Rohan Kanhai made 61. It was described thus: 'Kanhai opened his wings and delighted the crowd with his all-round batting exhibition and was very punitive when opposing the spinners'.[47] Kanhai identified his performance in this match as the foundation of his selection to represent British Guiana in

Barbados: 'A haul of 62 runs [probably 61] and five catches [behind the stumps] in the trial brought me a call for the second and third trials, both of which were rained off...So on the strength of that one performance, I found myself in the British Guiana party to fly to Barbados for a couple of games in [January/] February 1955...Unfortunately Ivan Madray and Joe Solomon...[the latter, strangely, was not selected for the trials] didn't make it, much to my surprise...[for while] I considered the elegant Butcher the kingpin of our club [Port Mourant]...the other two [were] not far behind'.[48]

Kanhai said he had never seen a first-class match until he went to Barbados in January 1955. He did not keep wicket in his debut match on 5 February 1955; Clifford McWatt, the established wicket-keeper who first played for British Guiana in 1944, did. Batting at no. 6, Kanhai had scores of 14 and 1. His team-mate from Port Mourant, Basil Butcher, batted at no. 7 and was much more impressive, with scores of 34 and 62. Barbados won by 144 runs. Butcher had made his debut in the previous match against Barbados, a week before, when he made 0 and 9 and British Guiana were ignominiously defeated by an innings and 102 runs. It was not a memorable beginning for Kanhai, but he was learning the ropes. Butcher's half-century in his second match was suggestive of possibilities providing the men from Port Mourant were not shunted back to the backwoods. They were not.

As will be seen in the next chapter, in April 1955, three Port Mourant men – Ivan Madray, Basil Butcher and Rohan Kanhai – were playing first-class cricket, at Bourda, against the invincible Australians. To comprehend this phenomenon, it is necessary to go to the grassroots, to locate some of those seemingly minor contests, which were the foundation of the basic technical competence being built up by these indefatigable young men from Port Mourant. One of these was club cricket organised by the Berbice Cricket Board of Control. It is noteworthy that these clubs were to a great extent based on the sugar plantations. The new spirit of reform from the early 1950s in the sugar industry, pioneered by Jock Campbell, following the eradication of malaria through the work of the malariologist, Dr George Giglioli, bred a palpable self-confidence and optimism among younger people on the plantations. This was accelerated because of the uncompromisingly radical (Marxist) politics of the young dentist turned politician from Port Mourant, Dr Cheddi Jagan. He had done much since 1947, when he was elected to the legislature, to enhance the political consciousness of many Indians on the sugar estates. There was paranoia in the colony that Cheddi believed in 'god-less communism', and that if he were to win the first elections under universal adult suffrage in British Guiana, in April 1953, he would tie the colony to the totalitarian USSR. The *Guiana Sunday Graphic*, subsidised by the Sugar Producers' Association, was prominent in the vitriolic assault on Jagan. This was resented, particularly on the Corentyne, the home of many of the emerging Indo-Guyanese cricketers. In March-April 1953, on the eve of the elections, the paper carried headlines such as:

YOU CANNOT BE A COMMUNIST AND BE A GUIANESE[49]
NO LOYAL GUIANESE ARE IN THE PPP (JAGANS PARTY)[50]

In March 1953, during the Test match against India at Bourda in Georgetown, that paper had carried a brief report that must have aggravated the Indo-Guyanese response to the local establishment, while enhancing their adulation of Cheddi and magnifying their identity with the visiting Indian cricket team. Indo-Guyanese would soon define their emerging cricketers, whether they liked it or not, in terms of their political aspirations. They were already being framed as instruments for change, weapons for asserting their place in Guyanese and West Indian society, an extension of the crusade of Cheddi Jagan, now perceived as a virtual Nehru. Rampant allegations of communism and charges that Jagan would make the country a satellite of the USSR, destroying free speech and religious freedom, had no resonance with them. They were staunch Hindus and Muslims, and no one, including Jagan, could take that away from them. The *Graphic's* piece was provocatively captioned:

Answer to the PPP Challenge
BERBICE JOINS CAMPAIGN AGAINST COMMUNIST ACTIVITIES
SUPPORT FOR ORGANISATION TO COMBAT MENACE[51]

> A militant band of respectable and loyal people in New Amsterdam [the main town in Berbice] are ready to join in any all-out fight against the current spread of Communist activities in British Guiana...They see in these communist activities a Godless ideology that strikes at the very root of law, order and decency, and thereby against the moral, social and industrial progress of the colony.

However, the fact that the enemies of Cheddi Jagan were invariably seen as belonging to the old order, including Booker and the 'sugar gods' as he dubbed them, enhanced his reputation as a fearless champion of the Indian sugar worker pitted against the Goliaths of privilege. So that when the British suspended the constitution and removed his democratically elected government, in October 1953, passions were gravely inflamed. Port Mourant, baptised as Bolshevik, 'Little Moscow', by many foreign journalists looking for 'reds', became the repository of a good deal of pent-up emotions. At the end of 1954, the *Berbice Weekly Argosy*, also openly hostile to Jagan, editorialised thus:

> The constitutional crisis of October 1953 left a legacy of apprehension and doubt which were capitalised on by the ousted People's Progressive Party (PPP) captains [Jaganites]...[T]he April disturbances on the Corentyne and elsewhere in the colony, disturbed production plans – especially of sugar – and created a tension unmatched even by that which existed in October 1953. Firm and tactful handling of the situation by the police and the military avoided possible bloodshed. And, along with the restricting of the PPP leaders and their subsequent imprisonment [including Jagan], paved the way for the restoration of confidence. The labour front, however, remained turbulent, with Port Mourant – the home of Cheddi Jagan – the chief sore spot. From the 'underground' came news that fanatical members of the Party planned to blow up the estate and other principal buildings, and these reports gained credence when the statue of Queen Victoria in Georgetown was decapitated by an explosion...[52]

The volatile temper at Port Mourant in particular was exacerbated when it was announced that its sugar factory would cease grinding from December 1955. Booker explained that the plantation would continue to produce cane, but that it would be ground at the neighbouring estate, Albion, which was being expanded and modernised. The people of Port Mourant were not receptive to any such rationalisation: they saw the closure of the factory as punishment for their support of their native son, Cheddi Jagan. It is conceivable, therefore, that the exhilaration and dejection occasioned by the volatile political environment were channelled into their cricket. It is also arguable that Indian youths on other plantations had a similar experience; their inflamed emotions, too, were canalised into club cricket. Many Indo-Guyanese perceived the people of Port Mourant as consummate rebels; they themselves had no doubts they were. They felt they were better than other Indians, particularly those from other sugar plantations. The cricketers of Port Mourant were inspired by the rebellious temper; but it had a price: they were being saddled with the hopes and aspirations of the Indo-Guyanese people as a whole.

Berbice won the inter-county championship convincingly, in October 1954, in Essequibo. Most of the Berbice players were from plantations: Rex Ramnarace (captain), Rohan Kanhai, Basil Butcher, Ivan Madray (Port Mourant); 'Cobra' Ramdat (Providence); Sonny Baijnauth (Albion); Sonny Moonsammy (Skeldon), Vic Harnanan, Ancel Hazel (Rose Hall); Charles Paul (Blairmont).[53] In the first game, Essequibo v. Berbice, the latter made scores of 174 and 211; Essequibo's response was feeble: 88 and 29. Berbice won by 268 runs. Sonny Moonsammy made an impressive 102 (retired) in Berbice second innings, while Kanhai made 54. Hamil Murray got a hat-trick; Mal Teekasingh (brother of Johnny Teekasingh) and Sonny Baijnauth got two wickets each.[54] In the final, between Berbice and the holders of the cup, Demerara, the former won by 6 wickets in a match of low scores. Demerara were 'routed for 73', in 165 minutes, in their first innings: '...their batting broke down against the swing and spin of the left-arm Baijnauth and the left-arm spin of Ramdat'. Berbice showed no appreciable resolve: they made 71, having capitulated to the off-spin of Lance Gibbs: 5 wickets for 11. Demerara made 84 in their second innings, having succumbed this time to 'Cobra' Ramdat, who got 7 for 13. Set 87 to win, Berbice made it for the loss of 4 wickets with 90 minutes to spare: Kanhai 19; Hazel 20; Madray 21.[55] The *Daily Argosy* of 18 October 1954 reported Berbice's hour of glory under the following caption:

BERBICE EMERGE INTER-COUNTY CHAMPIONS DEMERARA ROUTED TWICE AS RAMDAT RETURNS ANALYSIS OF 13 WICKETS FOR 38

The *Berbice Weekly Argosy* was jubilant, attributing the victory primarily to their bowlers, particularly the spinners. They were not circumspect in the least. They felt that in 'Cobra' Ramdat and Ivan Madray Berbice had two potentially world-class spinners; they were also most optimistic of Basil Butcher. Rohan Kanhai received no mention! The paper editorialised:

> [W]e are convinced that in Joe Ramdat ['Cobra'] (left-arm spinner whose 13 for 38 is a record in these games) and Ivan Madray (right-arm leg-spinner), the county has produced a spinning combination which would, we are sure – if given the opportunity – in time be as destructive and as popular as any pair of bowlers in the world today – including Ramadhin and Valentine! Another player who we think would be of use to the colony is Basil Butcher, a fine all-rounder, whose forceful batting and brilliant fielding, would find favour with the Georgetown crowd. These men...may, with the help of more seasoned players, give British Guiana an opportunity to bask in the sunshine of victory once more.[56]

'Cobra' would disappear from the remarkable odyssey of Berbice cricket but, as noted earlier, Butcher and Kanhai were selected to represent British Guiana in Barbados in a little over three months. A couple of months later, in April 1955, Madray would join them in the British Guiana team against the formidable Australians. Three Port Mourant men were now in the team. Basil Butcher has no doubt that the inter-county championship brought them to the attention of the Georgetown elite; without this competition they would probably have languished in rural adulation, anonymous beyond the villages and plantations of Berbice. Butcher, writing around 1966, argues:

> The revival of Guyanese cricket in recent years has been the direct consequence of the organisation, a dozen or so years ago [1953-4], of annual representative matches between the counties. For the first time it became virtually impossible for a young player of real promise to go unnoticed. Quite possibly neither Rohan Kanhai, Joe Solomon, nor I would have reached Test cricket under the old system. All three of us won a place at national and international level as a result of playing in the inter-county tournament [in 1954]. (Lance Gibbs, being a Demerarian, would not have been overlooked). [In fact, Lance had made his debut in the British Guiana v. MCC [England] match, at Bourda in February 1954, aged 19.][57]

Butcher explains why, hitherto, it was virtually impossible for Berbice cricketers to make an imprint on the national consciousness, which meant, in reality, the attention of the Georgetown elite: 'It may be difficult for the reader unfamiliar with Guyana to believe that such great players as Joe [Solomon] and Rohan [Kanhai] could be overlooked in any country, but any cricket writer who ever visited Guyana…will tell you how unbelievably far Rose Hall [or Port Mourant], Berbice, is from Georgetown. The map says it is merely a hundred miles, but distances…in Guyana especially, are not measured merely in miles'.[58] It is possible that Butcher is alluding to social distances, too, for the 'czars' of Georgetown, prior to the arrival of the Barbados and West Indies batsman, Clyde Walcott, in British Guiana in October 1954, rarely ventured beyond the capital and instinctively looked down upon estate 'coolies'. Appointed by the Sugar Producers' Association, following the recommendation of Jock Campbell (the progressive Chairman of Booker), Walcott was 'responsible for organising cricket and the coaching of cricketers on all the sugar estates of the colony'.

Gordon Rohlehr explains the political context of reforms on the plantations. This is useful in comprehending how Walcott was able to canalise the rebellious temperament on the plantations, converting it into excellence within the boundary:

> Alarmed at the continual striking since 1945, and especially at the [Plantation] Enmore strike in 1948 when the police opened fire

> on a group of workers, killing five and wounding twelve, the sugar bosses followed the cue of the Colonial Office [the Venn Commission Report of 1949] and entered on a programme of conspicuous welfare, which if it did little to alter the plantation system, sought to modify its natural by-product of degraded and tension-ridden human relationships. Thus welfare officers were appointed on each estate...cricket clubs were encouraged for the men...sewing classes for the women. Traditionally cricket on the sugar estates had been, like electricity or the riding of horses and mules, a status symbol distinguishing...[the] white managerial elite from the Indian workers. Now that cricket was being used to sublimate the violent energies and protest generated by plantation society, clubs arose out of the estates, and rapidly developed into powerful centres of social activity in communities which had been devoid of physical recreation. A new area had been created in which social prestige could be won.[59]

This process, as I have argued, was long in the making at Port Mourant because of Manager J.C. Gibson's uniquely enlightened ideas on management and the discernible self-assurance of its people. Consequently, Walcott's impact was felt immediately, and most profoundly, on that plantation. He recalls the experience with evident satisfaction: 'In the mid-1950s when I arrived and saw the facilities I realised what a mammoth task I faced to develop the game on the plantations. I had to organise the clubs and the competitions and advise on improving facilities, persuading the owners to put down concrete pitches in the outlying areas that would survive the harsh climate. New grounds were built and such was the enthusiasm of the Indian population that immense strides were made in a very short time'.[60]

And as Basil Butcher observes, this constituted a virtual revolution in Guyanese cricket: '[An]...important factor in the raising of standards...was the arrival of Clyde Walcott, the great (in more senses than one) Barbadian, as cricket coach which automatically made him friend and mentor of all young cricketers. As captain of Guyana and player of vast experience, Clyde's coaching and advice have done much to encourage promising youngsters. Not that "coaching" in the West Indies means what it means in England. I think "guidance" is a better word...Walcott quickly became a one-man Court of Appeal for village, community centre and sugar estate clubs'.[61] Butcher recalls that he introduced 'shrewd coaching methods' often imparted subtly, but effectively, in the dressing room. He emphasised the imperative of supplementing stroke-play with discipline and the primacy of powers of concentration: it was not enough to get a half-century.[60] Joe Solomon told me that if Walcott had not gone to British Guiana, all the Port Mourant players would have remained anonymous club cricketers: Basil Butcher, Rohan Kanhai, Ivan Madray and himself.[63]

Walcott's technical and ethical standards were high, and he sought continually to inculcate a culture of discipline and respect for the traditions of the game. But above all, his was a towering presence that infused cricket in British Guiana with a sense of purpose and a resolve that had eluded it for most of its existence. Imbued with the moral compass of the black Barbadian middle class, a product of the elite school, Harrison College, he was the ideal man for the volatile Guyanese political environment of the 1950s, rendered even more hazardous by the intractable race issue. Ivan Madray has retained the greatest respect for Clyde Walcott: '[He]...had no time for race, pettiness or spite...high[ly] cultured...[he] took a man for what he was worth. Nothing more...I could have walked to the end of the earth for Clyde Walcott'.[64]

In a very short time, Clyde had visited all the sugar plantations in his official capacity as cricket organiser for the Sugar Producers' Association. As early as November 1954, he was inspecting cricket grounds on these estates, speaking to cricketers and officials in order to ascertain the quality of play and the potential of the best cricketers. He was brilliant at engaging people, as he sought to harness the heightened rage engendered by the turbulent politics. He did it quietly, with a lightness of touch and much dignity. He made rural players, the backwoodsmen, feel as if they mattered. He was already on a 'coaching assignment' at Leonora and Uitvlugt in the third week of November 1954.[65] The next week Walcott and Robert Christiani, the former West Indies and British Guiana batsman (now Personnel Manager at Port Mourant), met cricketers and officials at Plantation Skeldon, on the Upper Corentyne. His aim was to promote more inter-estate cricket in order to raise the standard of the game. He addressed a 'largely attended' meeting on the 'difficult shots and how they should be played', as well as on aspects of bowling and fielding. Walcott's talk was illustrated with a short film in which he demonstrated the technical skills he was imparting to the enthusiastic young cricketers on the plantation.[66]

It is clear that Walcott was impressed with the potential of several of the players on the sugar estates. There were many in the past who had withered on the vine; the rest of cricketing British Guiana and the West Indies were oblivious of their potential, their natural gifts. He was categorical that the principal thrust of his work on the plantations was to ensure that 'one day the British Guiana team and the West Indies team would comprise players from the sugar estates'. Speaking at Plantation Uitvlugt, Walcott expanded on 'the finer points of the game' with supplementary use of his film on 'batting, bowling and fielding technicalities'. He counselled the young players on the centrality of 'cricket discipline', the necessity to respect the decision of the umpire in spite of the 'predominantly low standard of umpiring'. Walcott concluded with 'a comprehensive outline' of the programme he had for 'unearthing hidden talents' on the sugar estates. His approach was already assuming the character of a mission. It was based on a fundamental – recognition of what was axiomatic in rural British Guiana: substantial talent had long existed there. However, this was invariably dismissed as a mirage by the city-bound authorities in remote Georgetown.[67] His mission was given the highest, though tangential, commendation when it was announced in December 1954 that the West Indies Cricket Board of Control had exempted him from the mandatory residential qualification rule: he could now represent British Guiana in the inter-colonial tournament, in his native Barbados, in February 1955.[68]

Clyde Walcott would therefore play with – and monitor – the development of talented young players in the British Guiana team. They, in turn, would learn from the eminent cricketer and come to share a monumental respect for him: the cornerstone of their rapid elevation in 1955-7. These three years were the watershed in the colony's cricket; it would see the emergence of an enviable core of players for British Guiana – Kanhai, Butcher, Solomon and Lance Gibbs being the foremost, with Ivan Madray, Sonny Moonsammy, Saranga Baichu and Leslie Amsterdam not far behind (all but Gibbs were from sugar estates). Indeed, as early as April 1955, as noted earlier, three Port Mourant players had represented British Guiana in their match against Australia: Kanhai, Butcher and Madray. Butcher believes that the best players at Port Mourant were drawn quickly to Walcott's attention because of Robert Christiani's knowledge of their ability and potential for excelling at the highest level.[69]

But Walcott was never complacent. He continually emphasised that Berbice could not rest on their laurels. He was not happy with their standard of fielding, having observed their play in the inter-county final against Demerara at Bourda in November 1955. Moreover, he admonished them for being satisfied with scoring 40 or 50 runs and acting as if they were 'on top of the world'. He observed that inter-colonial (first-class) and international (Test) players were expected to make 140 or 150. He underlined his belief that discipline and continuity of focus were fundamental to success at the highest level. Walcott gave credit when he thought it was earned, but he was averse to lavishing superlatives on the basis of merely adequate performances. He was opening the horizons of rural cricketers, initiating them into his professional frame of reference that had taken him to the pinnacle of batsmanship.[70]

Berbice had defeated Demerara (essentially Georgetown) convincingly in the inter-county championship of 1954, in Essequibo. In 1955 they were substantially less impressive, although they narrowly retained the Cup on the proviso that the first innings of the match was not completed. If they had lost on first innings, they would have lost the Cup. Demerara outplayed them, having scored 441 for 8, with the colony's opening batsman, Glendon Gibbs, making 171, while Berbice held on precariously to the end: 260 for 9. Kanhai made 19, Butcher 46, Solomon 54, Amsterdam 45; but it was leg-spinner Madray's resolute 38 not out that ensured their retention of the Cup.[71] This less than emphatic performance had prompted Clyde Walcott to question whether they were really better than 'Georgetown' (Demerara), as many were claiming. It was his provocative way, Butcher says, of challenging people to aim higher. He therefore counselled Berbice to focus on improving their all-round play, particularly their fielding. He was blunt: 'they did not look a good team in the field'. He reportedly 'stressed that

Berbice had a lot to learn to improve their game', while conceding that the facilities in Georgetown were much better. But he was certain that the facilities on the plantations in Berbice were improving, and he implored the Berbice cricketers to work harder to improve their play.[72]

Earlier the *Berbice Weekly Argosy* had intervened in defence of the Berbice team, arguing that they 'laboured under severe handicaps before a ball was bowled' in the final in Georgetown. The paper was assertive: '…let it be remembered that some members had to be up at two or three o'clock on Saturday morning, and that each member had to travel 70 and 120 miles, then, with some two hours rest, commence this important and exacting fixture – in which they straight away lost the toss'. On the contrary, they contended that Berbice should be commended for the 'guts' they demonstrated under patently adverse circumstances: they possessed the 'calibre' of champions. They felt that Leslie Amsterdam and Joe Solomon, the top-scorers, had made an 'intelligent appraisal of the crisis' and responded unselfishly and courageously.[73]

Robert Christiani (from Demerara), the Berbice captain and former West Indies batsman, responded similarly to Walcott's criticisms. He reportedly countered thus: 'Mr Walcott had forgotten the very important point that the team had to travel to Georgetown on the same day of the match. No one, he stressed, would be 100% physically fit after such a journey; and he thanked the players for standing up to the pressure'. And Christiani underlined the point: lack of funds meant that they could not afford to travel earlier; he hoped that there would never be a recurrence of this situation. But he recognised that 'Mr Walcott had a special cricket interest in the rural areas; [and] that he was looking [for], and he was sure he would find, players like Ramadhin and Valentine'. This was an allusion to the two West Indian spinners, with only a couple of first-class games each to their credit, proceeding to England in 1950 and vanquishing the mighty English team: the first time the West Indies won a Test and a series there.[74]

But it was Walcott's perceived even-handedness, coupled with the fact that he was not a Guyanese and therefore above the partisan, increasingly polarised, political atmosphere of British Guiana from the mid-1950s, that made it possible for him to proffer critical judgment while earning the respect of those criticised. He was almost a unique example, in this highly politicised and racially charged colony, of an individual asking the right questions and moving efficaciously from diagnosis to resolution, circumventing the Guyanese penchant for grandiloquent rhetoric. Many in the colony could discern a new spirit, a contagious effervescence that had reached many of the club cricketers in the county of Berbice, especially on the healthier Corentyne Coast. At the end of 1955 the sports editor of the *Berbice Weekly Argosy*, Charles Chichester, was buoyantly assertive in his verdict on their cricket that year:

> This year will probably go down as one of the most significant in the field of sport as far as Berbice is concerned...Berbice achieved her full stature – I nearly said nationhood – during this period and, what is more, the promise of the future – even the immediate future – are many and roseate....[T]his has been such a glorious year for Berbice that one might well be forgiven for terming it all fantastic. One year ago Berbice did not have one player in the colony side [an Indo-Guyanese leg-break bowler, Sonny Basdeo, from the county of Essequibo, did play against England in 1954, his only first-class match, but bowled only 5 overs while conceding 36 runs]. Today Berbice has three 'musts' [Kanhai, Butcher, Madray, who played against Australia in April 1955] and three others, who will in all probability be in the next team [Joe Solomon, Sonny Moonsammy, Saranga Baichu]. In January [1955] both Butcher and Kanhai were included in the team to tour Barbados...Kanhai played in the second match only, was not particularly impressive [with scores of 14 and 1], but his compatriot, Butcher, was fine in two dynamic innings during the same game [34 and 62].[75]

He noted that in the British Guiana v. Australia match, in April 1955, four Berbicians were selected: Butcher, Kanhai, Madray and Charles Paul. That reassured them (although the colony lost by an innings and 134 runs) that Berbice was destined to dominate cricket in the colony, with bounteous potential for West Indies cricket. Chichester recalled that Butcher played a fine innings (of 46) while Madray demonstrated that he was 'our best leg-spinner [3 for 122]'. But it was Rohan Kanhai for whom the bouquet was reserved on this occasion: '...[his] two dazzling knocks [of 51 and 27] commanded most attention and, had he been used as the colony's wicket-keeper [Clifford McWatt was preferred], he might well have played for the West Indies in the Test match here [at Bourda]'. Such was the spirit emanating from the backwoods of Berbice in the mid-1950s!

The improving quality of play was reflected in the two main competitions in Berbice: the established Davson Cup and the recently inaugurated, Rohlehr Cup. It was a match between City Stars (a junior Port Mourant club) and Police Sports Club of New Amsterdam, in February 1956, which impelled Charles Chichester of the *Berbice Weekly Argosy* to underline the quality of play permeating much of first-division cricket in the county. Police, with respected players such as Pat Murray, his brother, Hamil, Lloyd Benjamin, Lloyd Stewart, Morris and Duff, were the stronger side. But the resolve, the will to win of City Stars (their 'sole figure of note was Ivan Madray'), allied with their 'brilliant fielding', produced a result, in the closing minutes of the game, that elevated the underdogs. Chichester elaborated:

> I can recall having witnessed few tussles that commanded so much attention as the fortunes of the match see-sawed all day Sunday, the final day…Indeed, were I to single out the factor which mostly contributed to victory for City Stars, I would say it was their fielding. Madray excelled, and on his performance during the match, he must be considered one of the finest fieldsmen in the colony today. He brought off two nice catches, but his best effort was that stupendous piece of work in which he dashed across to negative a Pat Murray on-drive and then, all in one action, threw back the ball to the wicket-keeper with admiring Murray well out of his crease…[B]efore a ball was bowled in this competition, Madray had expressed his confidence to me that his side would win. I can only add this – that they fully deserved to win.[76]

Chichester was sanguine that the best teams in Berbice, from sugar plantations such as Port Mourant and Blairmont, were 'the equal of any in Georgetown'. He suggested, therefore, that the premier cricket clubs in the capital, the Georgetown Cricket Club (GCC), British Guiana Cricket Club (BGCC), Demerara Cricket Club (DCC), Malteenoes (MSC) and the East Indian Cricket Club

(EICC), should challenge the best teams in Berbice. That would redound to the advancement of the game throughout the colony and accelerate the development and recognition of their best cricketers beyond British Guiana. He reminded the authorities in Georgetown, as he sought to jolt them out of their narrow universe: 'Do not forget that Port Mourant boasts such players as Butcher, Kanhai, Madray and Solomon…while Blairmont calls upon [Leslie] Amsterdam, Sipchand (a really promising batsman), Hoosain, Milne and Nelson Paul'.[77]

Reflecting the optimism permeating Berbice cricket in 1955-6, Chichester demanded that at least two Berbicians be selected by the West Indies to play in the imminent unofficial Test, against E.W. Swanton's touring team, in April 1956. Having seen Kanhai's performance against the Australian bowlers, he was assured that the Berbician had all the requirements for success at the highest level: 'good eyes, sound defence and…[getting] right behind the ball'. His was not a case of all flamboyance and a cavalier approach. In Basil Butcher, too, he saw the potential for similar achievement, deeming him 'the brightest star in the British Guiana firmament'.[78]

It is correct to say that Berbice cricketers did not rest on their laurels after Walcott's reproof. For instance, in 1956, before Kanhai, Butcher, Solomon, Madray and Sonny Moonsammy (he was 12th man) participated in the Quadrangular Tournament against Barbados, Jamaica and Trinidad, in October of that year, Berbicians appeared in first division cricket through the established Davson Cup (with three zones encompassing the whole county), the newly-founded Rohlehr Cup, as well as inter-county cricket (against Demerara and Essequibo). In addition, Indo-Berbician cricketers, such as Kanhai, Solomon, Madray, Moonsammy and Saranga Baichu, played in the Flood Cup (encompassing Indians in the three counties), as well as the Kawall Cup between Indians in British Guiana, Suriname and Trinidad. It was an environment that harnessed the new confidence by facilitating various platforms for advancing standards and honing skills. This, as seen above, materialised in the context of the sugar planters' apprehension of communist subversion, fomented by the Indo-Guyanese hero from Port Mourant, Cheddi Jagan. It was a desperate, but serious, endeavour to canalise the rage on the sugar estates. The potential for 'subversion' was refocused into cricket in the rural areas, in an unprecedented manner, after 1953, with the suspension of the constitution by the British Government. As I have argued elsewhere, Jock Campbell, the progressive Chairman of Booker (owner of over 80% of the plantations), imbued with Fabian socialist ideas, introduced a comprehensive programme of reforms, of which the Berbice cricketers were among the beneficiaries.

The Davson Cup, in Berbice, was very keenly contested. In the first round in March 1956, Plantation Providence defeated Saints Sports Club (from New Amsterdam) by 29 runs. In a match of low scores – all the pitches were uncovered – Providence made 86 and 78, but Saints could muster only 66 and 69. 'Cobra' Ramdat was virtually unplayable on such pitches: he had 5 for 11 in the first innings and 3 for 10 in the second. In that same round powerful Port Mourant were defeated on first innings by neighbouring Plantation Albion. Port Mourant, captained by Basil Butcher, made 190: Joe Solomon 36, Johnny Teekasingh 25. Sonny Baijnauth, the former British Guiana left-arm medium pacer, got 3 for 44. Albion did better, scoring 213, with Baijnauth, the captain, making 114.[79] Rohan Kanhai did not play in the Davson Cup that year; he was honing his skills in first-division Case Cup cricket in Georgetown, representing East Indian Cricket Club. His rising stature was transparent: he made the first century in the competition in 1956: 234 against the premier club in the colony, Georgetown Cricket Club (GCC).[80]

Kanhai was clearly capable of playing long innings, based on a wide range of strokes fortified by solid defence, although he was only twenty years old. He could also be mercurial. All these elements contributed to his being designated a potentially great player in international cricket. In April 1956, as Chichester had recommended, Kanhai played for the West Indies in the unofficial Test against Swanton's XI, at the Queen's Park Oval in Trinidad. He did not do well. He made 23 in the first innings, stumped off the bowling of the Cambridge and Sri Lankan leg-spinner, Gamini Goonesena. It was described thus: 'The cheeky young batsman was baffled by Goonesena and danced down the wicket to offer a stroke. He was out of his crease and Blake collected and smartly whipped off the bails'. In the second innings he made 5 and was dismissed in a similar fashion off another spinner, Oakman: '…the young Guyanese player danced down the wicket and was neatly stumped by Blake for the second time in the match'.[81] But he was soon in fine form again. In the fifth round of the Case Cup he scored 127 not out for EICC, in their match against DCC; he shared a long partnership with the former British Guiana batsman, Ganesh Persaud, who made 114. The match was affected by rain, but EICC dismissed DCC for 74, with Wilfred Edun getting 3 for 18, and the Berbician medium-pacer (from Springlands), Saranga Baichu, 2 for 22.[82] At the same time, his colleagues in Berbice continued to gain valuable experience. In a match against New Dam, Butcher, the Port Mourant Cricket Club's captain, made 45 and took 5 for 16, bowling leg-breaks. At the same time, Ivan Madray, playing for City Stars of Port Mourant against Fyrish Village, got 11 wickets in the match for 120.[83]

In the sixth round of the Davson Cup Port Mourant defeated Albion by 3 wickets: the latter made scores of 86 and 17, with off-spinner, Indal Persaud (who would play later for the colony), getting match figures of 8 for 66. The veteran Johnny Teekasingh also played. Basil Butcher made 29 in Port Mourant's first innings score of 99; in their second innings, Joe Solomon made 42 in their winning total of 111 for 7, while Baijnauth bowled very well for Albion: 6 for 29. In the same round City Stars defeated Whim Village by an innings and 39 runs. The victors made 209; Whim's response was inadequate: 59 and 111. Madray, as was the pattern, was unconquerable. He got 7 for 58 in the match. Sonny Moonsammy, playing for Plantation Skeldon against Crabwood Creek, contributed largely to their victory by an innings and 46 runs. He made 77.[84] Meanwhile, in the Case Cup in Georgetown, Kanhai continued his masterly batsmanship, week after week – now the star of that competition.

It was common for a player such as Kanhai or Saranga Baichu to appear one week in the Davson Cup, in Berbice, and two weeks later in the Case Cup, in Georgetown. This was a demanding schedule, but it gave these Berbice cricketers a solid foundation to develop skills, stamina and concentration. Though not professionals in a technical sense, they were mastering the rudiments of professionalism. As noted above, Baichu was playing for EICC in Georgetown, in late April 1956; in early May, he represented Springlands against Skeldon, taking 5 for 54 in a match won by the latter by 138 runs: Moonsammy (Skeldon) made 39. He, too, played for EICC occasionally.[85] In the Davson Cup zonal final for the Upper Corentyne these two teams met again, with Skeldon defeating Springlands on first innings, but Saranga Baichu got 10 wickets for 67.[86] As Ivan Madray recalls, Baichu was a 'tremendous frightening bowler, similar to Eric Atkinson [of Barbados], a medium-pace cutter. Saranga cut it viciously: off-cutters, outers as well – in and out. He had a very short run, but he really pinned the ball down, and he bowled at the stumps'. It sounds as if he would have been a most impressive bowler in England, but it was not an age when backwoodsmen could easily escape their anonymous fate, however gifted. Madray believes that with four Berbice players in the British Guiana team (Kanhai, Butcher, Solomon and himself), the Georgetown centre of gravity was so disrupted that other ascendant Berbician cricketers were bound to suffer. Moonsammy and Baichu were among the victims. Madray explains: 'Both Saranga [Baichu] and Moon [sammy] should have been selected, but that would have meant dropping two more players from Georgetown. We had already replaced four of them'.[87]

Those four who were now in the British Guiana team seemed determined that they should never be stigmatised as interlopers: included to palliate advocates of Berbice cricket. They brought the skills and commitment honed through rigorous cricket, a variety of contests, often on impaired pitches, and the long sense of hurt from perennial exclusion, into the colony's cricket. In July 1956 Port Mourant, Skeldon and Blairmont (all Berbice sugar plantations) were locked in the struggle for supremacy in the Davson Cup, but several of their top players were also engaged in trials, in Georgetown, preparing for a tour of Antigua to play against Jamaica and the Leeward Islands. Such was the range of challenging cricket being played, the foundation of the skills of the emerging Berbice players. They were not merely desirous of representing British Guiana, the old benchmark; they were determined to reach the summit. Excluded for so long from 'big cricket', they yearned to get into the West Indies Test team. And the active involvement of Clyde Walcott in their apprenticeship, transformed this goal from a fantasy to a virtual imperative.

In Antigua, against Jamaica, Kanhai and Butcher built on the reputation they had been establishing since 1954. In reply to Jamaica's 336, British Guiana made 365: Kanhai's score of 83 was deemed 'scintillating'; he 'completely dominated the show'. Butcher 'also in fine form' made 96 not out, while Solomon contributed a typically solid 34.[88] It is hardly surprising, therefore, that when 28 players were invited to practise for the inter-colonial tournament scheduled for October 1956, several were from Berbice: Kanhai, Butcher, Solomon, Madray, Indal Persaud (an off-spinner) (Port Mourant), Sonny Baijnauth (Albion), Sonny Moonsammy (Skeldon), Saranga Baichu (Springlands) and Leslie Amsterdam (Blairmont).

Baijnauth was coming to the end of his first-class career, but Leslie Amsterdam (1934-99) and Indal Persaud (1940-94) would play several matches for British Guiana in the early 1960s, when they also represented the formidable Mental Hospital team in the Davson Cup. In September 1956 Berbice retained the inter-county championship for the third consecutive year, having defeated Demerara by 49 runs. Baijnauth, the veteran medium-pacer, got a hat-trick as Demerara were dismissed for a meagre 85 in their second innings: three of these were West Indies batsmen, Pairaudeau, Clyde Walcott, and the wicket-keeper, Clifford McWatt. The match was played at the small ground at Plantation Rose Hall, East Canje, Berbice, but the crowd estimated at 3,000 was described as being 'mad with excitement' and 'running riot'. The match, however, was not without some controversy: Bruce Pairaudeau, the Demerara captain and West Indies opening batsman, was reportedly disturbed by the apparent tampering of the wicket at both ends, and indicated that he would lodge a report on the matter. However accurate his suspicions, it was not uncommon for home teams to zealously seek to change the character of the pitch overnight. Such skulduggery permeates cricket lore in Guyana.[89]

1956 still had a little over three months to go after the inter-county games. As will be seen in the next chapter, British Guiana were engaged in the inter-colonial tournament against Jamaica and Barbados at Bourda, from 11-16 October and 19-25 October respectively (comprising two 5-day matches), in which they emerged the regional champions: an unusual experience for the colony. The Port Mourant men, Kanhai, Butcher, Solomon and Madray, were largely responsible for this victory. Yet in early November the Kawall Cup final between British Guiana Indians and Trinidad Indians was played at Bourda. Donated by Guyanese businessmen, Francis Kawall, in 1941, as the symbol of cricket supremacy among Indians in the West Indies, Trinidad had won on four occasions, British Guiana twice, the last time in 1952. Now the latter had the advantage, with several first-class cricketers in its ranks: Kanhai, Solomon, Madray, Wilfred Edun (the medium-pacer who toured New Zealand earlier that year with the West Indies), and the veteran colony batsman and bowler respectively, Ganesh Persaud and Sonny Baijnauth. Captained by Dr Ali-Shaw of EICC, British Guiana were supreme. After the first day's play the *Daily Argosy* reported it under the following dramatic caption:

BG INDIANS RUN UP 343 FOR 2 IN RUN SPREE
MOONSAMMY 114, GOPAUL 111 NOT OUT, KANHAI 84 SEND TRINIDAD ON A LEATHER-HUNTING ASSIGNMENT
TOURISTS' FIELDING BUCKLES AS BATSMEN OUTPACE CLOCK IN CAVALIER DISPLAY

British Guiana Indians had scored their 343 runs in 270 minutes. The opening batsmen, Kanhai and Madan Gopaul (of EICC), shared a partnership of 110, while Gopaul and Sonny Moonsammy participated in a second wicket partnership of 197. Moonsammy's 114 was 'chanceless', and it was claimed that he 'had been given a raw deal in local cricket'. (This was probably an allusion to the fact that he was a know supporter of Dr Cheddi Jagan's PPP, seen as a communist organisation by most in the hierarchy of the British Guiana Cricket Board of Control.) Kanhai's innings was described as 'a scintillating 84' by the 'West Indies prospect', with the tour of England scheduled for the summer of 1957. Gopaul's innings was considered a 'painstaking undefeated 111'. British Guiana made 523 for 7 declared; Trinidad made 204 and 184, thus losing to British Guiana by an innings and 135 runs. All the British Guiana bowlers were instrumental in this victory: Baijnauth, Madray and Indal Persaud.[90]

A few days after the completion of the Kawall Cup final, a British Guiana XI, comprising all the top non-Indian cricketers in the colony played a Combined Indians XI, comprising the best from British Guiana and Trinidad. The colony team included Bruce Pairaudeau (captain), Clyde Walcott, Lance Gibbs, Glendon Gibbs (the opener), Basil Butcher, Leslie Amsterdam, Clifford McWatt, Pat Legall and Charlie Stayers (the latter two were the fast bowlers). British Guiana made 392, with Walcott scoring 138 and Glendon Gibbs 97. The Combined Indians made 305 and the game petered out in a draw. Nyron Asgarali, the Trinidad opening batsman (soon to play for the West Indies), made 44, Gopaul 33, Kanhai 16, Solomon 23, Moonsammy 44. But it was left to the leg-spinner, Ivan Madray, to mount a belligerent rear-guard assault, an innings of 61, in a vain effort to overtake the colony's score. It was described as 'dazzling' by 'a West Indies candidate for the forthcoming tour of England'. The report explained: '...in a determined display in which Madray attempted to demoralise the bowling, he clouted the bowlers all over the field. He unleashed two six hits in his knock – one off Lance Gibbs, whom he pulled towards the western stand, and the other off Glendon Gibbs whom he knocked out of the ground...'[91] The Combined Indians had not disgraced themselves, the quality of their play a testimony to their arrival. Clyde Walcott's work, over the previous year, was bearing fruit. He helped to facilitate a greater amount of cricket in order to raise standards; he discussed the finer points of the game with players; he decisively shifted the spotlight from its long static focus on Georgetown towards rural Guyana, particularly the sugar plantations of Berbice. In the process, he had brought out the best in cricketers such as Kanhai, Butcher, Solomon, Madray, Moonsammy, Baichu and Amsterdam. It is true that 'Cobra' Ramdat, inexplicably, had slipped out of the net, and Baijnauth and Ganesh Persaud were approaching the evening of their careers. But Joe Solomon believes that playing regularly against such high quality players, several of whom (like Ramdat) never represented British Guiana, lifted the quality of his play immeasurably.[92]

Following the completion of the inter-colonial tournament in October 1956, Duncan McGregor Stuart, President of the Berbice Cricket Board of Control (who had brought good tidings to Kanhai in 1954), spoke for all Berbicians when he commended the performance of their county's heroes: Kanhai, Butcher, Solomon and Madray. He said:

> Berbicians are justifiably proud of the achievements of their representatives at the recent quadrangular cricket tournament in

> Georgetown...It has been a long and arduous task in building cricket in this county, and we are sometimes discouraged when some of our best products are denied selection. We are very grateful to the Sugar Producers' Association for making available such talented cricketers such as Clyde Walcott and Robert Christiani, who succeeded in polishing some of our rough edges in their coaching, and the Booker Estates who are providing the type of grounds on which cricket should be played. This, I may say, is very important to our rapid improvement.[93]

This had become a matter of national importance, the amazing rise of Berbice cricket. There was a growing unease in Georgetown – the rest of Demerara, like Berbice and Essequibo, hardly mattered – that the Berbicians were 'posing a threat' to players from the capital. This had elicited a forthright appraisal from Kenny Wishart, Secretary of the British Guiana Cricket Board of Control, who proceeded to reprimand most of the Case Cup players (in first-division cricket in Georgetown), for their apathy, contrasting it with the energetic pursuit of the game in Berbice. Wishart reportedly said: 'He was most concerned about the apathetic attitude of players – the players taking part in the...[first-division Case Cup]. They had been showing little or no concern in the game. As a result their brothers in the country [Berbice] were gaining more and more places in the British Guiana side....[T]his [was] reflected in the standard of cricket in Georgetown. This was not good enough. He did not wish to create the impression that there was no talent in the players from the country [Berbice]...[but] he was aware that there was a lot of talent in Georgetown...[and] would therefore urge the players to show more interest in the game and only by so doing they would reach the top...'

Wishart concluded that if the cricketers from Georgetown did not show better discipline and application they would be superseded soon by the Berbicians: '...[they] would continue to get more and more representatives and, like Demerara in years gone by, the whole side would be from Berbice'. It is conceivable, therefore, that several Berbician players, such as Amsterdam, Baichu and Moonsammy, were victims of the apprehension, in Georgetown, that the backwoodsmen were single-minded in their resolve to oust the Demerarians. Consequently, the old assumption that Berbicians could not expect a fair deal from the British Guiana selectors was hard to dissipate, the presence of Clyde Walcott notwithstanding.[94]

Towards the end of 1956, Hilbert Spence, President of the Berbice Chamber of Commerce, was reflecting on general progress in the county over the previous year. It is unthinkable that he was not influenced by the astounding progress of the cricketers from Berbice in his overall assessment of the economic health of the county and their success in 'every field of endeavour'. The *Berbice Weekly Argosy* captioned their report on his Christmas message thus:

BERBICE CONTINUES TO ASSERT ITSELF FOR PROSPERITY REPRESENTED IN EVERY FIELD OF ENDEAVOUR

Spence's message was illuminated by the sense of possibilities that often bloom when those who are kept back for a long time suddenly discover that the playing field is becoming leveller: that it is now open to them. He remarked: 'We make bold the statement that whatever achievements – as a whole – have been recorded over the past few years [in British Guiana], have been accomplished to a very great degree through the energies and endeavours of the residents of Berbice. We cannot truthfully say that our efforts have been fully recognised proportionately, but at this time, we are conscious of the fact that with perseverance we will eventually assume our rightful position'.[95]

A few days later, the poet, A.J. Seymour, Chief Information Officer of the Government, commented on local radio on the energetic spirit he discerned among young people he had encountered throughout the colony. He attributed this to a revolution engendered by the eradication of the dreaded malaria, for centuries the scourge of the colony. On the sugar plantations in particular, as noted earlier, this revolution was magnified by the progressive attitude exemplified by Jock Campbell, Chairman of Booker. Partly as a means of countering Cheddi Jagan's communism and partly because of his own Fabian socialist instincts, a raft of reforms had been introduced to promote reading, healthy cooking and eating, as well as sports, among children of sugar workers. It was as if everybody was energised by the conquest of malaria, as Seymour argued:

> When we talk of this spirit of energy and self-reliance now expressing itself, don't let us forget, or take too much for granted, the amazing change in our national health since DDT slew malaria. Before 1946, a date which promises to be our 1066, malaria was an enemy within the walls of the human being, crippling our physiques, sapping our mental and moral and even our spiritual energies and, altogether, converting this country into a sort of walking hospital. But today the fundamental surge of good health increases the population…It is this health that lies at the bottom of our new-found community energy and which is an engine to power…social change. I have a chance officially to talk with and to young people in their groups and clubs, and it is tremendously heartening to see their probing minds and to hear the questions these young people ask as literally agents of social change.[96]

For Indians in particular, although they were more vulnerable to malaria than other ethnic groups, their birth-rate had been consistently better; the eradication of the dreaded disease, by the late 1940s, accelerated it, rendering Indian numerical superiority a major worry for others.

Crude Birth-Rates by Race: Indian and Other Races in British Guiana, 1911/20-1956/60 (per 1,000 Population of Racial Category)

Years	Indian	Other Races (excluding Amerindians)
1911-20	31.9	30.1
1921-30	34.9	31.1
1931-35	37.5	28.5
1936-40	38.4	27.9
1941-45	41.5	30.0
1946-50	46.1	35.1
1951-55	49.3	38.0
1956-60	49.4	38.6

Source: Jay R. Mandle, *The Plantation Economy: Population and Economic Change in Guyana, 1838-1960* (Philadelphia: Temple University Press, 1973), p. 103

This would have profound political implications; it was the foundation of Cheddi Jagan's increasingly unassailable position in

Guyanese politics, the source of rising Indo-Guyanese self-assurance, by the early 1950s. On the Corentyne Coast (in Berbice), where the malarial menace was never as virulent as in the two other counties, Demerara and Essequibo, it fed a self-belief that had ramifications in all spheres of endeavour. It spawned the phenomenal cricket culture of Berbice that came to fruition in the mid-1950s. The advent of Clyde Walcott, in 1954, did not create Kanhai, Butcher, Solomon, Madray, Moonsammy, Baichu, Amsterdam, Ramdat and several others of impressive talent; but it quickened the emergence of their gifts with a minimum of coaching ('guidance', as Butcher put it) and facilitated unprecedented access to local and regional cricket.

It was not fortuitous that the 'Sportsman of the Year' for 1956 in British Guiana was Rohan Kanhai, and that the runner-up was Clyde Walcott. They symbolised the new energy and the structured framework – the discipline and resolve engendered since Clyde's arrival in the colony in late 1954. They both believed in mastering the basics of cricket – technique and organisational continuity – from primary and secondary school to club, then first-class cricket and Tests. Speaking in Georgetown on 2 May 2008, the former Guyana and West Indies opening batsman and Chief Executive Officer of the West Indies Cricket Board, Stephen Camacho (born 1945), a beneficiary of the tradition established by Clyde Walcott between 1954 and 1970, argued that the technical foundations of that legacy have not been invalidated with the passage of time, however frayed the state of West Indies cricket. His definition of it did not depart from Walcott's guiding principles during his stewardship in Guyana:

> It must...be emphasised that first principles never change and I shall seek to illustrate this with two examples. Firstly, you cannot be a great batsman without a great defence. Rohan Kanhai and Sir Viv Richards played shots unknown to ordinary mortals, but this was complemented by a water-tight defence. Secondly, the great England opening batsman, Sir Jack Hobbs, who scored 195 first-class centuries and is one of *Wisden's* five cricketers of the 20th century, always advised young batsmen that footwork was the foundation of batsmanship.[97]

Camacho attributes the decline of West Indies cricket in recent years to its undermining in primary and secondary schools, as well as at the club level. His diagnosis of the roots of the problem underlines how sturdier were the foundations on which the skills of Kanhai, Butcher, Solomon, Lance Gibbs, Moonsammy, Amsterdam and Madray were built. He concludes: 'The clubs, so vital a link between schools' cricket and the game at first-class level, are also largely in decline. The major factors being uninspiring leadership, failing finances, reduced facilities and diminishing membership'. The age of Walcott and Kanhai feels like a golden age. It was.

NOTES

1. Hilary McD. Beckles, 'The Political Ideology of West Indies Cricket Culture', in Beckles and Brian Stoddart (eds.), *Liberation Cricket: West Indies Cricket Culture* (Kingston, Jamaica: Ian Randle Publishers, 1995), p. 151.
2. Clem Seecharan, 'The Tiger of Port Mourant', in Frank Birbalsingh and Clem Seecharan, *Indo-Westindian Cricket* (London: Hansib, 1988), pp. 50-1.
3. See Walter Rodney (ed.), *Guyanese Sugar Plantations in the Late Nineteenth Century: A Contemporary Description from the 'Argosy'* (Georgetown: Release Publishers, 1979), pp. 81-2, 97.
4. The *Daily Argosy*, 4 January 1939.
5. C.F. Andrews, 'Impressions of British Guiana', (mimeo.), p. 35, enclosure in the following Colonial Office file at the National Archives (Kew, London): CO111/689/75141 [1930]. See also Basdeo Mangru, ed., *C. F. Andrews, Impressions of British Guiana, 1930: An Emissary's Assessment* (Chicago: Adams Press, 2007).
6. *Report of the West Indian Sugar Commission* (Lord Olivier, chairman), Appendix 7, Vol. II, Evidence, etc., Relating to British Guiana: Memorandum by the British Guiana East Indian Association, p. 198.
7. The *Daily Chronicle*, 14 March 1933.
8. Interview with Ivy Jailall, Sea Well, Berbice, Guyana, 10 February 2003.
9. The *Daily Chronicle*, 21 February 1936.
10. Clem Seecharan, *op. cit.* [2005], pp. 54, 201.
11. Clem Seecharan, *op. cit.* [1997], p. 315.
12. The *Daily Chronicle*, 1 September 1937.
13. The *Daily Chronicle*, 12 January 1936.

14. The *Daily Chronicle*, 19 January 1936.
15. The *Daily Argosy*, 19 February 1957.
16. Clem Seecharan, 'Da Coolie Ga Mek Abi Hunt Ledda: Clem Seecharan in Conversation with Ivan Madray', in Frank Birbalsingh and Clem Seecharan, *Indo-Westindian Cricket* (London: Hansib, 1988), pp. 99-100.
17. Interview with Ivan Madray, London, 11 June 2008.
18. See *cricketarchive.com* for statistical details of John Trim.
19. Interview (by phone) with Basil Butcher, 25 July 2008.
20. See note 16, p. 108.
21. See *cricketarchive.com*
22. Learie Constantine, 'Cricket in the Sun', in Constantine and Denzil Batchelor, *The Changing Face of Cricket* (London: Eyre and Spottiswoode, 1966), p. 137.
23. John Arlott, *Days at the Cricket* (London: Longman, Green and Co., 1951), pp. 159-61.
24. *Ibid.*, p. 161.
25. 'Robert Christiani: Interview', in Frank Birbalsingh, *Guyana and the Caribbean: Reviews, Essays and Interviews* (Chichester, West Sussex: Dido Press, 2004), p. 131
26. See *cricketarchive.com*.
27. *Ibid.*
28. *Ibid.*
29. Frank Birbalsingh, *The Rise of Westindian Cricket: From Colony to Nation* (London: Hansib, 1997 [1996]), p. 163.
30. Interview with Ivan Madray, London, 11 June 2008.
31. Rahul Bhattacharya, 'The Indian Connection in the Windies', *Hindustan Times*, 6 March 2007.
32. Mihir Bose, *A History of Indian Cricket* (London: Andre Deutsch, 1990), p. 190.
33. See note 16, p. 111.
34. *Ibid.*
35. *Ibid.*, pp. 110-1
36. The *Daily Argosy*, 21 November 1954.
37. The *Daily Argosy*, 23 November 1954.
38. The *Daily Argosy*, 31 November 1954.
39. The *Daily Argosy*, 2 November 1954.
40. Kanhai, *op. cit.* [1966], pp. 19-20.
41. *Ibid.*, p. 20.
42. *Ibid.*
43. *Ibid.*
44. The *Daily Argosy*, 27 November 1954.

45. Kanhai, *op. cit.* [1966], p. 21.
46. The *Daily Argosy*, 12 December 1954.
47. The *Daily Argosy*, 13 December 1954.
48. Kanhai, *op. cit.* [1966], p. 21.
49. The *Guiana Sunday Graphic*, 19 April 1953.
50. The *Guiana Sunday Graphic*, 29 March 1953.
51. The *Guiana Sunday Graphic*, 15 March 1953.
52. The *Daily Argosy*, 29 December 1954.
53. The *Daily Argosy*, 13 October 1954.
54. See the *Daily Argosy*, 14, 15 October 1954.
55. The *Daily Argosy*, 17, 18 October 1954.
56. The *Daily Argosy*, 20 October 1954.
57. Basil Butcher, 'Guyana', in Garfield Sobers and J.S. Barker (eds.), *Cricket in the Sun: A History of West Indies Cricket* (London: Arthur Barker Ltd., 1967), pp. 45-6.
58. *Ibid.*, p. 46.
59. Gordon Rohlehr, 'Rohan Kanhai', in *Kanhai/Gibbs: Tribute to Two Great West Indians* (Port of Spain: Self-Published, 1974), p. 25.
60. Clyde Walcott, *Sixty Years on the Back Foot: The Cricketing Life of Sir Clyde Walcott* (London: Orion, 2000 [1999]), p. 65.
61. *Ibid.*
62. Interview (by phone) with Basil Butcher, 25 July 2008.
63. Interview (by phone) with Joe Solomon, 30 July 2008.
64. See note 16, p. 122.
65. The *Daily Argosy*, 16 November 1954.
66. The *Daily Argosy*, 24 November 1954.
67. The *Daily Argosy*, 9 December 1954.
68. The *Daily Argosy*, 29 December 1954.
69. Interview (by phone) with Basil Butcher, 25 July 2008.
70. The *Daily Argosy*, 16 November 1955.
71. See the *Daily Argosy*, 7, 8 November 1955.
72. The *Daily Argosy*, 16 November 1955.
73. The *Daily Argosy*, 9 November 1955.
74. See note 72.
75. The *Daily Argosy*, 28 December 1955.
76. The *Daily Argosy*, 15 February 1956.
77. *Ibid.*
78. The *Daily Argosy*, 14 March 1956.
79. *Ibid.*

80. The *Daily Argosy*, 28 March 1956.
81. The *Daily Argosy*, 10 April 1956.
82. The *Daily Argosy*, 23, 30 April 1956.
83. See the *Daily Argosy*, 14 April 1956.
84. The *Daily Argosy*, 24 April 1956.
85. The *Daily Argosy*, 11 May 1956.
86. The *Daily Argosy*, 19 June 1956.
87. See note 16, pp. 125-6.
88. The *Daily Argosy*, 9 August 1956.
89. The *Daily Argosy*, 12 September 1956.
90. The *Daily Argosy*, 2, 3, 5 November 1956.
91. The *Daily Argosy*, 12, 13 November 1956.
92. Interview (by phone) with Joe Solomon, 30 July 2008.
93. The *Daily Argosy*, 7 November 1956.
94. The *Daily Argosy*, 17 December 1956.
95. The *Daily Argosy*, 27 December 1956.
96. The *Daily Argosy*, 7 January 1957.
97. *Stabroek News*, 4 May 2008.

Kanhai between covers: his book of 1966.

CHAPTER FOUR

Rebellion and Racial Bitterness: the Age of Rohan Kanhai, the mid-1950s/60s

And how the Gods looked out
from within this little man.
Power, Grace, Majesty in collected divinity
...a fragment from heaven.
MacDonald Dash on Rohan Kanhai (1963)

I play my cricket in two ways – first as a means of enjoyment (both for me and the spectator, I hope) and second to win.
Rohan Kanhai (1966)

A batsman needs three things to succeed – guts, timing and concentration. Not many have all three and, to me, the one that is missing more often than not is guts.
Rohan Kanhai (1966)

Most Indo-Guyanese were buoyed, beyond the boundary, by the meteoric rise since 1947 of Cheddi Jagan, the handsome young politician from Plantation Port Mourant. An American-trained dentist turned Marxist, he was seen as the irrepressible champion of the sugar plantation workers and the gadfly of the plantocracy. Jagan's People's Progressive Party (PPP) won the first general elections under adult suffrage just five weeks after the cricketers from India had left British Guiana in 1953. This was a time of immense euphoria for Indo-Guyanese; African apprehension of their perceived ascendancy was tempered by the fact that Forbes Burnham, the rising African-Guyanese hero, was a member of the PPP, a loose coalition across the ethnic chasm. Ominously, however, the victory was sullied by a bitter leadership struggle between Jagan and Burnham. They did arrive at a compromise and formed a government; but after 133 days the British Government, driven by Cold War paranoia, suspended the constitution because of Jagan's supposed plan to create a communist state. For Indo-Guyanese, the suspension of the constitution and the presence of British troops in the colony enhanced Cheddi's stature as their hero, a virtual Nehru taking on the British Empire, destined to lead them to the promise land, in the footsteps of Mother India. Burnham left the PPP in 1955 to form his own political party. The racial divide between Africans and Indians, tempered under colonial rule, was now exacerbated by the mutual suspicion spawned by the imminence of Independence: who would inherit the colonial earth? Indians were perceived to be in the ascendancy – after the War – with their numerical advantage, greater cultural security and economic self-assurance that sprang from rice, cattle, commerce and the professions of law and medicine. Moreover, the freedom of Mother India, since August 1947, had helped to shape a sturdier pride in their Indian antecedents, conducing to a certainty, assertiveness and a deeper conception of their own possibilities.

Meanwhile, the sugar industry, particularly Booker under the progressive leadership of Sir Jock Campbell (1912-94), seeking to influence the predominantly Indian sugar workers towards moderation, in the aftermath of the political debacle of 1953, accelerated the pace of reform on the plantations. It included a comprehensive programme of social welfare, at the core of which was the provision of multi-purpose community centres and cricket grounds on all estates. In 1954, as seen earlier, the prolific Barbadian and West Indies batsman, Clyde Walcott (1926-2006), was appointed by Jock Campbell to promote the game on the sugar estates. He produced astounding results in a very short time by leaving 'fortress' Georgetown and venturing into the plantations of Berbice. At Port Mourant in particular, the high quality of their cricket, a legacy of Manager Gibson's pioneering work, was bolstered by Campbell's culture of reform, now accelerated to counter Jagan's perceived subversive Marxist challenge.[1] Walcott's greatest accomplishment was to use his immense authority, intelligence and imagination to facilitate the Port Mourant 'revolution'. By 1955 he had become the captain and a selector of British Guiana, in the inter-colonial tournament; and he deftly catapulted two young batsmen he discovered at Port Mourant into the team: Basil Butcher (aged 21) and Rohan

The Berbicians and their 'discoverer' (1956): left to right, Madray, Butcher, Walcott, Baijnauth, Kanhai and Solomon (Georgetown, 1956)

Kanhai (aged 19). These, along with Joe Solomon (also from Plantation Port Mourant) and Barbadians, Garry Sobers and Conrad Hunte (1932-99), would become the formidable batsmen of Frank Worrell's great team that toured England in 1963. 1956 was a momentous year: Walcott captained a gifted British Guiana team that was considered the best in the region; it included five players from the sugar estates: Kanhai, Butcher, Solomon (a solid middle-order batsman), and Ivan Madray, the leg-spinner (all from Port Mourant) – unearthed by Walcott in 1954-5 – and the veteran left-arm medium-pacer and left-arm orthodox bowler, 'Sugar Boy' Baijnauth (1916-85), from neighbouring Albion. By 1959 Walcott had discovered three more cricketers from the Berbice plantations; all represented British Guiana that year in the inter-colonial tournament: two batsmen, Sonny Moonsammy (Skeldon) and Leslie Amsterdam (Blairmont), and a medium-pace bowler, Saranga Baichu (Springlands). Walcott has modestly sketched what he did in British Guiana; but the legacy is monumental. He was a dedicated man inspired by, and inspiring in, an environment of challenge and change:

> My job was to develop cricket on the sugar plantations and improve the quality of Guyanese cricket in international competition. It was by far the most challenging task I had undertaken…There were several clubs on each estate and I decided to have them amalgamated into one club. If there were any disputes, I had to resolve them…Some very talented players emerged at that time, including Rohan Kanhai, Basil Butcher and Joe Solomon…None of the cricketers on the estate were coached, just as Shivnarine Chanderpaul today has natural talent. My job was to guide them and advise them on how to make the best possible use of that talent. Until then only two cricketers from the 'interior' had managed to break the monopoly of players from the Georgetown area in the British Guiana side, John Trim [from Port Mourant], who went on to represent the West Indies, and 'Sugar Boy' Baijnauth [from Albion]. Now they were to be followed by others.[2]

As seen earlier, John Trim was an inspiration to Madray and Butcher; but so, too, was Sonny 'Sugar Boy' Baijnauth (alias Bajou

Baijnauth or Ramcharan Ramcharitar). He never played for the West Indies and his first-class career was not crowned with glory. Yet he was a folk hero to many Indian boys in Berbice: he was the first Indian from a plantation in the county to represent British Guiana. In seven first-class matches, spread over 13 years, March 1947 to March 1960, he took only 9 wickets for 795 runs at an average of 88.32. But he bowled 305.2 overs at an economy rate of 2.60. Therein lay his strength. He could bowl unchanged for hours, maintaining a nagging length irrespective of whether he was bowling in the fast-medium or the left-arm orthodox mode. Two examples will illustrate his amazing capacity to maintain line and length on the most benign of wickets in British Guiana. One was at Bourda; the other at Plantation Rose Hall, in Baijnauth's county, Berbice. In October 1956, in the crucial match against Barbados, at Bourda in Georgetown, he did not get any wickets in the first innings, as Gibbs and Madray bowled the great side out for 211. But, as expected, he held his own, even against Sobers and Weekes: 24 overs, 10 maidens, 37 runs, 0 wicket. In his last first-class match, Berbice v. England [MCC], at Rose Hall, his figures were: 69 overs, 19 maidens, 182 runs, 0 wicket, an economy rate of 2.6. It was an extraordinary effort against a team that made 641 for 6, with Jim Parks, Ken Barrington and Rae Illingworth scoring centuries, and Geoff Pullar, M.J.K. Smith, Ted Dexter and Raman Subba Row getting half-centuries. Baijnauth's captain in that match was Joe Solomon, who made 201 not out, in a third wicket partnership of 290 with Basil Butcher (133 not out). An authentic feather bed! That puts 'Sugar Boy's' bowling into perspective: Solomon says that in the Davson Cup and other domestic competitions, he was highly respected for his virtually flawless bowling in different styles. It was, Joe recalls, an education to negotiate Baijnauth week after week. He, Kanhai and Butcher gained immeasurably from playing against such high-class bowlers.[3]

Trim and Baijnauth were primarily of the period just before Walcott's advent in Guyana. With Walcott's pioneering work and commanding authority there was a veritable torrent of plantation cricketers who entered the Guyana and the West Indies teams, between the mid-1950s and the early 1970s, when he returned to his homeland, Barbados. Rohan Kanhai was the finest of them all. Kanhai played his first Test in England in 1957; Madray his two

Tests in 1958, against Pakistan; Butcher and Solomon made their Test debut, in India, in late 1958. Butcher is an African-Guyanese; increasingly, however, the politics of race that poisoned the colony after the split between Jagan and Burnham, in 1955, was seeping within the boundary. For Indo-Guyanese, the flair and international acclamation of Rohan Kanhai would become an integral part of their political endeavour, fortifying their resolve even as their political fortunes slumped in the early 1960s. Perceptions of his mastery would be refracted through the political, necessarily a racial, prism. The two men from Port Mourant – Kanhai and Cheddi Jagan, the Indian political leader – became lodged in the Indo-Guyanese psyche, barometers of their identity, at the end of Empire. Butcher's achievement, though substantial – 3,104 runs in 44 Tests, at an average of 43.11 (with 133 at Lord's in 1963, and his highest innings of 209 against England at Nottingham in 1966) – never got the recognition from Indo-Guyanese (including the people of Port Mourant) it merited. Cricket, always an instrument of politics in the West Indies, was now unambiguously central to Indo-Guyanese identity. Kanhai and Jagan were constructed in terms of Indian religious iconography that bordered on deification; Butcher quickly slipped off their radar and would remain invisible in the Indo-Guyanese narrative.

Kanhai played in 79 Tests between 1957 and 1974, captaining the West Indies in his last thirteen. He scored 6,227 runs at an average of 47.53, including 15 centuries and 28 half-centuries. His highest score is 256, made at Calcutta in December 1958. He appeared in 61 consecutive Tests between 30 May 1957 and 20 February 1969, when a nagging knee injury forced him to withdraw from the tour of New Zealand. In his first-class career (1955-77), he scored 28,639 runs at an average of 49.29, with 83 centuries. He took 315 catches. But it is the way he scored his runs, the unconquerable flair of the man that has stayed with many admirers. As he stated in his autobiography of 1966, *Blasting for Runs*: 'When I bat my whole make-up urges me to destroy the opposition as quickly as possible and once you are on top to never let up. I've never been one for second best – that's why I never want fours, I want sixes. Once I've got the fielders with their tongues hanging out I aim to run them into the ground'.[4]

It was this bravado that made Rohan Kanhai the quintessential rebel answering the Indo-Guyanese quest to finally erase the 'coolie' stain. It paralleled Cheddi Jagan's radicalism, which sprang from similar promptings, and therefore could also be appropriated in the making of Indo-Guyanese identity. In spite of Manager Gibson's innovative approach that helped to shape a more self-reliant, assertive Indian persona at Port Mourant, it is noteworthy that Jagan recalls a different trigger that kindled his rebellious temperament:

> Between the white and non-white world there were distances – social (inhabitants of the two worlds did not associate) and physical (the mansions were out of bounds)...There was also a psychological distance. I recall vividly my great curiosity about the manager's mansion. I wanted to know what it felt like to be inside the gate...The opportunity came at Christmas time. I must have been about 8 or 9 years old [1926 or 1927]. I joined the creole gang [often child labourers] and went to share in the largesse of the manager. The manager's wife, Mrs Gibson, stood at the window of the top floor of this imposing mansion. She threw coins down at us and enjoyed seeing the wild scramble for the pennies. This was the way our manager's wife offered gifts to workers' children at Christmas time on the sugar plantations.[5]

The same rebellious temperament took shape in Rohan Kanhai; but it is necessary to repeat that it originated because of a comparatively more progressive environment at Port Mourant than on any other plantation. The rebel in Jagan and Kanhai was engendered by hope and possibilities of greater achievement – not despair or the death of ambition. That was why, in the Indo-Guyanese identity construct, Jagan and Kanhai were interchangeable. It had nothing to do with these two individuals from Port Mourant per se; it was rooted in their rebellious outlook, their abiding iconoclasm, and their meteoric rise – daring symbols of possibilities. Reform on the plantation fed the rebellious spirit with an insatiable appetite for change. And with the suspension of the constitution, six months after Cheddi Jagan's victory at the 1953 general elections, a robust and implacably rebellious posture took shape at Port Mourant, the spiritual home of Jaganism.

In early 1955 Michael Swan, a British writer, spent three and a half months in British Guiana at the invitation of the Colonial Office, in preparation for a book. He sought the advice of the security forces before he visited Port Mourant, and was quickly informed of their apprehensions:

> When I told Sergeant Mackinnon that I would be visiting Plantation Port Mourant, the birthplace of Cheddi Jagan, he told me not to miss going to the 'Rock Diamond' rum-parlour, where I would see some life. It was, he said, the place where the trouble-makers of the plantation met, and when the police wanted information they would send a man to eavesdrop at the 'Rock Diamond'. They were expecting trouble now, he added, since Booker had just decided to close down the sugar factory there, and the workers had got the idea that they had been punished for their support of [Jagan's] PPP [People's Progressive Party]...I asked about the threat of arson and the blowing up of key buildings and he said that while he knew of no proof that arson had been planned he knew for certain that caches of gelignite had been dug up at Port Mourant. He was whole-heartedly opposed to the PPP but, like everyone else I had spoken to, he told me if there were free elections tomorrow the PPP would be [re-]elected.[6]

Overseas reporters turned up continually at Port Mourant in the mid-1950s: 'Little Moscow'. To the people on the plantation, however, this spoke of their heroic challenge of the old order, something exhilaratingly provocative, subversive intentions that would change their world. It heightened their self-confidence, and sustained the perception of this plantation as a hotbed of young communists – rebels with a mind to do whatever they wished, ready to fight any authority no matter how sacrosanct. This was the spirit of place and temper of the time that fashioned the temperament of Rohan Bholalall Kanhai.

It was evident as early as April1955 when Rohan Kanhai played his second first-class match, against Australia. He had cross-batted the great Keith Miller several times on his way to a half-century, and was reprimanded afterwards by the famous man for playing across the line. Rohan was not daunted; he saw that as a challenge to continue to execute his strokes by his instincts, even if deemed risky and 'ungrammatical' by the purists:

> Keith Miller…got a bit upset at the way a green 19 year old was making a fool of the cricket manuals during the Aussies' triumphant tour of the West Indies back in 1955. I was a relatively new boy in the British Guiana side that tackled the Aussies at Georgetown that day. Miller was bowling his big out-swingers and I was clouting them regularly to the square-leg boundary. Nobody told me that I shouldn't do it – that I was committing the batsman's biggest sin by hitting against the ball. That was my favourite shot and it brought me a heap of runs. Big Keith was completely flummoxed. He knew the answer to every trick in the book, but I wasn't playing by the rules. The madder he got the more I innocently pulled him to the fence…At a party after the match, Miller came up to me with a rueful grin, wagged an accusing finger and said: 'The next time you play a shot like that kid you'll be in trouble'. Perhaps I should have taken his warning but I felt it was a pity to change when I was getting a few runs. And I haven't changed, you know.[7]

The *Daily Argosy* had discerned the special gifts of 19-year old Kanhai as early as that match, noting that only he and Clyde Walcott were 'able to meet the tourists on equal terms and show no regard for the bowling'. They attributed the defeat of British Guiana, by an innings and 134 runs, to 'fear' on the part of the young batsmen, rather than the extraordinary guile or hostility of the experienced Australian bowlers: Miller, Johnson, Davidson and Benaud. Two other Port Mourant players took part in that match: Butcher, who made 8 and 46, and the leg-spinner Ivan Madray, with figures of 23 overs, 0 maiden, 122 runs, 3 wickets: Neil Harvey, Peter Burge and Ron Archer. So there was probably more to the young men from Port Mourant than the paper recognised.[8] That was demonstrated emphatically in the quadrangular tournament, the following year, when all four players from Port Mourant were outstanding, thus raising the possibility that all could soon represent the West Indies. British Guiana won the tournament, having defeated both Jamaica and Barbados on first innings. In a score of 601 for 5 against Jamaica, the three batsmen from Port Mourant were superb: Kanhai 129, Butcher 154 not out, Solomon 114 not out. Jamaica made 469, with Madray's marathon bowling playing a key part in British Guiana's lead: 84 overs, 18 maidens, 168 runs, 4 wickets. Jamaica's bowlers included four top ones: Gilchrist, Dewdney, Collie Smith and the legendary Alf Valentine.

In the final, against Barbados, British Guiana made 581: Kanhai 195 (run out) and Solomon 108. Barbados were dismissed for 211; Madray got 4 wickets for 61; Lance Gibbs 4 for 68. The Barbadian batsmen included Everton Weekes, Garry Sobers, John Goddard (1919-87), Denis Atkinson (1926-2001) and Clairmonte Depeiza (1928-95), the latter two being the holders of the surviving world record of 347 for the seventh wicket, made against Australia in 1955, in the fourth Test in Barbados. The *Barbados Advocate* was generous in acclaiming the spin bowling of the Guyanese: 'Lance Gibbs bowled the off-breaks with a disconcerting turn and Madray spin the leg-breaks the other way, forming a new combination of the British Guiana "spin twins". They captured eight wickets between them for 129, a commendable achievement, the help which they got from the wicket [pitch] and which they put to good use notwithstanding...Barbados batting had cracked under the sustained spin bowling...'[9]

It was almost as if Port Mourant had beaten the masters of West Indies cricket. The *Daily Argosy* was effusive in its acclamation of the Berbician batsmen, particularly Kanhai and Solomon who, in a fifth wicket partnership of 251, had 'sent the Barbadians on a leather-hunting assignment for well over four hours':

> An estimated 12,000 crowd saw British Guiana run up the almost impregnable score of 582 for 9...The day's play was highlighted by two century innings by the Berbicians, Rohan Kanhai and Joe Solomon, coming after their two hundreds in the semi-final match versus Jamaica. Kanhai's effort...a magnificent knock of 195...further strengthened his claim for West Indies selection for the 1957 tour of England. He was run out from a beautiful throw by Frank King...Solomon's 108...was compiled mainly by elegant late cuts, fluent cover drives and almost contemptuous leg-glances. Gifted with a very good eye and a great deal of

> concentration, Solomon has also put himself among the candidates for West Indian touring caps.[10]

The role of Clyde Walcott, as I have shown, in the emergence of all these fine cricketers from Port Mourant simultaneously is one of the illuminating episodes in West Indies cricket. To Kanhai, Butcher, Solomon and Madray he imparted the confidence and a sense of proportion to develop the resolve, to erase flaws, while feeling secure to experiment and advance. But it was also his knowledge of the social and psychological forces that shaped these young men which endeared him to them. As a foreigner, a Barbadian, it was easier for him to empathise with the hopes and frustrations of the backwoodsmen from Port Mourant than the czars of Georgetown still marooned in class and colour prejudices. As Ivan Madray has stated, 'I could have walked to the end of the earth for Clyde Walcott. He always brought out the best in me. I never wanted to let him down'.[11] One could comprehend the foundation of this devotion to the man from the following appreciation by Walcott, in 1958, of Rohan Kanhai's 195 against Barbados in October 1956. It is largely about Rohan, but it also speaks of Walcott, the leader:

> The more I saw of these youngsters, the happier I became. After their success in the first round against Jamaica they showed no signs of over-confidence – one of the more dangerous states of mind one can bring to cricket – but a quiet determination to do as well as, or better than, they had done before. During a break which came just after Rohan Kanhai had topped his century I talked to him in the dressing-room. I explained that a century was something that came sometimes to quite ordinary players, but that a double century was a comparatively rare thing even for the very best player. If he reached the coveted target, I promised him, I would give him a bat. Well, Rohan was run out only a few runs short [five] and, when he arrived back in the dressing-room he collapsed from fatigue – both mental and physical. I think he felt that, as much as anything, he had let me down; that I wanted two hundred runs from him and that he had failed me. I talked to him – he was in a sort of daze and my words took some time to sink in – and told him not to worry, and

> that he had done very well indeed and would have plenty more chances to score double centuries in the future. At this he brightened up when, perhaps subconsciously, he realised that he had not let me down after all. A clever and likeable character, and one of great promise, he fully deserved the bat which, of course, I gave him though the 'conditions' had not been exactly fulfilled.[12]

Kanhai was determined to conquer Everest, and his means would not be dictated by circumspection or reserve. His iconoclastic approach often precipitated disasters but it was congruent with a seminal Indo-Guyanese aspiration – to produce a first-rate West Indies batsman imbued with passion and panache, the pillars of West Indian style. This was seen as the last milestone: the decisive final attribute, on the long road to belonging. Kanhai had entered the mansion and he was not going to genuflect. He had done so on his own terms and was resolved to create a new universe that bore his peculiar personality. He spoke for his people whether he was aware of it or not. So when he was selected to tour England with the West Indies in 1957, aged 21, the youngest member, a long-held dream was answered. The Trinidadian journalist, Owen Mathurin, had noted that Kanhai was 'already being tipped as likely to follow in the footsteps of the three W's';[13] and the tour brochure for 1957 was even more generous: 'Kanhai is reputed to possess the eyes of an eagle...a first-class bat in the making. He possesses a variety of strokes [and] is very smart in the field...The steep upward trend which British Guiana cricket has taken recently in relation to the other West Indian colonies is due largely to the efforts of this fine young player'.[14] But West Indies were conquered 3-0 – a catastrophic fall – after their glory of 1950; and Kanhai had an undistinguished tour. The batting was irretrievably fallible, Collie Smith's 161 at Edgbaston and Worrell's carrying his bat for 191 at Trent Bridge being rare exceptions.

The pain of Indo-Guyanese was palpable, however credible the explanation for Kanhai's failure in England. No batsman topped 40 in the averages: Collie Smith was first with 39.60; then came Worrell, 38.88, Sobers, 32.00, Walcott, 27.44; Kanhai was fifth with 22.88, followed by Weekes, 19.50. C.L.R. James, who saw the whole series, offered some consolation: 'West Indies were

Twenty-one year old Kanhai during his first tour of England, 1957

scrambling for openers and much of this responsibility was thrown on Kanhai [they used him thus in three Tests (apart from being wicket-keeper in three); Nyron Asgarali in two; Worrell in three; Sobers in two; and Bruce Pairaudeau in one]. He bore it without disgrace, with spasms of alternate toughness and brilliance which only later we were to learn were fundamental in his character…Altogether in 1957 it was the failure of Weekes, Worrell and Walcott to repeat the victorious cavalry charge of 1950 which threw such burdens on Sobers, Kanhai and Collie Smith. The burden fell most heavily on Kanhai. But the future batsman was there to be discerned'.[15] But this was a later assessment, in 1963.

That Indo-Guyanese were not overwhelmed with despair was occasioned by Cheddi's Jagan victory in the general elections of August 1957; it atoned, also, for the 1953 debacle. But a nagging doubt hovered; the old insecurities obtruded, in spite of the solidity of the political, economic and professional advances. Although all the great stars were eclipsed on that tour of 1957, the fear that Rohan may not get another chance was consuming. To produce a great West Indies batsman, that was the ultimate test. Indo-Guyanese nourished the hope that Rohan Kanhai, like Cheddi Jagan, would deliver soon. Kanhai's batting in 1958 against Pakistan built on the possibilities evinced spasmodically in England the previous year. He reached 96 in Trinidad and 62 at home in British Guiana, but his average of 37.37, though an improvement, paled against the Olympian batting of Garry Sobers, who averaged 137.33. Yet although Rohan was still to get his maiden Test century, J.S. Barker had seen much in his 96 to keep hope afloat: 'The virtues of foreign travel were clearly evident in this innings by Kanhai. His tour to England last year transformed him from a back foot to a front foot player and from a novice into a seasoned veteran'.[16] That was enhanced by the fact that Jagan was now firmly entrenched in government, while appearing this time to be more conciliatory, more mature, in his dealings with the British. Moreover, Rohan was selected to go on the West Indies tour of India, in 1958-9. It was seen as a kind of homecoming; he had to come good now: to do otherwise would give the impression, in Mother India, that the years had been squandered. Two other Port Mourant batsmen were also chosen: Basil Butcher and Joe Solomon. Three Indians were in the West Indies team: Kanhai, Solomon and Sonny Ramadhin.

Kanhai made 66 and 22 at Bombay, falling to the leg-spinner, Subhash Gupte, in the second innings. In the first innings of the second Test, at Kanpur, he was bowled by Gupte for 0; he made 41 in the second, but succumbed again to the mastery of this fine bowler, who got 9 for 102 in the first innings. Gupte was a brilliant exponent of the googly (some say two types of varying pace), but equally adept at bowling a range of deliveries in the same over, including the flipper, while maintaining impeccable control. And he bore his admirable skills with a palpable cockiness, unnerving in its timing and conducive to fallibility in his victims. In 1953, when he had lured West Indian batsmen into extravagance and sudden death – he got 26 wickets in the series – he was a hero of most Indo-Guyanese. Now Kanhai's vulnerability to Gupte was painful, unbearable; it evoked the reassertion of patriarchal authority: clipping the fledgling autonomy of youth. However, Kanhai's emphatic response to his 'Gupte problem', in the next Test, is a memorable testimonial to his strength of character. It reassured his Indo-Guyanese devotees; but the first response was a massive relief:

> India's Subhash Gupte was the greatest leg-spinner I have ever played against…Gupte was India's golden boy, the only real world-class player they had. In the first Test I presented him with his 100th Test wicket…In the next Test at Kanpur he bowled me…for a blob and as we came in for tea he sauntered up to me and sneered: 'Hello, Rabbit!'. The jibe brought a giggle from the rest of the players in earshot and set my blood boiling…[It] was not until we moved to Calcutta for the third Test that the rabbit turned. Garry Sobers went down with stomach trouble so I batted at no. 3 – and by the end of the day was 203 not out. I belted 34 boundaries in a stay just under five hours and shared an unbroken fourth wicket stand of 179 in 144 minutes with Butcher. My century, made in 132 minutes, was the quickest of the series. The next day I scythed my way to 256, unaware that I had topped Frank Worrell's record Test score against India – 237 in Kingston…[B]ut mastering Gupte was my prize.[17]

The Indian cricket writer and commentator, Dicky Rutnagar, covered the series for the *Hindustan Times*. He was enthralled by Kanhai's epic at Eden Gardens; and he drew the conclusion that Gupte had wilted under his 'punitive blade': 'The gaiety of the yuletide was distinctly present in the batting of Rohan Kanhai…[His] correct yet cocky innings was invaluable to his side, for besides providing such a large share of the total…it completely demoralised the Indian attack and nobody more than Gupte, so far the biggest thorn in the side of the West Indies batting'.[18]

But the other two men from Port Mourant also were outstanding. In that third Test in Calcutta, Butcher made 103, Solomon 69 not out. In the fourth Test, at Madras, Kanhai and Butcher were prolific again, scoring 99 (run out) and 142 respectively. Joe Solomon made 86 in the Kanpur Test and100 not out in New Delhi; he topped the batting averages (117.00). He recalls the innings in Delhi for another, no less significant, reason: it was watched by one of his heroes, who complimented him for the 'maturity' of his batting – Jawaharlal Nehru (accompanied by his friend, Lady Mountbatten). The *Hindu* described Solomon's century thus: 'With an excellent cover-drive for four and a well-run single, Solomon reached 100 – a feat which was well and truly acclaimed. It was a faultless knock, characterised by soundness in defence and good strokes…'[19] But it is his first Test match, in Kanpur, in mid-December 1958, that Joe cherishes most: West Indies, batting first and mesmerised by Gupte, were 76-5 when he came in, and soon 88-6, before he (45) and Alexander (70), put on 100 crucial runs for the seventh wicket. West Indies made 222, the innings when Gupte got 9 for 102; India responded with 222 as well. Sobers's 198 (run out) in the second innings and Joe's 86 (run out) contributed to their victory by 203 runs.[20]

Rohan's epic at Calcutta was the Indo-Guyanese gift to Mother India. It was a vindication that they had done well over the years – indeed, that the years had not been squandered. Joe Solomon recalls that India took Rohan to her heart: a gifted returning son. After his 256 in Calcutta, Kanhai was the recipient of an accolade that Indo-Guyanese could claim as a symbol of their progress as a whole in British Guiana: 'The President of India, Dr Rajendra Prasad, made a nice gesture presenting me with a stuffed tiger's

Port Mourant conquers 'Mother India': Kanhai (256) and Butcher (103) at Eden Gardens, Calcutta, 31 December 1958-1 January 1959

head in appreciation of what he called "a fine innings played in the right spirit"…I shipped the tiger's head home in a huge box and today it hangs proudly in my mother's home in British Guiana'.[21] The 'Tiger of Port Mourant', and the 'triumphant fall', Kanhai's unique shot, would become symbols of their own journey from the poverty of Mother India, to the 'logies', the former slave ranges on the plantation, and now towards the spaces of freedom being carved out by Kanhai, within the boundary, as well as by their political hero, Cheddi Jagan, beyond the boundary. 'What do they know of cricket who only cricket know?', asks C.L.R. James.

Ian McDonald, the Guyanese poet, tells a story that resonates with Indo-Guyanese; it helps us understand why, after Rohan Kanhai's 'epic at Calcutta', they virtually enthroned him amidst their pantheon of Gods. A senior Indo-Guyanese politician related it to Ian while on a visit to the Corentyne in 1955. This man had a brother who was a doctor; another was a famous lawyer; his sister was at university overseas. His father had started as a cane-cutter at Port Mourant; his grandfather was a 'bound coolie' from India. I first heard the powerful tale on the radio in Guyana, told by Ian thirty years later:

> When he was a boy, an old man, it may have been his grandfather, used to tell him about the time he came across the 'black water' from India. It seemed like months, if not years, the voyage lasted. And the one clear memory the old man had was that each night on the deck he looked at the stars blazing in the sky and gradually, as night succeeded night, his eyes, coached by the imagination, gradually picked out the shape of a tiger leaping in the sky amidst the constellations. That was what he recalled in the hardship and the monotony and the homesickness of the journey – a tiger leaping in the sky amid the stars. And he told it to his grandson and his grandson told it to me and during the Corentyne weekend traced himself for me that tiger-shape still blazing in the sky. And now at nights, at certain times of the year, I still look up and I think of the old man on his long voyage, and the generations who have done well after him, and it seems to me the tiger leaping in the stars must have become for him a sort of symbol of pride and strength and beauty which he could not then hope to possess but

> which perhaps he could yearn for in his new land one day. And it seems to me, also, that the generations have not misplaced the symbol or the old man's yearning.[22]

After India, the West Indies played three Tests in Pakistan. It was not a happy tour. Shortly before they entered Pakistan, their best bowler, Roy Gilchrist (1934-2001), whose pace was unconquerable against India (26 wickets at 16.11), was sent home because of irreconcilable problems with his captain, Gerry Alexander, stemming from his behaviour. Kanhai believes that the absence of Gilchrist, in conjunction with the coir matting on which two of the Tests were played, led to their defeat by 2-1. In their fast-medium bowler and captain, Fazal Mahmood (1927-2005), Pakistan had a marvellous exponent of bowling on the mat. The first and second Tests, in Karachi and Dacca, were played on the coir mat: Fazal got 19 for 224. West Indies won the final Test, in Lahore, by an innings and 156 runs. This was played on a conventional turf pitch; Fazal took 1 for 99 in West Indies only innings. Kanhai reflects on their defeat in Pakistan. Although he was not enamoured of the mat, he felt that the outcome could have been different: 'Gilly [Gilchrist] would have demoralised the Pakistanis in the same way as he did the Indians…[W]ithout Gilly, the combination of the mat and its master, Fazal Mahmood, was too much for us. I've never liked playing on matting wickets [pitches]. Although great care is taken in laying and taking up the mat nothing can prevent the soil underneath from loosening, causing bubbles on the coir surface. There are other problems. Bowling, for instance, becomes a different art. The mat extends beyond the wickets so…a bowler with a reasonably lengthy run-up, like Wes Hall, hits the mat in mid-stride and can be thrown out of his rhythm. Ordinary spikes, of course, cannot be worn for obvious reasons and the bowlers had to take the field in rubber-soled boots'.[23]

Kanhai clearly did not enjoy the mat. In Karachi and Dacca his scores were: 33, 12, 4 and 8. Butcher and Solomon fared better in Karachi: 45, 61 and 14, 66 respectively; but they, too, had succumbed to the mat at Dacca: 11, 8 and 0, 8 respectively. The West Indies manager on the tour of India and Pakistan was the Guyanese, Berkeley Gaskin (1908-79). He was unequivocal: '…coir matting wickets [pitches] in this year of grace, 1959, should be outlawed. This was mainly responsible for our defeat in the series against Pakistan'. As one who had supported the exclusion of Gilchrist from the tour, he did not reflect upon the implications of his absence. But the fact that Pakistan won the Dacca Test by only 41 runs (Fazal got 12 wickets for 100), lends credence to Kanhai's assertion that even with Fazal and his mat, the inclusion of the demon fast bowler Gilchrist, only 24 and at the peak of his powers, could have altered the results. Gerry Alexander, also, was not pleased that they had to play two Tests on matting, particularly the coir variety: 'We were not prepared for the particular type of matting on which we played. From the point of view of batting, it required a great deal or fair amount of luck to survive, and the matting did not permit free stroke-play. Apart from that we were up against Fazal Mahmood, a leg-cutter who could exploit these conditions more than, possibly, any other'.[24] Alexander, too, did not reflect upon Gilchrist's absence in Pakistan.

After West Indies were destroyed by Fazal at Dacca for a paltry 76, a sports editor in Guyana, Cedric Wiltshire, had referred to the 'putrid' performance of the batsmen against the 'babes of Test cricket': 'Perhaps it was the coir matting to which we were unaccustomed. Perhaps it was the Gilchrist incident'.[25] But the curator of the Bourda ground in British Guiana, 'Badge' Menzies, had no reservation in attributing West Indies woes against Fazal to the coir matting. He thought West Indies would have encountered no problems with the finer jute matting (used in Trinidad); it was the coarser coir that posed insurmountable problems for players accustomed to playing on turf.[26]

Alexander was, however, impressed with the consistency of Butcher and Solomon in India and Pakistan, and he expected them to continue to advance. He was, indeed, complimentary of all four of the Guyanese players: '...without exception, they performed well up to expectation. Both of Kanhai's double centuries [256 in Calcutta; 217 in Lahore] were beautiful to watch, a fact which undoubtedly stamps him as a classic player. Lance Gibbs did not get much opportunity in India, but in Pakistan he bowled extremely well'.[27] In the third Test in Lahore, the West Indies batsmen thrived. They made 469: Kanhai 217; Sobers 72; Solomon 56. Their victory by an innings was also attributable to their bowlers: Hall's 5 for 87 in the first innings, including the hat-trick; and in the second innings, Eric Atkinson's 3 for 15, Sonny Ramadhin's 4 for 25 and Lance Gibbs's 3 for 14. But it was Kanhai's double century that stole the accolades.

Kanhai's innings of 217 was watched by General Ayube Khan, the Pakistani President. A.H. Kardar, who captained Pakistan in the West Indies in 1958, was deeply moved by Kanhai's epic, a chanceless innings with 32 fours. He wrote:

> It is an innings that will live with us…It shall live with us as will its every stroke, each defensive forward and offensive back-foot stroke between mid-wicket and mid-on. It shall live in our memory as a reminder that in this age of cricketing prudence, indiscretions are as welcome as they are rare…Joined by Sobers [with the score at 38 for 2], Kanhai gave up the role of a back-bencher and took up arms like a lord setting his lands in order [an apt analogy in Pakistan]. In a partnership of 162 runs…Kanhai's batsmanship spoke of the thunder and told of the blood-shaking of his heart. The innings was existence itself and presence at the ground a privilege. This Kanhai-Sobers association…was cheered wildly all the while by a knowledgeable crowd. We were privileged to see two princely cricketers in artistic performance…Kanhai's was an innings to which all hearts – and the Lahore crowd always has a big heart for the visiting team – responded gaily…We…shall remember for a long time this masterly innings. It shall continue to shine with increasing brilliance and shall be remembered, reviewed and recreated whenever a Test is played at the Bagh-i-Jinnah ground.[28]

In June 1959, the editor of the *Nation*, in Trinidad, C.L.R. James, reproduced an article by India's Dicky Rutnagar from the *Playfair Annual* (England), in which he made an assessment of where he thought Kanhai had reached following the long tour of India and Pakistan in 1958-9. He was meticulous in demonstrating that the flamboyant play was now grounded in admirable technical competence, demonstrated in his application in mastering the formidable craft of Subhash Gupte, the versatile Indian leg-spinner. Rutnagar argued: 'Almost half of Kanhai's aggregate of 538 runs for the series came in one dashing innings, at Calcutta

[256], but this should not mislead one into thinking that Kanhai was not consistent. In fact, it is he who gave the first indications that Gupte could be mastered long before the series ended. Kanhai's nimble footwork always placed him well over the ball and he drove with consummate ease off the front foot. Getting his nose right down, he reached well forward to defend against the ball that held out the slightest threat of coming off the wicket awkwardly…'

And he was pleased, indeed, that Rohan's command of the basics did not inhibit his instinctive exuberance:

> If Kanhai did not leave India with a superior Test average, it was because he took far too many risks. Nothing seemed to curb the adventurer in Kanhai. At Kanpur he was out for a 'duck' in trying to sweep Gupte, and yet, in the second innings, he attempted the stroke within a few minutes of his arrival at the wicket. Surer fielding hands could have made Kanhai pay heavily for his exuberance in the early stages of his monumental innings at Calcutta, but he was absolutely irrepressible and scored at a rate which enabled the West Indies to finish the match before lunch on the fourth day. One is grateful that Kanhai, after the first two Tests against England, in 1957, was not persisted with as an opener, for the added responsibility would almost certainly have flattened the champagne that is Kanhai's batting.[29]

England toured the West Indies in early 1960. This was a sterner test than the subcontinental experience. Garry Sobers was magnificent as usual: an aggregate of 709 runs and another Olympian average: 101.28, with a highest score of 226. Frank Worrell, returning to Tests for the first time since 1957 (he was studying at Manchester University), had an average of 64.00; Hunte was third with 41.57. Kanhai was fourth, having scored 325 runs in the five Tests, with the 110 in Trinidad his best; his average was 40.62. The great strides made in India and Pakistan were somewhat faltering against England's fast bowlers in 1960, Trueman and Statham. He made two half-centuries and a six-and-a-half hour century, at Port of Spain, designed to chisel away at massive time. But the heroic resistance could not save his team from defeat by 256 runs. His two Port Mourant colleagues had an abysmal series. Butcher and Solomon played two Tests each and were dropped: Butcher scored 31 runs in three innings with an average of 10.33; Solomon was marginally better in four innings: 50 runs at an average of 16.66. Butcher would miss the tour of Australia in 1960-1 and not reappear until the summer of 1963 (at the age of nearly 30), in England. He was out of Test cricket for three years and four months. C.L.R. James had launched his campaign to get the West Indies captain, Gerry Alexander, replaced by, in his estimation, a vastly superior leader, Frank Worrell. Butcher's failure in the two Tests in 1960, with scores of 13 in Barbados and 9 in each innings (lbw b Statham in both) in Trinidad, had led James to question Alexander's ability to provide counsel to rectify the problems of a potentially first-rate batsman:

> [Butcher] was obviously mentally upset and unable (a) to wait; and (b) after waiting, to go through freely with his stroke. Butcher is a far finer player than his performances in the second Test would indicate. Here is where the knowledge and the authority of the captain come in. Frank Worrell could tell Butcher exactly what was wrong (his right foot is pointing too much to extra-cover and his elbow is out of place). Things like this happen to all batsmen at certain times, even the greatest. It was, it is Alexander's business to put Butcher right in the nets by having his fast bowlers bowl to him, standing behind and showing him what was wrong. Alexander cannot do this. He doesn't know. And even if he did, he hasn't the authority. Clyde Walcott [Butcher's coach in British Guiana] will have to put Butcher right. That is the mess we are in.[30]

The sole redeeming feature of the England tour of 1960 as far as the Port Mourant men were concerned was Kanhai's marathon 110, in his vain endeavour to save the second Test. With four Tests drawn, that victory by England proved to be decisive. Alan Ross, cricket correspondent of the *Observer*, had a small bouquet for Rohan's resistance that nearly secured a draw; he considered his innings a 'courageous' one, marked by 'correct, poised methods adorned by sudden scarlet spread of wings...'[31] It was essentially 'dogged, resourceful and finely calibrated'. The occasional 'spread of wings', particularly one over against Trueman described by

Ross, underlined that it was primarily a back-to-the-wall effort: 'Suddenly, without warning, Kanhai struck back at Trueman. He crashed him off the back foot to the long-off boundary, drove the next ball to the sightscreen, pulled him into the crowd at square leg. A glance and a place for two each made it...sixteen off the over'. But after the marathon, he gave it away, as was often the case: the flaw was ever lurking in the genius. Ross again: 'Kanhai off-drove Dexter to the Coca-Cola board [in his second over]. The third ball of his third over was a full toss on the leg-stump and Kanhai, hitting it hard but a shade early, saw it curve right to Smith at mid-wicket. He banged his bat in understandable irritation. This was the crucial wicket'.[32] The Test was lost.

MacDonald Dash, a Guyanese cricket correspondent, was so enchanted by Rohan's range of strokes, although subdued by circumstances, that he was drained of superlatives: 'They say that his 256 at Calcutta was a gem; this was a pearl. Kanhai was master of the cover-drive; master of the late-cut; he played superbly off the leg stump...[M]aybe I will never see another innings steeped in such majesty...'[33]

Kanhai was very proud of that innings; maybe, because it was uncharacteristic of his style he cherished it – another string to his bow. This is his recollection:

> England...declar[ed] with nine wickets down...leaving us 10 hours to make 501 for victory. It would have been easier to climb Everest in sandshoes. Being partial to a good fight I decided to put Kanhai the slasher into cold storage and play a subdued, back-to-the wall innings. Yes – I can do it if the occasion demands. Six-and-a-quarter hours I stayed at the wicket until the English bowlers had bitten their nails right down to the bone in exasperation. I made 110 painstaking runs in that time, but unfortunately my contribution failed to save us from a 256 runs defeat. Playing against the grain like that takes some will-power...[34]

C.L.R. James recognised the two dimensions, the marathon defensive play and the odd oasis of ferocious assault, around which the innings of 110 was constructed. His verdict on the lost Test was frank and sincere: '...the better side won...There is no question about that at all...[But] we saw one of the greatest innings ever played by a West Indies batsman, the innings of Kanhai. That is something we shall always remember'.[35] Like Dicky Rutnagar's observations on Rohan's defensive play at Calcutta, James was equally impressed by the technical foundation of the innings against a superior bowling attack (Trueman, Statham, David Allen, Rae Illingworth): 'I saw Kanhai stretching forward, almost overbalancing in order to place a sloping bat over the near half-volleys Illingworth was serving up to him. Kanhai was taking no chances and my respect for him was immensely increased by the restraint which he showed. The circumstances demanded it'. [36] James could not let Kanhai's innings pass, for a few weeks later he was still pondering on its merits: 'I would not exchange Kanhai for any batsman on the England side…[He] is a great batsman. In concentration, in defence and at the same time seizing every opportunity to make a succession of brilliant strokes, Kanhai in making 110, played one of the finest innings I have ever seen. And the best has not been seen of him yet'.[37]

Kanhai's epic at Calcutta would be repeated in Australia in 1960-1. This tour would release all the gifts that many knew were immanent in his cricketing brain. He was second in the Test averages (50.30), and had the highest aggregate in all matches: 1,093; he topped the first-class averages (64.29). Kanhai scored a century in each innings of the Adelaide Test and had a few other fine innings: one of 84 in a West Indies score of 181, in the second Test at Melbourne, encapsulated all Kanhai's maturing gifts. Bill O'Reilly, the great Australian leg-spinner of another age, watched the match. Kanhai was at the crease early, two wickets having fallen for one run:

> He dropped Davidson's hopes with a magnificent square-cut; followed immediately by a morale-busting on-drive which went straight back past the left-hander like a bullet. Benaud's spinners had no effect. Kanhai moved down the pitch and hit hard into the covers where he kept O'Neill and Harvey busier than they appreciated. Johnny Martin, bowling his left-handed off-spinners, had no hope of stopping the rhythm of Kanhai's on-side hitting…To rub in the obvious knowledge that he was in full control, he occasionally lofted the ball high to unpatrolled sections of the outfield. The volatile little batsman is a worrying problem

> for Australian bowlers. He constantly accepts the risks involved in hitting into the ball, but his bat moves at such unusual speed that even if he does mis-hit, the ball generally is bound to fall safely out of danger from the in-fieldsmen...Kanhai has become a commanding cricket personality in this country. One cannot fail to admire the courageous manner in which he accepts his batting responsibilities which he carries out with the confidence and pugnacity of a man who knows all the answers and is keen to reveal the fact.[38]

The Australians scored just as fast as the West Indians but the latter made the greater impact. With the series 1-1 after four Tests (one drawn; one tied), 90,800 went to the Melbourne Cricket Ground (MCG) on the Saturday of the final one. But, as Don Bradman recalled, it was the quality of the runs, the style, a magical flair that West Indians displayed time and again that captivated Australians on that tour: 'It is not only a question of speed of scoring or how many runs are hit. Personality comes into it. A batsman like Rohan Kanhai grips your interest. The sight of him winding up to hit with all his might stirs onlookers more than a boundary hit by an orthodox stroke'. John Priestley of the Melbourne *Herald* concluded: 'It was Kanhai who came to Australia with the reputation of not having the temperament to succeed in Test matches. Yet against the battle-hardened Australians he answered his critics with 503 runs in the Tests'.[39]

Jack Fingleton, the former Australian batsman and cricket writer of distinction, saw all of Kanhai's innings in Australia in 1960-1. At the end of the tour he reflected on his attitude to the game:

> He was a run-hungry young man and he knew how to go about building a big score. He seemed to hate bowlers, to hate the ball, and his whole being seemed to explode in spite as he got the stroke out of his electrified system. He hit so hard to leg that often he fell over in the middle of his stroke and once, in his 252 [against Victoria at Melbourne], hit a perfect sweep when prone on the ground [the first time he played 'the triumphant fall'?]. Even so early as Melbourne, Kanhai had his own ideas who was the best batsman not only in the West Indian side but in both sides. His bat flashed like his dark eyes....If not faster, Kanhai was at least as fast

> as Don Bradman between the wickets – and that is praise indeed… Sobers was the batting star of the early part of the tour; Kanhai undoubtedly was so in the later games and often as I watched him, particularly when he made his two centuries at Adelaide, I thought I was watching the best batsman in the world. Undoubtedly I knew that in Kanhai I was watching the world's best fieldsman, so fast was he in running, gathering and in straight throwing…He is a batsman of dynamite, probably over-anxious to light an immediate fuse against the best bowlers without working up to it. He got himself out more often than the bowlers did.[40]

Richie Benaud, the Australian captain in 1960-1, while recognising Sobers as the best all-rounder in the world even then, gave Kanhai the edge as a batsman on that tour:

> One of the great players to come from the West Indies since the three W's were in full cry is Rohan Kanhai who is a complete individualist with the bat but at the same time, when the bowler is good enough, is a highly orthodox batsman. In defence he is very straight and if he has a weakness it is that he sometimes chooses the wrong ball to attack – a ball that a batsman of lesser confidence would play with the greatest care. He was virtually unknown when he came to England in 1957…but although much was expected of him he was unable to live up to the talk that had preceded the team. But it was after this tour that he really began to make a name in world batting lists, and by the time he came to Australia in 1960-1 to play on a series of good batting pitches he was reckoned to be one of the best players in the world. By the time the tour was over there were many in Australia who listed him as the best…When West Indies came to Australia there was something of a battle between Sobers and Kanhai to decide the world's best batsman, and it says much for Kanhai that…I thought he just shaded Sobers in that series.[41]

Benaud explained the basis of his judgement several years later, towards the end of the decade of the 1960s: 'The most vital point about his batting is his ability, like Sobers, to hit not only the bad ball for four but also the one the bowler considers to be a good delivery. An example of the bad ball is the full toss I bowled to him first ball after lunch in Adelaide – he hit it for six from around ankle height when most batsmen would have been having a sighter and pushing it past mid-on for two. There were plenty of good deliveries that series that went flashing to the boundary, deliveries from Davidson, myself, Meckiff, Martin and Kline, and at team meetings before and after each Test match, one of the main points of discussion would be "whether or not it was possible to keep Kanhai quiet". The best way we found of keeping him quiet was to attack and try and get him out because when he is in the mood I doubt whether there is any bowler who could keep him quiet by defensive means…I will defy anyone to produce a more exciting cricketer when things are running for him. Sobers is one of the most brilliant in the world and Kanhai loses nothing by comparison…His play, I am certain, must be along the lines of Bradman but Bradman allied consistency to devastation…'[42]

This abundance of talent permeated Kanhai's batting in the controversially drawn fourth Test at Adelaide, between 27 January and 1 February 1961. Benaud dismissed him in both innings, but Rohan's scores were 117 and 115. The young master at work made a fine impression on Percy Beames of the Melbourne *Age*. The following are excerpts from his report on Kanhai's 117. The first wicket (Conrad Hunte) fell on 12; Kanhai then came to the wicket: 'What the Australian bowlers had feared in each Test took place today, with Kanhai cutting loose…The brilliant 25 year old stroke-player quickly settled in…The greatness of this atomic-hitting player was demonstrated time and again as he brilliantly hit fours from balls that normally would have commanded respect. Kanhai's batting when turned on at full pressure, is given an even greater ruthlessness because he is so willing to hit the ball high and hard into the air to defeat close-in fieldsmen…'[43]

Lindsay Kline, the slow left-arm chinaman bowler, ended his Test career with a brilliant economy rate of 1.96, but he had encountered Kanhai on one of 'his most fearsome days'. He was therefore forced into a very defensive mode, yet his figures for that innings were: 21 overs, 3 maidens, 109 runs, 0 wicket. But even the vastly experienced Benaud had to endure the insuperable Kanhai: 'batting with the touch of brilliance shown in making 252 against Victoria, he sailed into Benaud's first 14 balls so enthusiastically that he collected 18 out of 19 runs'.[44] Cammie Smith's wicket fell at 83 and Garry Sobers (bowled Benaud 1) at 91. Rohan, joined by his imperturbable and reassuring captain, Frank Worrell, could not be contained. They had a fourth wicket partnership of 107 in 72 minutes. Percy Beames reported:

> But Kanhai, with his blazing fireworks, and helped by quiet, methodical support from Worrell, soon burst the bubble of Australian jubilation. The bowler the two West Indies batsmen began to carve up was Lindsay Kline. Kanhai who had moved past his half century in 73 minutes, with five 4's and one 6, three times crashed Kline for boundaries. [At lunch on the first day of the Test, West Indies were 133 for 3: Kanhai 76 not out; Worrell 15 not out.] In the first over on resumption, Kanhai lifted a no-ball from [Des] Hoare over the mid-on boundary, then followed it up by cracking boundaries off Benaud and Kline. Twenty minutes after lunch he moved on to his century. It was a glorious effort in which he had proved his brilliance with equal facility against both spin and speed. His century had taken 126 minutes and included 14 fours and two 6's. Kanhai went on to 117 before Benaud ended the batting massacre by having him caught at first slip [by Bobby Simpson]…The West Indies captain [Worrell] was never able to match Kanhai's versatility or power of stroke-play, but he hit the ball with his usual confident touch.[45]

Yet Kanhai was 'bitterly disappointed' with the outcome of this Test to which he had made such an emphatic contribution: it ended in a draw. Set an improbable task – 460 to win – Australia were 207 for 9, with an hour and 50 minutes left in the match. Kanhai and the other West Indian players were certain that Sobers, fielding at silly mid-off, had taken the catch to dismiss Ken Mackay. They were all walking off: the Test had been won; they were going 2-1 up in the series. Not so! Mackay refused to move, and when, belatedly, the West Indians appealed to the umpire, Colin Egar, he turned it down. Mackay and Kline then proceeded to bat to the end thus achieving a draw. Kanhai was unequivocal and angry: 'Now this was never a bump ball and everyone knew it except Egar and Mackay. Sobers and Hall, who had been fielding close at silly mid-on, and the others swore afterwards that it was a straightforward catch. No doubt Mackay and Egar acted sincerely but they were wrong. Even the rest of the Aussie players watching from the pavilion thought it was all over'.[46] But Ken Mackay would never concede that he was caught by Sobers. In 1961-2 Wes Hall played for Queensland in the Sheffield Shield; one of his team-mates was Ken Mackay, yet Wes could never get him to admit that he was caught by Sobers: 'I was fielding at silly mid-on and was convinced it was not a bump ball; but with over an hour to play we felt we had plenty of time to shift…[Mackay or Kline]. A year later, during my stay in Queensland, I repeatedly ribbed Ken with the words: "Come on Slash, you can admit it now. You know you were out". "No, Wes", he would reply solemnly. "If I thought I was out I would have walked. I was sure it had hit the ground, so I stayed and let the umpire give his decision"'.[47]

It is noteworthy that in his book, *Willow Patterns*, Benaud gives three pages to this controversial Test[48], but not a word on the incident that would have virtually given the West Indies the series. It was tied at 1-1, after four Tests. (The final Test, in Melbourne, was won narrowly by Australia, by 2 wickets, amidst suggestions of a potentially decisive decision again going against the West Indies, as another climactic match oscillated to its end.) Even the respected Australian commentator, Johnnie Moyes, dismisses the unanimity of perception by the West Indies cricketers, as well as the consensus of several English cricket writers of vast experience, such as John Woodcock of the *Times*, that Mackay was out at Adelaide.

In his 'critical study of the tour' of 1960-1, Johnnie Moyes attributed Australia's survival from the brink to poor tactics by the West Indies:

> The last part of the story is simply told. Mackay and Kline stayed until six o'clock and Australia gained a draw. Every bowler was tried, some of them two or three times. They hurried through their overs, far too quickly as a matter of fact because two well-conceived overs are better than two bowled in haste. Now and again the ball went into the air, but it fell safely though there was *a sensation of a kind* when Mackay played forward to Worrell, Sobers grabbed the ball, and he and others began to walk off the field.

> Mackay stood firm and went on chewing his gum. This brought an appeal which Umpire Egar promptly rejected...[emphasis added][49]

Moyes then accuses the English journalists of partisanship against Australia, although they were in no position to assess the merits of the West Indian claim that they had caught Mackay. He considers the integrity of Mackay and Egar unimpeachable:

> [T]he Mackay incident hit the headlines when some visiting English writers didn't hesitate to question the umpire's decision. They were 'convinced' that Mackay was out and that the West Indies had been robbed of victory by an Australian umpire. I haven't any doubt that some of the West Indies players thought that Mackay was out. I also haven't any doubt that this fine man was satisfied that he was not, and that the umpire was also perfectly certain on the point. Mackay is too well known in Australian cricket for anyone to doubt his integrity and Umpire Egar in his first season had gained golden opinions. The one man who was stationary during the incident was the umpire. He had a clear view from about 20 yards away. The English writers were some 70 yards or so away at square leg, and for them to express an unqualified opinion was sheer impertinence.[50]

He asserts that he was better placed than them (being a radio commentator), behind the wicket, yet he could not arrive at a conclusive judgment on Sobers's claim to have caught Mackay: 'It would not have been so bad if the writers had expressed the view of the West Indians – if given for publication [such things were not done during tours] – and had also said something favourable to Mackay and Egar; as it was the whole thing left a nasty taste in people's mouth, though we had previously had occasion to resent and deplore outburst from some of the same writers when they were in Australia with Peter May's team [in 1958-9]'.[51] Principal among the English journalists Moyes was reproaching was John Woodcock of the *Times*. Shortly after the tied Test, in December 1960, Woodcock had characterised the tortoise-like play of the man at the centre of the Adelaide controversy, ironically dubbed 'Slasher', thus: '...as a Test cricketer Mackay is evidently as immutable as the central Australian desert and equally indifferent to the passage of time'. His strokes were described somewhat inelegantly: 'dabbing, prodding, chopping'.[52] With regard to the controversial incident at Adelaide, Woodcock had no reservations about the legitimacy of Sobers's claim that he had taken the catch to win the match:

> Mackay pushed forward to a ball from Worrell, and Sobers, one of the most active close to the wicket fieldsmen in the world, caught it at silly mid-off, four yards from the bat. The West Indies to a man thought Mackay was out. Those of them who were close to the wicket began to leave the pitch...But the umpire thought differently. Without consulting his colleague he ruled that Mackay was not out, apparently on ground that it was a bump ball. Some West Indians will believe till their dying day that Sobers in fact caught Mackay then and won the match. The scorebook, however, does not support their views.[53]

It was a measure of the sportsmanship and dignified leadership of Frank Worrell – some spoke of his statesmanship on that tour – that he responded to what was a heart-rending experience, after their failure to remove Mackay and Kline in the remaining110 minutes, with equanimity and humour. Woodcock observed: 'Worrell took the disappointment with magnificent calm and gaiety, sitting in the dressing room laughing about the misfortunes of the day and suggesting that there should be a sixth Test, to be played in Honolulu'.[54] One could conjecture that he was alluding to the possibility that Hawaiians were more adept at distinguishing a genuine catch from a bump ball. Given the character of Worrell, however, such an interpretation would have been unwarranted.

Nevertheless it is important to note that in Kanhai's second century of the controversial match, Johnnie Moyes had detected even greater virtues than in the first one, because it had a discernibly better technical foundation. He observes: 'Anything not exactly right in length or direction was punished relentlessly by this little man who varied things a fraction by hitting a ball from Mackay over the head of extra cover for four runs. Then he turned his attention to Benaud and took two more fours, one to fine leg and the other between mid-off and extra cover, a stroke of real beauty. He had 53 in an hour and this was finer cricket than in the first innings because his technique was more adequate'.[55] Moyes deemed Rohan 'an impertinent little player, cheeky, possessing tremendous natural gifts. We enjoyed his batsmanship so much, the most gifted player to visit Australia in many years...In the field [also] Kanhai was often dazzling, as when he caught Simpson at Sydney and...when he threw McDonald out at Adelaide. Quick to the ball he had a lovely swift throw'.[56] As a commentator on ABC Radio, being beamed ball-by-ball to the West Indies, Moyes's assessment of Kanhai as the tour progressed, was familiar to many Indo-Guyanese. His sentiments were certainly congruent with their feelings about the 'Tiger of Port Mourant', by the end of the tour in February 1961. He concluded:

> Kanhai will long be remembered in Australia. When he arrived, he had nothing like the reputation of Sobers but, by the time he left these shores, he had firmly established himself in the hearts of all who love scintillating batsmanship. This little man who sometimes reminded us of Macartney – that is no light praise – had such superb natural skill. He had the ability to please. Like Macartney he was never prepared to allow the bowler to call the tune and so he had a grand tour, with more than 1,000 runs and a century in each innings at Adelaide setting the seal on his fame. All in all he was far more consistent than Sobers. He always seemed to me to handle spin bowling with greater skill and, judging him on his form and performances in Australia, he was certainly a finer batsman and a greater menace than his left-handed colleague, who was too spasmodic in his brilliance.[57]

This was judgement of the highest order from one who was the voice of Australian cricket in the age of the radio: the John Arlott down under. To compare Rohan Kanhai with C.G. Macartney (1886-1958), the New South Wales and Australian batsman who played 35 Tests between 1907 and 1926, was 'no light praise', indeed. Moyes's cherished impressions of Macartney were well-known. In his book of pen-portraits, *A Century of Cricketers*, he was perceptive and assured in assessing the merits of the legendary batsman: 'In the pavilion at Chatswood Oval, Sydney, there hangs a photograph of a cricketer, standing erect with bat raised, who glares defiantly from under the peak of his cap as though daring the bowler to do his worst. It depicts to the life Charlie Macartney's outlook on the game, for no more impertinent [the same word he reserved for Kanhai] batsman than Macartney ever lived...[He] was a genius that brooked no opposition. There was no bowler to whom he would pay deference: even the mighty [Sydney] Barnes [1873-1967], greatest of all English bowlers, could not daunt his spirit'.[58] The latter, a fast-medium bowler, played only 27 Tests for England, between 1901 and 1914, but he got 189 wickets at an average of 16.43. Moyes considered him the best English bowler he had ever seen.

At the start of the tour, in November 1960, the Trinidadian journalist, Michael Gibbes, had remarked on what he considered the peculiarity of West Indian batsmanship: '[It] has a glorious heritage. The current tour reinforces the conviction that our star performers possess the distinguishing mark of the truly great – never to be merely content with the dry bones of batsmanship, but to be ever seeking to put flesh on those bones by way of audacious (even improvised) stroke-play, and an uncommon quickness of eye, flexibility of wrist, a quick-silver quality of footwork, that carries the challenge to the bowler'. Rohan Kanhai, in the eyes of most West Indians, possessed all these attributes. He had arrived; and he was carrying his Indo-Guyanese devotees as well with him.[59]

On the eve of the West Indies tour of Australia, Neville Cardus had expressed hope that Test cricket could be lifted out of the doldrums (into which many believed it had sunk), by the 'style and brilliance' of stroke-players such as Sobers, Worrell and Kanhai. He was prophetic: 'Things crucial to the immediate future of the game could happen in the Tests'.[60] At the end of the tour in early 1961, he was a very satisfied man in his measure of the West Indian achievement, but he lamented the paucity of their spirit of play in English cricket of the early 1960s:

> The rubber between Australia and the West Indies this winter [1960-1] will be long remembered, not because it was won or lost by one side or the other, but because it revived Test cricket. A few months ago, a mere mention of Test matches provoked a yawn, threatening lockjaw. The superb play of the West Indies against an Australian XI, which only the other year [1958-9] wiped the floor with England on Australian wickets, has put new life and

> new hopes into the future of cricket...Often the West Indies plundered Australia's bowling to the extent of five runs an over...Last autumn I forecast a hard struggle when the West Indies went into action on Australian cricket fields. But I did not dream that the West Indies batsmen could produce a range and brilliance of strokes unsurpassed even by Bradman, May, Compton, or any other cricketer.

However, Cardus could not look to England for more sunshine in the summer of 1961, during the Australian tour:

> It is now up to England to ensure that in the coming rubber, Test cricket is not allowed to drop back into the old familiar doldrums. But frankly, I cannot hope to see England cricketers of post-1945 training giving us anything like the stroke-play of the West Indies artists. Most English batsmen play from a rooted background...A sort of palsy, a miasma of self-doubt, seems invariably to fall over an England innings. Even born stroke-players in the English team are reduced to tentative pushers and pokers in a Test match...The West Indies have exposed the deficiencies in Australia's cricket resources...[They] are lucky to have genius in their ranks – Sobers, Kanhai, Worrell.[61]

It is comprehensible, therefore, why Indo-Guyanese worshipped Rohan Kanhai even more after that tour of Australia. They needed no persuasion that he was the greatest batsman in the world. No debate was necessary. They brooked no arguments to the contrary. The commentaries were carried all night on local radio in British Guiana, in 1960-1; we all listened to Johnnie Moyes and Alan McGillivray – all night. And Rohan's peculiar stroke, a cross between a pull and a hook that invariably brought him flat on his back as the ball disappeared into the crowd on the backward-square boundary – what Sir Neville Cardus memorably christened the 'triumphant fall' – accompanied by the hauntingly beautiful clapping of white Australian hands, the magic accentuated by the palpable remoteness, the crackling of the air-waves, made Indo-Guyanese feel that they mattered. Little boys would attempt to play the 'triumphant fall', although they had never witnessed its execution. And as the solid darkness claimed the villages, big men and little boys would continue, late into the night, talking about the great man from Port Mourant. He was at the centre of their lives; but they could not see that they had actually elevated the man into the pantheon of Hindu gods. Little boys would crudely extract pictures of Kanhai from the *Argosy*, the *Chronicle* or the *Graphic* and casually paste them amidst the framed pictures of Hindu deities on the walls of their homes. And each morning, as their mothers communed with the gods, burning incense, sprinkling fresh water and reverently placing flowers on these pictures, Kanhai, caught among Shiva, Krishna and Hanuman, received obeisance from Indian women in British Guiana.

Joe Solomon was always in the shadow of Rohan Kanhai, but as V.S. Naipaul observed, the people of Plantation Port Mourant, which he visited with Cheddi Jagan in early 1961, were extremely proud of their cricketers, as they were of Cheddi. The heroic feat of Solomon, who had hit the stumps side-on, from square-leg, with the second last ball of the match, to run out Ian Meckiff in Brisbane in December 1960, thus producing that first tied Test, was still fresh in their memories. Naipaul was not allowed to forget the magical moment:

> Port Mourant is a sugar-cane estate of flat, hideous vastness, miles long and miles deep. The people are proud of the vastness, and believe that Port Mourant produce the finest Guianese. They are only slightly less proud of their cricketers than they are of Dr Jagan. The house of Joe Solomon, who miraculously threw down the last Australian wicket in the tied Test at Melbourne [Brisbane], was pointed out to me more than once by people who had known Solomon ever since he was a boy.[62]

As early as 1956, in the British Guiana match against Jamaica, in which four Guyanese scored centuries, their captain, Clyde Walcott, had discerned Joe's peculiar place among the titans – the man for a crisis:

> British Guiana had been in the cricket doldrums for some time, and was in theory still the weakest of the colonies…We won the toss and scored over six hundred in our first innings [601 for 5]. Four of our batsmen scored centuries: Bruce Pairaudeau [111]

> and three sugar estate players – Rohan Kanhai [129], Basil Butcher [154 not out], and Joe Solomon [114] – whose coaching had been largely in my hands. This was one of the most pleasing things of all. Not only had these players reached three figures, but they did it in an utterly convincing way, and looked mature and confident in the process. Pairaudeau, Kanhai and Butcher had the ability to excel…but Solomon had less natural ability, so deserved more credit for his innings. His shots, by West Indies standards, are extremely limited, and his innings was a fine example of concentration and what I can only describe as 'guts'…[Against Barbados, a few days later,] [o]ut of a total of nearly six hundred [581] Rohan Kanhai [195 run out] excelled his previous innings…Joe Solomon played his dogged, immensely valuable part with another hundred [108]…[63]

A little over ten years ago Joe told me of the fundamental difference in style between Rohan and himself: 'Rohan was an aggressive player…flamboyant, full of flair that took you to the edge…I was quiet…He was born aggressive and it came out in his cricket. He respected no bowler…I often had to struggle against the great bowlers. I think you cherish it more when you struggle for it'.[64] Joe Solomon played 27 Tests and his average was only 34, with one century and nine half-centuries; but it was the solidity of his approach that had endeared him to his hero, Frank Worrell: Joe played in 14 of the 15 Tests captained by him. In Worrell's scheme Joe had a crucial role to play in the lower order, at no. 6 or even 7 (following the great stroke-makers), eking out a crucial 70 or 80 runs with the bowlers – in an age when lack of pretensions to batsmanship by bowlers was tolerated. As J.S. Barker once said of Joe, he was 'the best maker of 60 in the business'.[65] Alan Ross phrased his steadying hand in the lower order more elegantly: 'comfortable intractability'.[66]

Joe says that Worrell was not one for histrionics although he was elegant in most things. He did not believe in exaggerated celebrations when a batsman was dismissed, even when a big partnership was broken or a prized wicket taken early. He knew that there were still wickets to be fought for; the job was not done; the focus should not slip because, often, complacency allowed mediocre batsmen to add valuable runs. Worrell was always at ease: rational. Joe is of the same temperament: unflappable and in control of his emotions. He believes that Frank recognised and appreciated those qualities in him, judging them as being congruent with the approach he expected him to adopt in shepherding the bowlers to garner every possible run late in the innings. Joe adds that Worrell would often counsel them to expect long partnerships from their opponents from time to time. It is in the nature of things. It was for them to take adversity in stride, control their emotions, maintain focus on the task and strive to complete the job.[67]

Worrell saw Solomon's role as a stabiliser in a team of wonderful stroke-makers. But it is primarily for that magical throw at Brisbane, on 14 December 1960, for which Joe will be remembered. It is therefore entirely appropriate that I reproduce the Australian captain's version of that monumental moment. Richie Benaud writes:

> The game was tied with two balls to go! One run to win...and last man Kline joined Meckiff. Hall bounded in to bowl the second last ball of the match to Kline. He knew he must be deadly accurate...[T]he only way to prevent the batsmen getting the run that would mean victory for Australia was to bowl at the stumps...to spread-eagle them if possible. There was not much sound in the ground at that moment, and even less as Hall let the ball go. It pitched in line with the middle and leg stumps and Kline played it with the full face of the bat to forward square-leg. The crowd screamed as the two batsmen set off for the winning run. They crossed as Joe Solomon was just about to gather it in both hands...[H]e picked up as Meckiff got within about six yards of the safety of the crease. Solomon, the quiet one...good and dependable...the sort of man for a crisis! Was there ever a more crisis-like moment in a game of cricket than this? There sure could never have been a better throw. The ball hit the stumps from the side-on with Meckiff scrambling desperately for the crease. Umpire Hoy's finger shot to the sky...A TIE...the first in Test history.[68]

An Australians victory seemed a formality, at 226 for 6; but with 8 runs required, Joe had run out Alan Davidson for 80, with a direct hit, which Garry Sobers describes as 'a match-saving piece of fielding brilliance'. That was followed by a miraculous piece of

Joe Solomon: the immaculate throw that tied the Test at Brisbane, 14 December 1960: 'Solomon is one of the few of…[Worrell's] colleagues who share his calm…' [John Woodcock, 1961]

fielding on the boundary and a magnificent return, from deep mid-wicket 90 yards away, by Conrad Hunte to wicket-keeper Gerry Alexander, to run out Wally Grout, with the scores tied: 232-9. Then came Solomon's moment of magic! Sobers recalls Joe's second direct hit, to run out Meckiff thus achieving the first tie in Test cricket:

> ...the scores were tied with the Aussies on 232 for 9. They needed one run from the last two balls to win as their last man, Lindsay Kline, joined Meckiff...Frank again went over to the excited Wes Hall and this time said to him: 'If I move Solomon [at square leg] two steps to his right and then two back to his left, the field will remain the same but the batsman will not know what I have done'. It may have looked meaningless to the spectators, but he was cleverly sowing the seeds of doubt in the minds of the batsmen. He also reminded Wes he would never be able to go home to the West Indies, never mind Barbados, if he bowled a no-ball. When Wes let it go [the second-last ball of the match], in that heady atmosphere, I prayed that if the ball came to me at leg slip, it would be in the air and not on the ground; but Lindsay Kline played it off his legs towards square leg and set off for the winning run. Meckiff hesitated just a fraction and that was enough for the deadly Solomon to run him out.[69]

Sobers concedes he was relieved that he was not in Solomon's position: 'I don't think I would have hit the stumps in those circumstances. They picked the wrong man – there was no one better than Joe and even though he could see just one stump, he threw the wicket down with Meckiff diving full length and only just failing to make his ground'.[70] No wonder when Joe was given out in the next Test (hit wicket b Benaud 4), in Melbourne, after his cap fell on the wicket and dislodged a bail, 67,000 Australians booed Benaud, who was bowling to him at the time of the appeal. 'Johnnie' Moyes, the veteran Australian writer and commentator, took an officious stance on the matter, but the masses were on the side of Joe on this occasion, having fallen already for the ebullient spirit of West Indian play, under Frank Worrell – 'apostles of a new look in cricket' (Moyes): 'Little Solomon...dropped his cap on the wicket while playing a stroke and the off bail fell to the ground.

Grout could be seen pointing to it and umpire Hoy gave the batsman out "hit wicket" as, under the Law, he was bound to do…The crowd, many of whom had doubtless not watched cricket except on public holidays and did not know the Laws, took the decision very much to heart and booed Benaud in a manner which was not only unjust, but was almost entirely without reason. Whenever he started to bowl the yelling would continue and not for some time did the unruly mob cease the turbulence. It was a nasty scene and most discreditable'.[71]

Moyes's final verdict on Solomon, whose average in the Tests was only 27.77, grasped his centrality in a team of gifted strokemakers: his solidity in the lower order, as well as his fine fielding:

> The little man was one of those honest craftsmen with unlimited patience. He was not blessed with many strokes although at times he produced some very good ones, his value lying in the fact that the situation of the game didn't worry him, nor did the reputation of the bowler. An obdurate soul, he was an ideal man half-way down the list, someone who knew his limitations, would in general not go beyond them – once or twice he did when sent in first – and a good man to stay while a more brilliant player got among the runs. This happened at Brisbane, where Solomon made 65 [hit wicket] and 47 and helped materially in building up the total both times. Then at Melbourne he was sent in first. It didn't work out [he scored 0 and 4 ('hit wicket' – with cap)], and in subsequent Tests he was back at the old address. Twice in the series he was out 'hit wicket' and in the fifth Test he was twice run out [for 45 and 36], a lot of excitement for such a quiet chap. This handy player was also a fine field and he will never be forgotten when the story of the 'tie' is retold, as he threw out Davidson who looked like winning the game for Australia, and then knocked down the stumps with the scores level. His place in history is assured.[72]

John Woodcock, as usual, saw things that eluded even seasoned writers and observers of the game. He discerned the chemistry between Frank Worrell and Joe Solomon, as early as the first Test captained by Frank Worrell, the tied Test. In that match both Frank and Joe made significant scores in both innings: Worrell 65 (c Grout b Davidson) and 65 (c Grout b Davidson); Solomon 65

Worrell's exceedingly popular team in Australia, 1960-1 – two from Port Mourant: Kanhai and Solomon (front row, centre); on Kanhai's right is Conrad Hunte and on Solomon's left is Seymour Nurse. Worrell is seated between Kanhai and Solomon (second row)

(hit wicket b Simpson) and 47 (lbw b Simpson). Australia's lead of 52 in the first innings had assumed ominous proportions when West Indies lost their fourth wicket in the second innings (Rohan Kanhai for 54) to an irresponsible stroke. As in the first innings, Kanhai drove outside the off-stump at a Davidson away-swinger and was caught by wicket-keeper Grout. Woodcock observed that with the match swinging perilously away from them, no West Indian should have 'found it physically possible' to execute Rohan's reckless stroke. He noted, however, that Worrell and his faithful disciple, Solomon, grasped the gravity of the situation and proceeded to construct a partnership of 83, 'with infinite care, like men dismantling a bomb'. Woodcock has left a perceptive observation that explains why Solomon played in 14 of the 15 Tests captained by Worrell; it underlines his gift of equanimity however testing the circumstances. In a team of brilliant, but often mercurial, men, Joe's 'comfortable intractability' was indispensable to Frank's conception of the unity of the whole:

> Worrell...conducted himself, in a critical situation, with all the experience and technical dexterity at his command...[He] is the world's most imperturbable batsman. He never pulls his cap or fiddles with his pads; he remains in all circumstances calm, dignified and polite. Once today he smiled when he was in the middle of coming down on a Davidson yorker. If he could distribute some of his composure to his men, he could have a much more effective team under his command. *Solomon is one of the few of his colleagues who shares his calm, and Worrell could not have had a better partner.* Solomon, indeed, his sleeves rolled down, smiling all the while, all afternoon, played Benaud...with notable skill, never allowing himself a rash stroke [emphasis add].[73]

J.S. Barker, the journalist with a fount of admiration for the West Indian style, was perceptive enough to detect Worrell's wisdom in bringing the prosaic Solomon into the pantheon of stars in his firmament; so did Benaud. Barker recalls: 'Solomon...Richie Benaud had told me in Australia, would be the first man he would prefer to bowl to last. Neat, unflurried pushes, a dab here, a touch there, and an occasional authentic flash of aggression...Solomon is never other than almost detachedly calm and coolly efficient in everything he does, on and off the field'.[74] In Joe's final Test series, against Australia in 1965, he made a vital 76 in the first Test in Jamaica that was crucial to West Indies victory. In the next Test in Trinidad he made 31 not out and 48. Richie Benaud had remarked on the latter as a measure of Joe's true value in the West Indies team of the early 1960s: 'The best stroke-play of the day came from the self-effacing Solomon, after the crowd had slow-handclapped him…Solomon's driving and forcing off his pads was a delight to watch, and I reflected again what a valuable performer this little man had been for the West Indies'.[75]

Although most Indo-Guyanese put Rohan Kanhai on a pedestal – they, but only they, could boo him when he failed – they were quietly proud of Joe's unprepossessing manner, his good manners, his remaining close to his roots although he had reached the pinnacle and dined with eminent people all over the world. It was frequently told how he met the great Jawaharlal Nehru after the fifth Test match in Delhi in February 1959, when Joe made his only Test century. Moreover, Nehru allegedly had put his hand around his shoulder and complimented him thus: 'My son, I admire the way you fought for the runs. I admire your strength of character'. Rohan had taken Indo-Guyanese to Everest; he made them feel they had earned the right to belong to the West Indies; but Joe's calmness, accessibility (he was a coach on Walcott's team on the sugar estates) and humility spoke of imperishable values, incorruptible by success and fame. Joe's conduct seemed to epitomise unchanging Indian values.

By the early 1960s Indo-Guyanese had arrived, and they owed it to their two heroes from Port Mourant: Kanhai and Cheddi Jagan; but Joe Solomon, too, was there somewhere. He kept his place in Worrell's highly respected team, less triumphantly than Rohan – unobtrusively. Indo-Guyanese thought they were on the 'threshold' of independence. Little could they surmise that their world would soon be turned upside-down; that Jagan's belief in communism and his declared support for Fidel Castro, after 1960, would precipitate an obsession by President Kennedy that Guyana must not become independent under Jagan. However, Jagan still had a chance to redeem himself, in the aftermath of the Bay of Pigs debacle of April 1961, when he met Kennedy on 25 October that year. But he left the President with no doubt that he was a communist and that

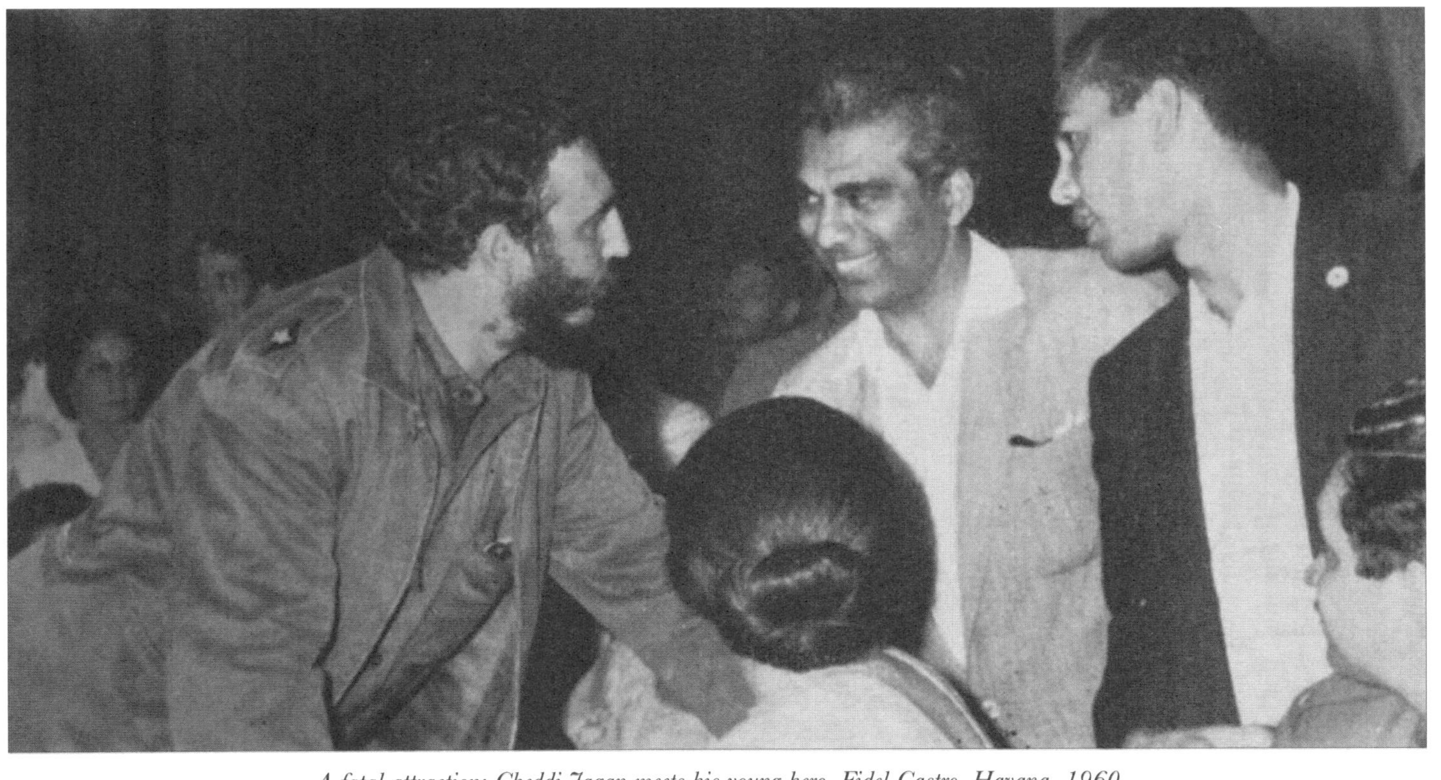

A fatal attraction: Cheddi Jagan meets his young hero, Fidel Castro, Havana, 1960

America's security would be jeopardised if he were to rule an independent Guyana. The CIA soon became enmeshed in the internal affairs of the colony, assisting the predominantly African-led People's National Congress of Forbes Burnham and the rabidly anti-communist United Force of Peter D'Aguiar (a Portuguese businessman), in 1962-3, to foment a campaign of terror against Jagan's government in order to make the place ungovernable. Jagan was mortally wounded. Thus was Kennedy emboldened to pressure the British government personally, in 1963, to change the electoral system to proportional representation, in order to secure the defeat of Jagan. Although the Macmillan government resisted for some time, they eventually caved in. Cary Fraser argues that 'British collaboration with the United States represented...recognition that its colonies were passing into the American sphere of influence in the Caribbean. For the Americans, the campaign against the PPP reflected policy driven by a fear of ideological pluralism in the Caribbean and the traumatic effect of the Cuban Revolution upon American policy-makers. The [local] anti-PPP forces...exploited the growing influence of the Americans and the American fear of the PPP to full advantage'.[76] By early 1964 Jagan was aware that he had virtually seized defeat from the jaws of victory. He resorted to his own phase of terrorism as he belatedly sought to force the British to reverse their decision. It was utterly futile. Burnham, in a coalition with D'Aguiar, would lead Guyana to independence in 1966.[77]

Indo-Guyanese political aspirations, which seemed so secure in late 1961, after Jagan's victory at the polls in August, were ruined by Jagan's lack of imagination, his sleepwalking Guyana into the Cold War on the side of Castro. Now it was the mastery of Kanhai in England in 1963, his unsullied excellence, which sustained many Indo-Guyanese as they impotently surveyed the decline of Jagan. They lived through their master batsman's ebullience and seductive flair. Kanhai's batting became a catharsis for their depleted sense of purpose and receding vision. It could shoulder that burden – although he could not – because his style was infused with a profoundly West Indian spirit, the character of his art having been recognised by all West Indians. His explosiveness was theirs; it compensated for their cowering before Burnhamite terror and the CIA-funded general strike of 1963 that brought Jagan virtually to his knees. The 'Tiger of Port Mourant' did not score a century in the Tests but he had the highest aggregate of 497 at an average of 55.22; only Conrad Hunte did better. But the quality of his play, the mature elegance and the continual flirting with danger that were so exhilarating, sustained the fascination with him, in England, in 1963. He had scored 90 (run out) at Manchester, 73 at Lord's, 92 in the first innings of the fourth Test at Leeds, bowled by Tony Lock. He made 44 in the second innings, and the veteran correspondent of the *Times*, John Woodcock, encapsulated the impression made by Rohan's style: 'Kanhai [is] a player of impudent genius…There was a hint of Bradman in [his] batting. Fortunately for present day bowlers, however, the temperaments are different. Kanhai when he was leg-before, swiping at Shackleton [for 44], looked more disgusted with the umpire than himself. Bradman would never have played the stroke'.[78]

In the second innings of the final Test, at the Oval, which gave the West Indies a 3-1 victory over England, reminiscent of their supremacy in 1950, Kanhai played an innings of 77 in 90 minutes, which was deluged with encomiums. It was enthralling to listen to it on the radio; there was no television in British Guiana yet the spirit of the innings was not lost, as many urgent domestic chores were ignored that day in August 1963. The *Daily Mail's* Ian Wooldridge captured the character of Rohan's 'glitteringly brilliant' innings, a veritable tribute to his captain, Frank Worrell (1924-67), in his last Test match:

> Now Kanhai came to say farewell as only he conceivably could. It was his greatest innings of the summer – 77 runs in an hour and a half, hit to all points of the Oval with shots fit to lay before an audience of emperors. He started with a supreme glance down to fine-leg off Shackleton and then, stroke by stroke, moved round the compass until he was lashing an unstoppable four just wide of the slips. And then he came back again, hesitating only to linger over the sheer pleasure of smashing ball after ball into the covers. It was almost pointless to bowl to him. In desperation Dexter called up Close…Close called Lock out of the leg-trap and sent him over to reinforce the covers. Kanhai watched him calmly and then, three times in the next six balls, crashed unstoppable shots through the human fence out there on the off…Amid it all Hunte…had been almost forgotten. Kanhai had given him a two and a half

Worrell's triumphant team in England, 1963 – three from Port Mourant: Butcher (back row, second from right); Kanhai (middle row, second from left,); Solomon (front row, centre), between Deryck Murray to his right and David Allan to his left. Worrell is seated behind Solomon.

> hour start and caught him in 88 minutes. The shot that brought their scores level was his famous falling hook. Kanhai was lying full-length in his crease as the ball crashed down forty yards beyond the boundary. It was his last runs of the series. Two balls later, trying a still more audacious sweep, he was caught knee-high by Bolus at mid-wicket and went out laughing hugely. That valedictory innings will never be forgotten by anyone who saw it.[79]

In assessing the quality of play of the West Indian cricketers since the tour of Australia in 1960-1, the coming to fruition of the team with style, it is essential to locate Frank Worrell in this process. At the start of the tour of England, in May 1963, Irving Rosenwater paid tribute to him: 'Worrell is one of the aristocrats of cricket. He betrays the stamp from the moment his lithe figure emerges from the pavilion. In his walk to the wicket – the nearest approach to feline grace on the cricket field – and in his commanding, upright stance there is unmistakable elegance: it becomes dynamic when he drives and cuts, though age may have dimmed the lustre of some of his former brilliance. Lissom as a panther, languorous but very wide awake, he remains – as Richie Benaud has called him – a man of stature'.[80]

After the final Test in late August 1963 the *Guardian* thought it necessary to comment on the meaning of this tour for the future of West Indians in England. They observed that with bat and ball their cricketers were paving the way for them in a manner no one else could have done: 'There has been a Homeric touch about the whole series…Who will forget that last half-hour of the second Test [at Lord's], which led up to a climax that fulfilled all the laws of drama?...[O]ne of the results of this series is that the West Indians who live here have become a part of the English scene in a way that they never were before…It now means that the West Indians and the British now have something to chat about; too often West Indians arriving here have found their neighbours apparently surly and unfriendly, not realising that the average inhabitant finds it more or less impossible to talk to any foreigner simply because he does not know in the least what to talk about. Sobers, Butcher, Kanhai and the rest have changed all that. Most Englishmen may still not be too sure where exactly the West Indies are, but at least they know who they are'.[81]

The *Cricketer* was even more celebratory of West Indian contribution to the series, within and beyond the boundary. In 1963, at several of the grounds, during the Tests, there were probably as many West Indians as Englishmen. The journal saw the whole experience as 'a victory for cricket' – a victory for race relations. The team under Worrell had continued to enthral, in the manner they set Australia ablaze in 1960-1:

> Now we can say that cricket lives again and we must pay tribute to all those who have brought this about. First we salute Frank Worrell, a captain who, by his demeanour both on and off the field, has given the game dignity and resolution. He has led his team – surely one of the finest of modern times – with the firmness and understanding which are the hall-marks of good captaincy. Moreover, his tactical handling of his considerable resources is an object lesson…But perhaps we shall remember more than anything else the wonderful crowds who for the first time in Test matches in England were nearly evenly divided in their loyalties…[But] however tense the struggle became there seemed to be a great love for cricket running through the cheers and the groans, the laughter and the sorrow. And for this, England supporters must thank the great number of those who have come to live amongst us from the Islands in the Sun and brought to this famous series the colour and the warmth with which cricket will forever be associated. Frank Worrell and his men will be leaving soon. We thank them for what they have done for cricket.[82]

The greatest cricket writer of them all, Sir Neville Cardus, has left a verdict on Kanhai that secures his place in West Indies cricket eternally. It was written in 1966 (after the fall of Cheddi Jagan in Guyana); but it captures the unconquerable spirit of Rohan and suggests why his mastery could carry the psychic burdens of Indo-Guyanese:

> In captain Sobers alone the West Indies can boast three brilliant exponents in one single ebullient personality: an accomplished batsman, a seam-bowler with the new ball and a 'googly' spinner. He is already acclaimed as the greatest all-round cricketer of the post-Grace period…But of all the delights West Indies cricket has

> showered on us, the galvanism of Constantine, the quiet mastery of Headley, the tripartite genius of Weekes, Worrell and Walcott, the enchanted improvisations of Ramadhin and Valentine, none has excited and delighted me, sent me so eagerly on the tip-toe of expectation as Kanhai, upright or flat on his back...[He] often seems to have only one object in life – to hit a cricket ball for six into the crowd at square-leg, falling on his back after the great swinging hit. The impetus of the hit, its sheer animal gusto, brings him down to earth, but *it is a triumphant fall* [emphasis added].[83]

Beyond the boundary, in Guyana, the African leader, Forbes Burnham's self-assurance since November 1963, following British acquiescence to American pressure to change the electoral system to proportional representation, was at a high point. In an interview with the *Daily Telegraph* of London (1 May 1964), he reflected upon the Guyanese situation with unapologetic triumphalism: 'If it came to a showdown, the East Indians must remember that we could do more killing than they could. Everyone knows that there are more East Indians than negroes...but let me say that in an all out race war...Dr Jagan's numerical superiority would not be reflected in the results'. Most Indo-Guyanese, mired in Cheddi Jagan's quagmire and demoralised – the antithesis of their own triumphalism in wake of his victory of August 1961 – would have concurred.

Indo-Guyanese now saddled Kanhai with the task of 'liberator'. He had to atone for the perceived impending fall of Jagan, following his signing a fatal document in London in October 1963. Jagan was tricked by the British, at the behest of President Kennedy, obsessed that Jagan would create another Cuba in the hemisphere. Consequently the inter-colonial match, between British Guiana and Barbados, in February 1964, assumed unprecedented significance for Indo-Guyanese. Burnham had virtually won the war; this battle within the boundary was their quest for a degree of redemption. Kanhai was about to encounter the combined might of the two fastest bowlers in the world: Wes Hall and Charlie Griffith. They had tormented several English batsmen of renown the previous year into recurring fallibility. Wes Hall had broken Colin Cowdrey's arm, at Lord's: this remained a fresh iconic image of England's demise and West Indian

President Forbes Burnham of Guyana meets West Indies captain Garry Sobers, March 1971, Bourda (Georgetown). On Sobers's right is Everton Weekes; on his left are Lance Gibbs and a perceptibly cynical Rohan Kanhai

ascendancy. The fear now stemmed from anxiety whether the Guyanese batsmen could cope with the pace – like fire – of the two Barbadian fast bowlers. This was the ultimate test of batsmanship. Could Kanhai rise to the occasion? The racial bitterness of local politics had thrust Rohan into something he could hardly have contemplated – he certainly did not comprehend it.

The battle took place in Bridgetown, Barbados, in February 1964. British Guiana was soon 13 for 3: Vic Harnanan 0, Colin Wiltshire 0, Basil Butcher 0. Griffith bowled Kanhai for 0. Divine intervention! It as a no-ball! Hall and Griffith were ferociously fast, unleashing a barrage of short-pitched deliveries; they, too, saw this as the ultimate challenge: the destruction of the nos. 3, 4 and 6 batsmen in the West Indies team – Kanhai, Butcher and Solomon: the men from Port Mourant. The captain of British Guiana, Joe Solomon, told me that Griffith was in a bitter mood because the night before the match he, Kanhai, Butcher and Lance Gibbs (the senior players), were drinking at the hotel in Barbados, reflecting on Griffith's dubious bowling action: they concurred that he was throwing. The barman, who had heard every word, apparently communicated the gist of the conversation to Griffith. But reprieved, Kanhai proceeded to dominate the pace attack: he hooked and drove Hall for three consecutive fours in his sixth over; he improved on this in Hall's eight: four fours. There were 10 fours in his first fifty; his score of 108 comprised 17 fours. Meanwhile, the other man from Port Mourant, Joe Solomon, defended stoically, heroically, for 63, although he was hit on the finger from a Griffith delivery. Kanhai had conquered.[84] And throughout the three hours that he ruled, Indo-Guyanese saw each boundary hit as a blow against Burnhamite terror, a compensation for the impending Jagan fall. The other Port Mourant man, Basil Butcher, made 105 in the second innings. Basil's performance, however, does not belong in the Indo-Guyanese narrative, now totally immersed in the racist imagery of Guyana at the end of empire.

Burnham ascended to power in December 1964, as expected. Perceived as the lesser of two evils, the Portuguese leader, Peter D'Aguiar, joined him in a coalition to pass the proportional representation post and form a government. Jagan was vanquished. Indo-Guyanese languished in despair. Kanhai, their other hero, did not start well against the touring Australians of 1965. He failed in

Jamaica, in the first Test: 17 and 16. But West Indies won by 179 runs; this series was seen as the contest for the unofficial championship of the world. Before the second Test in Trinidad, Kanhai appeared for that island in their first-class game against Australia. C.L.R. James, covering the series for the *Times*, observed how keenly many were following Kanhai's state of play and state of mind because of the intrinsic value of his art. On the eve of the second Test James noted: 'Perhaps the atmosphere surrounding this match is seen best in the attitude to Kanhai. He scored only 52 and 34 in the recent game [Trinidad v. Australia], but his friends expect him to recover his finest form in the Test match. This form is anticipated not for what it will do to the Australians but for the delight of batting for its own sake'.[85] The man's gifts were elevated to another plane: 'the delight of batting for its own sake'.

Kanhai's arrival in Georgetown in April 1965, to play against the Australians in the third Test, assumed extraordinary proportions, too oppressive to bear, because of Jagan's fall in December 1964. Indo-Guyanese lifted themselves for the occasion though tormented by fear of another failure. Kanhai did not disappoint. Not quite! Rohan made 89 in the first innings; and they applauded, drank rum and chanted as each stroke was executed. Even his defence was infused with a touch of grandeur, as desperate racial promptings intruded on their vision. It was a splendid performance, and Richie Benaud (now a journalist) described it as 'one of the finest innings in modern-day Test cricket'. He elaborated: 'Kanhai's stroke-play was tremendous…He was known as "the little wizard" or "the little master" in Australia; and those who watched him bat in 1960-1 and were so delighted, would have seen an exact replica in his innings at Bourda on this day. Off the front foot he was sure in defence and savage in attack, and if forced on to his back foot his timing was superb and he sent the ball flying away to the boundary. He pulled Philpott [the leg-break/googly bowler] for six through mid-wicket and then played two magnificent off-drives off McKenzie that had the fast bowler removed from the attack. When Philpott overpitched, Kanhai hit him a scorching drive through the covers, and then when he dropped shorter, forced him away between cover and point with his own particular brand of subdued violence'.[86]

C.L.R. James, too, was impressed with the innings. Kanhai and Butcher shared a partnership of 135 as they consolidated after two

Kanhai executes the on-drive against Australia, 1965: a study in mobility, timing and concentration

wickets had fallen quickly. Kanhai 'dazzled' as of old, imposing himself on all the Australian bowlers: Graham McKenzie, Neil Hawke, Laurie Mayne, Peter Philpott and Norman O'Neill. This was how James saw it at Bourda, in Georgetown, British Guiana, on 14 April 1965:

> Kanhai and Butcher, both native sons, opened up after the luncheon amid a jubilant expectation somewhat tempered by the unexpected loss of two wickets in quick succession [Conrad Hunte and Bryan Davis]. An off-drive and a hook by Kanhai to the boundary off successive balls from McKenzie unloosed irrepressible celebration. Kanhai also cut Philpott to the boundary, and it became clear that as long as he remained at the wicket there should be no shortage of dazzling strokes. Kanhai underlined the hundred [partnership] by driving McKenzie through mid-off. Hawke was now bowling round the wicket with a solitary slip, the field well spread out. The batsmen were contented with sharp singles. Kanhai lifted Philpott over square-leg for six off a ball that was barely short of a length. It is a forte of his that once in position he is abnormally quick with the bat, as quick as Bradman was on his twinkling feet. Rain stopped play when the pair had turned [the score from] 68 to 121, Kanhai making 37 and Butcher a watchful 19…[When play resumed at 4 pm] Kanhai hooked Hawke for four almost at once. O'Neill seemed to get his leg-spin to bite. The crowd started to applaud Kanhai's 50 from the time he had reached 48, and he sent them into delirium by hitting O'Neill to the off boundary three times in an over. A square-cut by Butcher to the boundary raised the 150…[87]

Kanhai was 88 not out overnight; next morning Hawke bowled him with a magical away-swinger, for the addition of a run. The amazing delivery is etched in Kanhai's memory: '…the ball from Neil Hawke that nailed me for 89…is the best I've ever faced (I know this is a big statement). It started off diagonally towards the pads, swung late, pitched leg stump, and struck the top of the off-stump. Even allowing for the fact he was using the new ball, it was the prince of out-swingers'.[88] But the magic of the master had been savoured!

Then came the second innings! It, also, is etched in Kanhai's memory – for less savoury reasons:

> When I appeared for my second knock I was cheered all the way to the wicket by the wildly delighted fans. But this time, unforgivably, I was bowled third ball by McKenzie for a blob, trying to turn an off-cutter to mid-wicket. What a difference! I was booed, yes booed, the whole way back to the pavilion by the same fans who minutes earlier had cheered themselves hoarse on the reverse walk. It was a strange, frightening noise I had never experienced before and [I] never want to again.[89]

James described the moment slightly differently: 'a sharp in-swinger (from McKenzie) which Kanhai, who disdains to play himself in, was driving through extra-cover [Kanhai says mid-wicket], bowled him for nought'. But James said nothing of the booing: his discerning mind would have grasped its futility, its desperate prompting, and stay quiet.[90] Butcher recalls the dreadful experience and felt sorry for Kanhai, but he could not comprehend the reason for it; Joe Solomon could.

Indo-Guyanese were demoralised and haunted by Cheddi Jagan's fall in December 1964 – no 'triumphant fall' this! It evoked an image of Humpty-dumpty. Kanhai's brilliance against Australia, on 14 April 1965, just four months later, brought some relief; it could do no more, but it was productive of brief triumphalism. Because of that tawdry display of racial pride during the first innings, Rohan's failure in the second provoked double shame. But it would have been unimaginably more painful if African-Guyanese had booed Kanhai, for he was now the highest symbolic self-representation of his Indo-Guyanese compatriots. They, therefore, were pre-empting blacks by doing so: a psychological stroke of ultimate despair. Frank Birbalsingh has commented on the peaks and troughs Rohan Kanhai has inspired in his bewitched fans, evoking exhilaration and triumphalism, on one hand, and melancholy, despair – even shame – on the other, in the blink of an eye:

> Like the archetypal West Indian trickster, Anansi, Kanhai lived by his wits. When he came off there was nothing like him; when he did not, he and his admirers could be badly bruised, as Anansi often was. But never would he settle for the ordinary or the mundane, safety or correctness, as he struck lustily out, heading

> boldly, precariously, for the high road of manful risk and threatening danger. The wonder was that despite risk and danger, it was a road that took Rohan Kanhai, the plantation 'coolie boy' from Port Mourant to what [C.L.R.] James calls 'regions Bradman never knew'. Some plantation! Some coolie boy![91]

But it imposed an unconscionable burden on the 'coolie boy'. It made him bitter. He has never recovered. I do not believe that Kanhai played any first-class matches in his home county, Berbice, between 1961 and 1972. This was probably actuated by the construction of him as redeemer – the surrogate for Cheddi Jagan – with which Indo-Guyanese had saddled him. He was disdainful of the imposed responsibility, which he could not comprehend. The situation was made worse by deep-seated flaws in his personality. Kanhai was, and still is, capable of arrogance, rudeness and a casual disregard of the feelings of those who genuinely adore him, especially his Indo-West Indian devotees. Oscar Ramjeet was a young cricket correspondent and friend of Kanhai from his seminal years in the mid-1950s, and he still regards him as a genius, one of the best batsmen he had the privilege to see: a shaper of beauty. But he recalls two incidents that demonstrate his mercurial temperament.[92] The county of Berbice, in British Guiana, was playing England (MCC), in March 1960, and Kanhai was scheduled to bat at no. 3. He was having a cold drink (a 'Watkins' stout) with Oscar and two other friends in the pavilion at Rose Hall, Canje, when the first wicket fell [Alvin Bacchus b Greenhough 28]. He handed Oscar his drink and said: 'Keep this, I'll be back'. He hit three fours and a single in a short time, and his Indian compatriots, young and old, who had travelled many miles from as far as the Upper Corentyne, to see their hero, were ecstatic. But he was soon bowled by off-spinner David Allen for 13, playing a 'rash stroke'. His devotees were crest-fallen: their 'god' had let them down. He retrieved his drink from Oscar and apparently soon left the ground. He did not field when England batted in a marathon innings of 641 for 6. He took no further part in the match. No explanation was given. This was the first first-class match I ever saw. I was only 10 years old, but I do remember being taken to Rose Hall to see the second day's play, hoping to see my hero,

Rohan Kanhai, for the first time. He was not on the field. I was very upset about this. I wanted to cry.

Oscar could not recall the details of the matter, so I went to the British Guiana newspapers in order to piece together Kanhai's role in the match. After the first day's play Berbice, which included two other Test players, Joe Solomon and Basil Butcher, were in a commanding position: 286 for 2. This is how the *Guiana Graphic* told the story:

MCC [ENGLAND] BELTED BY BERBICIANS
SOLOMON SLAMS 150, BUTCHER BATS FOR 88 – BOTH NOT OUT

Joe Solomon and Alvin Bacchus opened for Berbice, before a crowd estimated at 7,000 (most impressive for a small ground). At lunch they had an unbroken partnership of 70. Shortly after the resumption, Bacchus was bowled by the leg-spinner, Tom Greenhough, for 28, with the score at 77. An apparently reluctant Kanhai then came to the wicket. The *Graphic* reported:

> Rohan Kanhai…flattered only to deceive for after scoring 13 with two promising fours [off successive deliveries], he tried to hook David Allen out of the ground but was beaten and bowled by a sharp off-break.
>
> AS HE MADE HIS WAY SLOWLY AND SADLY BACK TO THE PAVILION A SECTION OF THE CROWD BOOED HIM [emphasis in the original].[93]

The *Daily Argosy's* Charles Chichester reported the incident thus: 'After lunch Bacchus was bowled playing back to Greenhough. Then Kanhai made a fine sweep and an on-drive off successive balls before being bowled trying to pull Allen. A section of the crowd booed him as he went back to the pavilion clearly of the belief that he had thrown away his wicket'.[94]

If Oscar's recollection of the incident is correct, it would validate the assumption of those who booed Rohan – drawn presumably from his numerous Indo-Berbician admirers – that he did not take the match seriously. As early as May 1959 the District

Commissioner of East Berbice, W.A. Angoy, had stimulated curiosity in this fixture by announcing it at Port Mourant, at a match in honour of Butcher and Solomon (Kanhai did not return to British Guiana), following their successful tour of India and Pakistan. Angoy said: 'Berbice owes a lot to Butcher, Solomon and Kanhai. They have not only won great laurels for themselves as cricketers, but they have put Berbice on the cricketing map of the world. In March next [1960] a MCC team [England] will engage Berbice for the first time in that county'.[95] So the fact that Rohan did not take the field, possibly piqued by the reaction of the crowd, was a great disappointment and it lent credence to the perception that his head had become swollen with his international success. He had grown too big for his humble, barefooted devotees from Port Mourant and other plantations and villages in British Guiana. Yet, paradoxically, the more he sought to be liberated from his roots, the more the roots imprisoned him, grasping at his gifts and his fame. Indo-Guyanese had elevated him, as his friend and colleague, Ivan Madray, put it to me many years ago, to a 'living god'.

In the match at Rose Hall in 1960, it is noteworthy that Rohan's more prosaic team-mates from Port Mourant, Solomon and Butcher, battling to retain their places in the West Indies team, did not let the spectators down. Berbice made 387 for 2, with Solomon 201 not out and Butcher 131 not out: '...Solomon drove and cut with both style and power...This performance must put him bang in line for an opening spot on the tour of Australia [in 1960-1]...Butcher...from the start was in command playing his strokes which have put him among the best in these parts. Solomon kept with him all the way and indeed increased in adventure'.[96] But, with Indo-Guyanese, the accolades were reserved for Kanhai, then and now. He was the pathfinder; his flair and panache are imperishable. He remains at the summit of their imagination – for all time.

Yet Oscar Ramjeet recalls another incident, possibly two years later, around 1962, which underlines Kanhai's indifference to the people who admired him most, Indians in his home county, Berbice. The match was a 'friendly' played at the Port Mourant Cricket Ground, just behind Rohan's family-home. Oscar explains:

> Rohan was asked to captain a Berbice XI against a Demerara XI led by Lance Gibbs. It was organised by some Hindus from the Corentyne District, with assistance from the Berbice Cricket Board, to raise funds to build a Hindu temple at Port Mourant. Kanhai was reluctant to play but eventually led the side. Gibbs won the toss but sent in the Berbice side because he probably figured that they had all come to see Kanhai primarily. Rohan was dismissed for 5, to the disappointment of the large crowd. Gibbs then declared early to enable them to have a second look at their hero. This was not to be: playing a very rash stroke, he made 0 this time.[97]

Oscar adds: 'Rohan returned to the pavilion mumbling something to the effect that he did not want to play. He promptly started to pack his gears and he told me that he was leaving. I responded: "Rohan, you cannot leave; the game is till in progress; you are the captain". He ignored me and stormed out of the pavilion. The next day I carried a report in the *Evening Post* that Captain Kanhai had failed twice and he left the game while the match was still in progress. Rohan saw me a few days later in New Amsterdam and rebuked me publicly that I had written "shit". I was tempted to write another article on his hostility to me, but Basil Butcher asked me not to follow up on the story as it would tarnish his reputation as an international cricketer. I complied'.[98]

Oscar seeks to comprehend the long-known attitudinal conundrum of this gifted, but flawed, man. He goes back to his early days at Plantation Port Mourant, when Kanhai, from humble background, learnt his skills playing with three other boys, all born in the first half of the 1930s: Joe Solomon, Basil Butcher and Ivan Madray. By 1957-8 they had all played Test cricket for the West Indies. This is what Oscar has come up with:

> The cricketers from Port Mourant honed their skills in the underarm, softball version of the game, on the turf near to the famous open-air market on the plantation. They played for eight hours each Saturday and Sunday. It was a ritual that engrossed the community. In the late 1940s Kanhai, Solomon, Butcher and Madray and a few others excelled. They never received any formal training, no coaching, yet their hand/eye coordination was brilliant. The talent on display was riveting, week after week.

> Rohan was the most flashy, definitely more impetuous even then, than Basil or Joe, who were seen as less flamboyant but reliable. Kanhai was always more aloof, somewhat difficult, some say arrogant. It is felt that he suffered from a bit of inferiority complex because, unlike the other three, he did not have the benefit of a secondary education. He had chips on his shoulders long before he became a world class batsman. Butcher, Solomon and Madray [all Christians] had better social skills, greater ease. I think that Rohan's perceived arrogance is a mask for deficiencies in character coupled with social stresses.[99]

Oscar may be right; but Kanhai's stature as the greatest Indo-West Indian batsman of all time is unassailable. For that they revere him until today, whatever his defects as a man. Moreover, his departure from Guyana after he became an international cricketer in the summer of 1957 (he has resided in England ever since) – aggravated by the unavailability of television coverage or films: the absence of visual images – multiplied the myths and deepened the fantasies around the man. There was always a racial/political dimension to the way Rohan was perceived by Indians in Guyana. As possibilities of regaining political power receded, after December 1964, with the ousting of Cheddi Jagan, communal vision evaporated; Indo-Guyanese (over 50% of them, in some villages over 80%) sought hope in flight, mainly to Canada and the United States. However, individual efforts to succeed did not dry up; and many of a certain age still say with pride that they owe their success around the world, in great measure, to the inspiration of the 'Tiger of Port Mourant', Rohan Kanhai.

John Woodcock of the *Times* covered many of Kanhai's great innings, so his final verdict on him has a feel of a deeply held truth about a work of art. He concludes: 'His cricket was all about self-expression, a good deal more so at times than was in the best interests of his side. When the urge took him, he would suddenly swing himself off his feet and fall spread-eagled across his crease in an attempt to cart the ball out of the ground. No batsman ever got himself out more than Kanhai, as distinct from being got out. In terms of pure talent he was in Don Bradman's class, and of much the same stamp – slight, eagle-eyed and incredibly quick-footed. When he applied himself he was a wonderful player on every sort of pitch. No one ever played the ball later or had more strokes'.[100]

Trevor Bailey, the England all-rounder, commentator and writer, was so famed for his dour batting, his immovability, that he was dubbed 'Barnacle Bailey'. He first encountered Kanhai in 1957 and was entranced by his mercurial batsmanship. He called him the 'magician from Guyana', and composed a celebratory portrait of him, reminiscent of scores of similar ones issuing from the pens of Englishmen mesmerised by Ranji before the Great War:

> Rohan Kanhai is not the greatest batsman I have bowled against but few, if any, have had the power to fascinate and satisfy me more. Just as the sauces can transform a good meal into a feast, it is the stroke execution that garnishes a Kanhai innings which would make it unforgettable even when his score is not particularly large. Rohan is a...[Guyanese] of Indian extraction and like the most exciting cricketers of Asian origin there is more than a touch of eastern magic about his batting. For, though slightly and almost delicately built, he has overcome this by a combination of timing, eye and the use of his wrists. He has the ability to flick, almost caress the ball to the boundary, which is especially attractive. On one occasion I fractionally over-pitched a ball on his off stump. He drove at it and at the very last moment impacted an extra touch of right hand, slightly angled the bat so that it streaked between mid-wicket and mid-on before either could move...

Bailey's admiration for Rohan's style, possibly because it was the very antithesis of his, is unequivocal:

> Rohan is essentially an extravagant and colourful performer. He is always liable to embark upon strokes which others would not consider, let alone attempt to execute. This flamboyant approach to batting has on many occasions brought about his downfall, but it is the reason why I find him so satisfying. When he is at his best there is more than a touch of genius about his play which has an aesthetic appeal. He reminds me of a great athletic conjurer whose tricks sometimes fail – not because of inability, but because he attempts so much, sometimes even the impossible – he is

> seldom mundane...Because Rohan is one of the finest, as well as one of the most exhilarating cricketers of his generation, he has in addition to his vast range of attacking shots a basically sound defensive technique...If I could choose how I would like to be able to bat, I would select Kanhai as my model.[101]

The poet and broadcaster, Ian McDonald, a Trinidadian, settled in Britain Guiana in 1955, after Cambridge, lured by the Booker Company led by the imaginative Jock Campbell. That was the year Rohan first played for British Guiana, against the Australians, so McDonald witnessed the rise of the 'Tiger of Port Mourant', in the mid-1950s, through his magnificent innings of the 1960s. His verdict on him is an ode to a body of work – art that illuminates life beyond the boundary: an aspect of the full life. The poet's own life is enhanced by the mastery of the artist conjuring fresh images of beauty with his bat, thus adumbrating new horizons for him:

> All the ingredients of greatness were there, like no other batsman. And mixed into that mixture already so supremely rich there was one final ingredient, a flair and a touch, that no one can define and no one can wholly grasp but which one knew was there and felt it as the man took the field and made his walk to the wicket – something uniquely his own, a quality that made excitement grow in the air as he came in, a feeling that here was something to see that made the game of cricket more than a sport and a contest, made it also an art and an encounter with the truth and the joy that lies in all supreme achievements.[102]

It seems to me that McDonald is framing Rohan's gifts in terms of Hazlitt's conception of the genius; but the construction of the latter is not realisable if the gift of tutored perception is missing – the taste. However, for Indo-Guyanese, including myself and boys growing up at the time of Kanhai's ascent, that taste was not a cultivated one; it came out of our unconscious craving for a great West Indian batsman to transport us to the heart of creole sensibility – West Indian authenticity. George Lamming has noted that '[there is] a psychic shame that burns the hearts of men whose lives have been a history of genuflection and an apparent subservience of spirit. This shame secretes dynamite, and it would be unwise to underestimate its explosive capacity'.[103] Rohan released that dynamite in many Indo-Guyanese because, I believe, his unique talent, acknowledged by all groups in the West Indies and beyond, offered them the means to wipe out the inferiority complex bred on the sugar plantation. In the process, they fortified their self-belief to chart individual paths to wider horizons.

That there were chips on his shoulders, which betrayed a lingering self-doubt that was never fully dissipated, is incontrovertible. Apart from the sense of hurt bred on the sugar estates, there was a deep-seated social inferiority that inhered in the rural Indian. It was actuated by the chasm between his social mores and those of the creole universe of white, Portuguese, black and coloured West Indians, steeped in a variant of British culture. The Indians were the latest of comers to the region, so people like 'Sugar Boy' Baijnauth and Rohan Kanhai, besides the pressure to succeed being pioneer Indo-Guyanese cricketers, had to continually negotiate massive social expectations, as well as alien social etiquettes. It tended to exacerbate the insecurities and the tendency to impute slights or prejudices into other people's responses when no such were intended. Ivan Madray speculates: 'Deep down, Rohan must have known that, as an Indian, if he failed he was out [of the West Indies team]. He never told me anything, but I think he always had this at the back of his mind, and that was why he tried to be better than all of them. And he wanted all Indians to be the same: attacking, attractive, dedicated West Indian cricketers'.[104]

Trevor Bailey has also reflected upon aspects of Rohan's personality that spoke of old complexes, the persecution syndrome rooted in the low status of the 'coolie' on the sugar plantations. It would also carry Cheddi Jagan's Marxism into the realm of unreality as he sought to expunge perennial imperial exploitation, while championing the superiority of the Soviet system. Bailey observes perspicaciously that black West Indians, already more socially secure by the 1950s, were less apt than Kanhai to be burdened by a hinterland of imagined slights:

> In his early days…[Rohan] was inclined to be suspicious of people, Anglo-Saxons in particular, which stemmed from his

> background and from being a little unsure of himself. He had moved into a world which was in many ways different from the one in which he had been reared and some of the differences confused, amused and occasionally angered him. He has always been sensitive so that he was liable to think that he had been slighted, and to take offence when none was intended. He was apt also to brood over a wrong, imagined or otherwise, for far longer than would a West Indian of African extraction. At one time I gained the impression that he had something of a 'chip on his shoulder' and that this occasionally led to clashes with authority which could easily have been avoided. The flashes of impetuosity and rashness in his batting are also part of his character, and his character, like his batting, can sparkle or simmer.[105]

The magnanimity and ease that characterised the cricket of the three W's, Weekes, Worrell and Walcott, caught the discerning eye of Jim Swanton: 'This Barbadian trinity will be recalled by all who saw them play not only as superb performers but as sportsmen of high degree. Brought up with a due sense of chivalry and good manners, they never slipped from grace, however tense the occasion, however strong the provocation'.[106] Like C.L.R. James, Grantley Adams, Norman Manley, Sir Arthur Lewis and many black and coloured people of distinction, deeply shaped by the British West Indian tradition of 'muscular learning', two of the three W's, Worrell and Walcott, went to the elite schools, Combermere and Harrison College respectively. Clyde Walcott recalls: 'When it was dark and supper was finished the uncles and aunts would join us to talk about the issues of the day, the state of West Indian cricket, the latest political crisis or whatever took our fancy. We learned a lot from these discussions. Sometimes the exchanges became heated but it was a way of learning about people and events. This is the West Indian way. We love talking'.[107] Lower middle class blacks and coloureds were all socialised within the West Indian variant of English civilisation. It made for a kind of confidence that was not readily apprehensible by the same generation of Indo-West Indians like Kanhai, Sonny Ramadhin, V.S. Naipaul and Cheddi Jagan. It showed.

The two most celebrated men in the history of Indo-West Indians are Rohan Kanhai and V.S. Naipaul, the Nobel Laureate in Literature in 2001. It is their art that counts ultimately; the perceptible flaws in their personality are excusable, indeed, deemed integral to their genius. Imprisoned by their gifts, and defined by Indo-West Indians as representative men, carriers of massive burdens dictated by race and identity, it was virtually impossible for them to resume assumptions to normality. Kanhai and Naipaul were the first world-class batsman and writer respectively to emerge from the community. Their rise to eminence, in the early 1960s, at the end of empire, embodied Indo-West Indian arrival – the validation of claims of belonging. They had, indeed, achieved distinction in the sphere of muscular learning; they had earned a place in creole sensibility. Neither man was comfortable with, or probably even comprehended, the massive burden with which they were saddled. Consequently, they often resented the responses, the overreaction, of their Indo-West Indian compatriots, to their art. However, from such unconscionable realities is the complex texture of identity woven; and although Indians were deeply pained by the frequent failures of Kanhai to convert good scores into centuries (he made 28 half-centuries in Tests), the mastery and style could sustain their passion for his craft – and the representative role thrust upon him. So whatever angst Indo-Guyanese experienced when Kanhai disappointed them, it could not diminish his iconic stature. For the same reason they would stick with Cheddi Jagan, their foremost political leader, for fifty years, his limitations as a statesman notwithstanding. Because Rohan was a batsman of extraordinary gifts, he occupied a place in the Indo-Guyanese psyche that was unprecedented. But he did much more, as C.L.R. James observed in 1966, on the eve of Guyana's independence:

> A great West Indian cricketer in his play should embody some essence of that crowded vagueness which passes for the history of the West Indies. If, like Kanhai, he is one of the most remarkable and individual of contemporary batsmen, then that should not make him less but more West Indian... [I]n Kanhai's batting what I have found is a unique pointer of the West Indian quest for identity, for ways of expressing our potential bursting at every seam...Here was a West Indian proving to himself that there was one field in which the West Indian not only was second to none,

> but was the creator of its own destiny...[Here was] a West Indian proving to himself that henceforth he was following no established pattern but would create his own...Kanhai...discovered, created a new dimension in batting.[108]

This is redolent of Ranji. It is recognition, indeed, coming from one of the greatest West Indian thinkers. Indo-West Indians now belong: they are West Indians. James certainly had no reservations about that. His classic book, *Beyond a Boundary*, was published on the eve of the West Indies tour of England, in 1963, one of the most accomplished teams to play in that country. It was captained by that civilise man from the Barbadian lower middle class, Sir Frank Worrell (1924-67). Around April 1963 James sent a copy of the book to V.S. Naipaul (he also sent a copy to Rohan Kanhai), and he felt it necessary to speak from the heart to reveal the innermost prompting of the work – something he has never said to anyone else and which most people still miss. He could only have shared this with one he considered a West Indian of unexampled intellect, however ironic this may appear. He was asking Naipaul to communicate to West Indians the significance of what he had done in *Beyond a Boundary* because he believed that the writer was the embodiment of West Indian intellectual distinction – 'what we are':

> I am not impertinent enough to tell you what you should think of the book. I prefer to tell you what I think. The book is West Indian through and through, particularly in the early chapters on my family, my education and portraits of West Indian cricketers of the previous generation, some of them unknown. The book is very British. Not only the language but on page after page the (often unconscious) literary references, the turn of phrase, the mental and moral outlook. That is what we are, and we shall never know ourselves until we recognise that fully and without strain...I believe that, originating as we are within the British structure, but living under such different social conditions, we have a lot to say about the British civilisation itself which we see more clearly than they themselves. I believe I have made that clear in the treatment of W.G. Grace...I hope you will like it and say something about it, something that West

> Indians will hear. Curiously enough, I have little doubt that in England it will be understood. It is the West Indies that I am concerned about.[109]

In May 1963 James thanked Naipaul for some preliminary remarks he had made on the book – rare insights not readily apprehensible by authors of their own works: given only to discerning readers from within a culture – and for his impending review in *Encounter*. He wrote: 'I felt not only that here was someone who understood it, but what is always more precious, someone who could show me things in it and evolving out of it of which the writer himself was not fully aware. That you should be doing such a substantial piece in *Encounter* is good luck indeed'.[110] Naipaul obliged. The review appeared in the September 1963 issue of the journal. He said: '*Beyond a Boundary* is one of the finest and most finished books to come out of the West Indies, important to England, important to the West Indies. It has a further value: it gives a base and solidity to West Indian literary endeavour'.[111] But Naipaul went further in exploring the foundations of the great work. I believe he helps us to comprehend why Rohan Kanhai became the 'Constantine' in Indo-West Indian identity construct. Two extensive excerpts from the review will testify to the power of the book in opening a window to the question of identity in the West Indies; the power, too, of Naipaul's discerning intellect:

> 'Who is the greatest cricketer in the world?' The question came up in a General Knowledge test one day in 1940, when I was in the fourth standard…Though I had never seen him play, and he was reported to live in England, no cricketer was better known to me than Learie Constantine. Regularly in the *Trinidad Guardian* I saw the picture of him: sweatered, smiling, running back to the pavilion, bat in hand. To me the bat was golden: Constantine, in a previous General Knowledge test, had proved to be 'the man with the golden bat' as, earlier, he had been 'the man with the golden ball'. But now – the greatest cricketer?...I saw it as a trap question…I wrote 'Bradman'. This was wrong; the pencilled cross on my paper was large and angry. 'Constantine' was the answer to this one too...The teacher was a Negro, brown-skinned, but this is

> a later assessment and may be wrong...It is possible to see his propaganda for Constantine as a type of racialism or nationalism. But this would only be a part of the truth. Racial pride pure and simple in the victories of Joe Louis, yes. But the teacher's devotion to Constantine was more complex. And it is with the unravelling of this West Indian complexity that C.L.R. James...is concerned. He has done his job superbly.[112]

And that job? Naipaul is most perceptive. He got to the soul of the notion of West Indianness, which would allow Indo-West Indians to belong :

> The West Indies, captained for the first time by a black man, did great things in Australia in 1960-1. A quarter of a million people came out into the streets of Melbourne to say goodbye to the cricketers [on 17 February 1961]: West Indian cricket's finest moment which Mr James sees as something more. 'Clearing their way with bat and ball, West Indians at that moment had made a public entry into the comity of nations'...To Mr James, Frank Worrell is more than the first black West Indian captain: 'Thomas Arnold, Thomas Hughes and the Old Master himself [W.G. Grace] would have recognised Frank Worrell as their boy'. This is the last sentence in Mr James's book, and this is his astounding thesis. To dismiss it would be...to fail to see that these territories are a unique imperial creation, where people of many lands, thrown together, 'came together within a system that was the result of centuries of development in another land'...Stollmeyer, Gomez, Pierre, Christiani, Tang Choon, Ramadhin: the names of West Indian cricketers are sufficient evidence. To be a nationalist, Mr James says elsewhere, you must have a nation. The African in Africa had a nation; so had the Asian in Asia. The West Indian, whatever his community, had only this 'system'; and my fourth standard teacher could only grope towards some definition of his position in the world by his devotion to Constantine...So...in Mr James's pages...[West Indies cricketers emerge]...with heroic qualities, for their success, as with Constantine or Headley, was the only triumph the society as a whole knew. And their failure, as with Wilton St. Hill who, achieving nothing in England in 1928, remained all his life a clerk in a department store, bitter tragedy.[113]

This is why it was imperative for Rohan Kanhai not to fail. He did not, neither did Naipaul; and, for a time, it appeared as if Cheddi Jagan, his Marxist fantasies notwithstanding, was unconquerable. By the early 1960s Indo-West Indians could walk with a spring in their steps. Not only had they arrived at the essence of belonging, muscular learning, but recognition had come from C.L.R. James, possibly the most intrepid, innovative thinker from the British West Indies, at the end of empire. The poet, Ian McDonald, constantly revisits what the genius of Kanhai means to him. He saw many of his great innings, and as recently as November 2006, he pondered again on the life-enhancing images his favourite batsman still evokes in him:

> When he came out to bat there was at once that expectant, almost fearful, silence that tells you are in the presence of some extraordinary phenomenon. Of course you could look forward to his technical brilliance. Was there ever a more perfect square cover drive? And has anyone in the history of the game made a thing of such technical beauty out of a simple forward defensive stroke? And, more than just technical accomplishment, there was the craft and art of Kanhai's batting – no mighty hammer blows or crude destruction of the bowler, simply the sweetest exercise of the art of batting in the world. But in the end I am not even talking of these things, important though they are.[114]

McDonald allows his imagination to craft an image of Rohan's originality that is resonant with those of H.A. Altham, Neville Cardus and Eric Gill, all enchanted by the genius of Ranjitsinhji:

> There was something much more about Kanhai's batting. It was, quite simply, a special gift from the Gods. You could feel it charge the air around him as he walked to the wicket. I do not know quite how to describe it. It was something that kept the heart beating hard with a special sort of excited fear all through a Kanhai innings as if something marvellous or terrible or even sacred was about to happen. I have thought a lot about it. I think it is something to do with the vulnerability, the near madness, there is in all real genius. It comes from the fact that such men – the most inspired poets, composers, artists, scientists, saints, as well as the

Rohan in England, 1963: surely a gift from the gods!

> greatest sportsmen – are much more open than ordinary men to the mysterious current that powers the human imagination. In other words, their psyches are extraordinarily exposed to that tremendous elemental force which nobody has yet properly defined. This gives them access to a wholly different dimension of performance. It also makes them more vulnerable than other men to extravagant temptations. The Gods challenge them to try the impossible and they cannot resist. This explains the waywardness and strange unorthodoxies that always accompany great genius. When Kanhai was batting with every stroke he played...one felt that somehow what you were experiencing is coming from 'out there': a gift, infinitely valuable and infinitely dangerous, a gift given to only the chosen few in all creation.[115]

Sunil Gavaskar (born 1949) grew up in the shadow of Rohan; he first saw him in late 1958, when the West Indies played India in the first Test in Bombay. It was a seminal experience for the nine year old Sunil, and it made him determined to master the art of batting, to become like his hero. The outcome needs no elaboration, but Sunil's portrait of Rohan, from the early 1980s when he himself was at the peak of his powers, is a testimonial for all time:

> Rohan Kanhai is simply the greatest batsman I have ever seen. What does one write about one's hero, one's idol, one for whom there is so much admiration? To say that he is the greatest batsman I have seen so far is to put it mildly. A controversial statement perhaps, considering that there have been so many outstanding batsmen, and some great batsmen I have played with and against. But having seen them all, there is no doubt in my mind that Rohan Kanhai was simply the best of them all. Sir Garry Sobers came quite close to being the best batsman...he was the greatest cricketer ever, and he could do just about anything. But as a batsman I thought Kanhai was just a bit better.[116]

Gavaskar explains the basis of his conviction. He revisits an innings he had the privilege of appreciating, being Kanhai's partner in a Rest of the World XI v. Australia 'Test', in Perth in December 1971. Sunil was 22, Rohan nearly 36, so the precocious student was still learning from the master. It was the best place to learn, in the eye of the storm. Perth was the fastest pitch in the world then; and Dennis Lillee, on his home ground, had reduced great players, such as Kanhai and Sobers, to mediocrity by his ferocious pace and infallible length. In response to Australia's 349 (Doug Walters made a century), the World XI were humbled for a paltry 59 in less than two hours: Lillee 8 for 29. Following on, Gavaskar lost his opening partner, Farokh Engineer, early, but he and Kanhai endeavoured to resist in this innings. They shared a partnership of 65: Sunil made 21, Rohan 118. The World XI lost by an innings and 11 runs, but the master left an indelible impression on his young protégé:

> I had a rare opportunity to stay...with him in a partnership. Earlier in that innings of his, a short ball from Lillee hit him in the chest. It was painful but he shrugged off all help and stood his ground. The next ball expectedly was another short one and Rohan imperiously hooked it wide of mid-wicket for four. That was a great shot, because Lillee was bowling genuinely fast and to have the time to get up on one's toes and smash the ball down like a forehand overhead shot in tennis requires some talent. Our partnership lasted about two hours and during that time one got an object lesson from Rohan Kanhai on how to play quick bowling. After I had flashed outside the off stump to McKenzie, he walked down the wicket and said: 'What are you trying to do? You just stay there; don't worry about your runs...just give me the support...I'll get the runs'.[117]

Sunil was enthralled by the range of skills and the fortitude that were the foundation of the innings:

> That's precisely what he did. He just smashed the ball to all corners of the field and scored 117 [118]. I've seen quite a few century innings, but that, to my mind, ranks as the best century I've ever seen. For sheer guts, for sheer technique, for the...audacity of the shots, that century was worth preserving on film. However, another hundred – a double hundred – in the same series completely erased from the people's mind Kanhai's hundred. But I feel Rohan's hundred was the greater...It was

Another version of Rohan's 'triumphant fall' (the Oval, 1966); Basil D'Oliveira (slip) and John Murray (wicket-keeper) are mesmerised

> played under more tension – it was...played when the bowling [of Lillee and McKenzie] was really fierce...I am not dismissing Sir Garry's 254. It was a great innings...but Rohan's...was just that shade better.[118]

Sunil named his son Rohan, so did another protégé of Rohan Kanhai, Alvin Kallicharran of Port Mourant (also born in 1949). This underlines the inviolable stature of the 'Tiger of Port Mourant'. On the occasion of Guyana's Independence, in May 1966, James Scott celebrated his style thus: 'To see Kanhai flat on his back – with the ball among the crowd beyond the square-leg boundary – after making one of his outrageous sweeps to a good length ball, is to watch a man capable of playing shots fit to lay before an audience of emperors'.[119] Nineteen years after his first first-class match, Rohan Kanhai played his last Test in March-April 1974, against England in Trinidad. Michael Gibbes wrote at the time: 'His niche in West Indies cricket...is assured, as is his place in the hearts of all who treasure human excellence in any form'.[120] It is not necessary to improve on this.

NOTES

1. I have addressed this in my book, *Sweetening 'Bitter Sugar': Jock Campbell, the Booker Reformer in British Guiana, 1934-66* (Kingston, Jamaica: Ian Randle Publishers, 2005).
2. *Ibid.*, p. 67.
3. Interview (by phone) with Joe Solomon, 30 July 2008.
4. Kanhai, *Blasting For Runs*, (London: Souvenir Press, 1966), p.16.
5. Cheddi Jagan, *The West on Trial: My Fight for Guyana's Freedom* (London: Michael Joseph, 1966), pp. 18-9.
6. Michael Swan, *British Guiana: The Land of Six Peoples* (London: Her Majesty's Stationery Office, 1957), pp. 101-2.
7. Kanhai, *op. cit.* [1966], pp. 11-2.
8. The *Daily Argosy*, 21 April 1955.
9. The *Barbados Advocate*, 25 October 1956.
10. The *Daily Argosy*, 21 October 1956.
11. See Birbalsingh and Seecharan, *op.cit.* [1988], p.115.
12. Clyde Walcott, *Island Cricketers* (London: Hodder and Stoughton, 1958), p. 126.

13. Owen Mathurin, 'The 1957 West Indies Team and its Prospects', in W.A.S. Hardy (ed.), *They Live for Cricket: A Souvenir Programme Featuring the West Indies Cricket Tour, 1957* (London: the Author, 1957), p. 5.
14. *Ibid.*, p. 17.
15. C. L. R. James, 'Kanhai: A Study in Confidence', *New World Quarterly* (Guyana Independence Issue, 1966), p. 13. This article was reproduced in a reader edited by Anna Grimshaw (see note 108).
16. *Trinidad Guardian*, 7 February 1958.
17. Kanhai, *op. cit.* [1966], pp. 37-8.
18. The *Hindustan Times*, 1 January 1959.
19. The *Hindu*, 10 February 1959.
20. Interview with Joe Solomon, Plantation L.B.I., Guyana, 27 August 1997.
21. Kanhai, *op. cit.* [1966], p. 37.
22. Ian McDonald, 'Tiger in the Stars', 'Viewpoint', Broadcast on the Guyana Broadcasting Corporation, Georgetown, Guyana, [May 1985], (mimeo.), p. 5. It was published in Joel Benjamin, Lakshmi Kallicharan, Ian McDonald and Lloyd Searwar (eds.), *They Came in Ships: An Anthology of Indo-Guyanese Prose and Poetry* (Leeds: Peepal Tree Press, 1998), pp. 271-4. The quote is on p.274.
23. Kanhai, *op. cit.* [1966], p. 47.
24. The *Guiana Graphic*, 8 April 1959.
25. The *Daily Argosy*, 14 March 1959.
26. The *Guiana Graphic*, 4 April 1959.
27. See note 24.
28. The *Pakistan Times*, 27, 29 March 1959.
29. The *Nation*, 5 June 1959.
30. The *Nation*, 12 February 1959.
31. Alan Ross, *Through the Caribbean: England in the West Indies, 1960* (London: The Pavilion Library, 1986 [1960]), p. 119.
32. *Ibid*, p. 117-8.
33. The *Guiana Graphic*, 4 February 1960.
34. Kanhai, *op. cit.* [1966], p. 60.
35. The *Nation*, 5 February 1960.
36. The *Nation*, 19 February 1960.
37. The *Nation*, 8 April 1960.
38. The *Sun-Herald* [Sydney], 1 January 1961.
39. The *Herald* [Melbourne], 21 February 1961.
40. Jack Fingleton, *The Greatest Test of All* (London: Collins, 1961), pp. 92-3; 87-8.
41. Richie Benaud, *Willow Patterns* (London: The Sportsmans Book Club, 1970

[1969]), pp. 115, 112.
42. *Ibid.*, p. 116.
43. The *Age* [Melbourne], 28 January 1961.
44. *Ibid.*
45. *Ibid.*
46. Kanhai, *op. cit.* [1966], pp. 75-6.
47. Wes Hall, *Pace like Fire*, (London: The Sportsmans Book Club, 1966 [1965]), p. 75.
48. Richie Benaud, *Willow Patterns* (London: The Sportsmans Book Club, 1970 [1969]), pp. 95-8.
49. A.G. (Johnnie) Moyes, *With the West Indies in Australia*, 1960-1 (London: The Sportsmans Book Club, 1963 [1961]), p. 125.
50. *Ibid.*, pp. 126-7.
51. *Ibid.*, p. 127.
52. The *Times*, 13 December 1960.
53. The *Times*, 2 February 1961.
54. *Ibid.*
55. Moyes, op. cit. [1963], p. 120.
56. *Ibid.*, p. 166.
57. *Ibid.*
58. A. G. Moyes, *A Century of Cricketers* (London: George G. Harrap and Co. Ltd., 1950), pp. 91-2.
59. The *Nation*, 11 November 1960.
60. Neville Cardus, 'This may be "Kill or Cure" Test Rubber', [November 1960], in his *A Cardus for all Seasons* (London: Souvenir Press, 1985), p. 188.
61. *Ibid.* (see his 'Wanted – A Dose of the West Indies Tonic', pp. 193-6.)
62. V.S. Naipaul, *The Middle Passage: The Caribbean Revisited* (London: Andre Deutsch, 1962), p. 133.
63. Clyde Walcott, *op. cit.* [1958], pp. 124-6.
64. Interview with Joe Solomon, Plantation L.B.I., Guyana, 27 August 1997.
65. J.S. Barker, *Summer Spectacular: The West Indies v. England, 1963* (London: The Sportsmans Book Club, 1965 [1963]), p. 84.
66. Alan Ross, *The West Indies at Lord's* (London: Constable, 1986 [1963]), p. 23.
67. Interview (by phone) with Joe Solomon, 30 July 2008.
68. Richie Benaud, *A Tale of Two Tests (With some Thoughts on Captaincy)*, (London: Sportsmans Book Club, 1963 [1962]), p. 38.
69. Garry Sobers, *My Autobiography* (London: Headline, 2002), 123-4.
70. *Ibid.*, p. 124.

71. Moyes, *op. cit.* [1963], pp. 60-1, 75.
72. *Ibid.*, pp. 168-9.
73. The *Times*, 14 December 1960.
74. Barker, *op. cit.* [1965], p. 44.
75. Richie Benaud, *The New Champions: Australia in the West Indies, 1965* (The Sportsmans Book Club, 1966 [1965]), p. 88.
76. Cary Fraser, *Ambivalent Anti-Colonialism: The United States and the Genesis of West Indian Independence, 1940-64* (Westport, CT.: Greenwood Press, 1994), p. 194.
77. See my *Sweetening 'Bitter Sugar', op. cit.* [2005], Chapters 31-2, for details of the turbulent political backdrop referred to here.
78. The *Times*, 29 July 1963.
79. Ian Wooldridge, *Cricket, Lovely Cricket: The West Indies Tour, 1963* (London: Robert Hale, 1963), pp.155-6.
80. The *Cricketer*, 10 May 1963.
81. Leader, the *Guardian*, 27 August 1963.
82. 'Comment', The *Cricketer*, 13 September 1963.
83. Neville Cardus, *A Fourth Innings with Cardus* (London: Souvenir Press, 1981), pp. 116-7.
84. *Guiana Graphic*, 16 February 1964; the *Daily Chronicle*, 16 February 1964.
85. The *Times*, 26 March 1965.
86. Richie Benaud, *op. cit.* [1966], pp. 100-1
87. The *Times*, 15 April 1965.
88. Rohan Kanhai, *op. cit.* [1966], p.117.
89. *Ibid.*, p. 72.
90. *Guiana Graphic*, 19 April 1965.
91. Frank Birbalsingh, *The Rise of Westindian Cricket: From Colony to Nation* (London: Hansib, 1997 [1996]), p. 180.
92. Personal communication, 31 March 2008.
93. *Guiana Graphic*, 19 March 1960.
94. The *Daily Argosy*, 19 March 1960.
95. The *Guiana Sunday Graphic*, 24 May 1959.
96. *Ibid.*
97. See note 92.
98. I have been unable to verify this. Kanhai does not give interviews.
99. See note 92.
100. John Woodcock, *The 'Times' One Hundred Greatest Cricketers* (London: Macmillan, 1998), p. 52.
101. Trevor Bailey, 'Rohan Kanhai: The Magician from Guyana', in his *The Greatest*

in my Time (London: The Sportsmans Book Club, 1970 [1968]), pp. 108-9.

102. Ian McDonald, 'Rohan Kanhai – Batsman Extraordinary', 'Viewpoint', Broadcast on the Guyana Broadcasting Corporation, Georgetown, Guyana, 5 February 1983, (mimeo.), p.2.
103. George Lamming, 'The West Indian People', *New World Quarterly*, Vol. II, No. 1 (Croptime, 1969), p. 69.
104. See note 11, p. 124.
105. Bailey, *op. cit.* [1970], pp. 113-4.
106. E.W. Swanton, 'The Three W's', in his *As I Said at the Time: A Lifetime of Cricket* (London: Unwin, 1986 [1983]), p. 68.
107. Clyde Walcott, *op. cit.* [1999], p. 5.
108. C.L.R. James, 'Kanhai: A Study in Confidence', in Anna Grimshaw (ed.), *Cricket: C.L.R. James* (London: Allison and Busby, 1986), pp. 165-6, 168-9.
109. C.L.R. James, 'Letter to V.S. Naipaul', in Anna Grimshaw (ed.) [1986], pp. 116-7.
110. *Ibid.*, p. 118
111. V.S. Naipaul's review is reproduced in his *The Overcrowded Barracoon* (London: Andre Deutsch, 1972): 'Cricket', pp. 17-22. This quote is on p. 23.
112. *Ibid.*, p. 18.
113. *Ibid.*, pp. 20-1.
114. Ian McDonald, 'Vote for Kanhai', *Stabroek News* [Georgetown, Guyana], 26 November 2006.
115. *Ibid.*
116. Sunil Gavaskar, *Idols* (London: Allen and Unwin, 1984), p. 224..
117. *Ibid.*, pp. 230-1.
118. *Ibid.*, p. 231.
119. James Scott, 'Let's now Hail our Champions', *Guiana Graphic* (Independence Souvenir), May 1966, p. 95.
120. Michael Gibbes, 'Rohan Kanhai: The Peter Pan of West Indian Cricket', in Gordon Rohlehr, *Kanhai/Gibbs: Tribute to Two Great West Indians* (Port-of-Spain: Self-published, 1974), p. 19.

CHAPTER FIVE

Aryanism, Race and Silences in the Indo-Guyanese Narrative: Madray, Moonsammy and Butcher

> The cricket field is a screen against which the drama of West Indian society is often starkly projected.
> *Hubert Devonish* (1995)

When I discussed Rohan Kanhai with his boyhood friend, Ivan Madray, in November 1987, he had eulogised him as 'my living god'.[1] Nearly twenty-one years later I read to Ivan the thoughts of Oscar Ramjeet on Kanhai's personality defects – his arrogance and frequent lack of civility, coupled with a resilient sensitivity to slights of decades ago – which virtually preclude any meaningful exchange with the man. (In fact, I was unable to meet with him although I sought to do so through my publisher and another intermediary, a friend of Kanhai.) Ivan thinks that Oscar's assessment is a remarkably accurate one, but he is certain that the arrogance and the mercurial temperament were part of the whole that made Kanhai's batting a work of genius. In the age-old pattern of many artists of distinction, the unique gifts are inseparable from the flaws. Ivan also believes that Rohan was badly damaged by the racial burdens with which Indo-Guyanese saddled him. He never forgot, nor could he forgive, the booing by his devotees in British Guiana: at Rose Hall in 1960 and at Bourda in 1965 – Indian spectators with deep-seated social insecurities exacerbated, in the latter case, by the raw political wounds inflicted by Cheddi Jagan's defeat in December 1964. Only the dark flipside of Rohan's iconic stature among Indo-Guyanese festers in his imagination. Madray thinks a stronger, more secure, man would have recognised, in retrospect, that his status as hero is unimpeachable, and that 'the booing was a piece of the territory'.[2]

The Indo-Guyanese narrative is so permeated by Cheddi Jagan and Rohan Kanhai (both Port Mourant men), that eloquent silences obtrude thus rendering it incomplete. This is hardly surprising, for the shaping of identity elevates selected memories and tendentious embellishments, in conjunction with the silencing of others, as Stuart Hall has pointed out. In British Guiana an imagined Mother India has played a major role in the making of Indo-Guyanese identity. But the real India whence they came, impoverished, disease- and caste-ridden eastern Uttar Pradesh and western Bihar, was long silenced within the collective imagination.[3]

The 'bound coolies' from India, aided by myth and amnesia, were able to erase that past of unimaginable pain. They constructed a new Mother India, culled from the *Ramayana*, a veritable golden age, augmented by an ancient India of high civilisation allied to Gandhi's unimpeachable India, seen to be in rebellion against foreign rule: a moral crusade. It constituted the invention of a motherland that was the antithesis of that which they had learnt to forget. From the 1890s, an India of ancient grandeur and glamour took shape among the educated elite (the most creolised): a construct of illumination, virtually peerless in its art, temple architecture, sculpture, philosophy and ancient literature – a monument to erudition. In the 1920s-30s, for instance, excerpts from articles, particularly by Europeans, that sought to substantiate this ancient glory were reproduced continually in the local press. The following quote from Sir Ariel Stein, a British archaeologist and explorer, appeared in the Indo-Guyanese intellectual, Peter Ruhomon's weekly column, 'Indian Intelligence by the Pandit', in April 1932:

> The vast extension of Indian cultural influences, from Central Asia in the north to tropical Indonesia in the south and from the border lands of Persia to Japan and China, have been fully revealed to the world at large and only during the last 70 years or so almost entirely through the researches of western scholars. They have shown that ancient India was the radiating centre of civilisation which by its religious thought, its art and literature was destined 2,000 years since to leave its mark on races wholly diverse and scattered over the greater part of Asia.[4]

Some aspects of the imagined India, part fact, part fantasy, did reach even the unlettered in colonial Guyana, as they tried to find an antidote to the 'bound coolie' stigma (the last batch of indentured labourers landed on 18 April 1917; the last indentures were not terminated until April 1920). One of the received ideas was the notion of Aryanism, in the late 19th/early 20th centuries: the assumption that Sanskrit was the source of ancient Greek and Latin, therefore Aryans in ancient India were related, by blood, to people of European stock, including the British. Aryans were light complexioned and they sought to insulate themselves from the black or the dark peoples they had conquered, while institutionalising their superiority through ritual validation. This was the foundation of the caste system: lightness of skin is highly prized in the Indian imagination; darkness or blackness evokes overwhelmingly pejorative associations.

In November 1932 Peter Ruhomon reproduced a quote from the German poet, critic and scholar, Friedrich Schlegel (1772-1829), which reinforced assumptions of the motherland's pivotal role in learning: 'The loftiest European philosophy is, compared with Oriental philosophy, like a feeble Promethean spark in the full blood of the heavenly galaxy'.[5] This perception of ancient India, while useful in countering the 'coolie' stain among Indo-Guyanese, also contributed to the shaping of a notion of cultural and racial superiority, grounded in Aryanism. In August 1936 the Indo-Guyanese poet, artist and cricket enthusiast, J.W. Chinapen, wrote a poem in honour of the distinguished Indian philosopher at Oxford, Professor Sarvepalli Radhakrishnan (1888-1975). It was permeated by Aryanism and a return to the 'golden age':

> Illustrious Son of Aryavarta [abode of the Aryans]
> Torch-bearer of the eternal Veda
> Sweet,
> The light which waked a univ-
> ersal frame
> Into one long celestial harmony,
> Long we have learnt to love thy
> Song and name,
> Have felt thy presence kindling
> in our hearts
> The Vedic flame. Illumine these
> corners dark

As did our Rishis [seers] in the bygone
days
When from the Motherland they
issued forth
To guide the nations to the
Throne of Grace [emphasis in original]
Art thou the herald of the days'
return
When Aryavarta again shall beckon
all
The world to drink of her im-
mortal breast?
All hail! The winds bear witness to thy word.

The star rose in the east and
travelled forth
Until it made a circuit of the
earth.
Once more 'tis rising on thy
sacred shore
With promise of the radiant gleam
of yore,
O mother, thou who wert the
world's delight,
Hail to the rising of thine ancient
Light.[6]

A few months earlier a local correspondent to the *Daily Chronicle*, Mohanlal Thakurdas, wrote a piece, 'The Origin and History of the Indian Race', echoing Professor Max Muller and extolling the Aryan antecedents of high caste Indians. It would have resonated with many Indo-Guyanese whatever their caste provenance, reinforcing their partiality for lightness of skin and European concepts of beauty:

> It may seem unbelievable, but it is nevertheless true that the high caste Indian and the Englishman alike have descended from a common ancestry of Aryan or Indo-Germanic stock; that they once inhabited the same country somewhere in Western Asia and

> that they spoke the same language, no trace of which can now be found but which is believed to have been closely akin to Sanskrit. Over a period of centuries, bands of the noble Aryans migrated east and west from their primitive homes in Asia...We know little about the habits and customs of the Aryans in western Asia, or the exact spot where they resided; but we do know that they spoke a language not much different from Sanskrit of the Vedas – the earliest Sanskrit literature in existence today.[7]

On the eve of the Indian centenary in British Guiana (5 May 1938), the *Daily Chronicle* thought it opportune to editorialise on what it saw as ominous trends in race relations in the colony. It was meant as a warning to Africans and Indians, although this was not stipulated:

> Some years ago, an American professor visited British Guiana and expressed the opinion...that where questions of race were concerned, we had in British Guiana a utopia about which more should be known abroad. But of recent years those who have eyes have seen beneath the surface currents which must be arrested before there develops a really serious undermining of colonial authority...[T]he causes have their origins in which the various peoples first entered this country a hundred years ago [mainly those from India]. At one time it was safe to predict that time would level all barriers. But...social forces have tended to produce the opposite effect. Don't let's waste time fixing the blame. Let it be the concern of all men of goodwill to give deep and anxious consideration to any scheme which would make for freer social intercourse among our various groups.[8]

The nationalist crusade in Mother India, coupled with a spate of Aryanism fostered by several visiting missionaries from India (Arya Samajists), lifted the self-assurance of Indo-Guyanese. A young scholar of Aryanism, Tony Ballantyne, has shown why it became so central to India's cultural resurgence and the emergence of a powerful *Hindutva* (Hinduness) strand in Indian nationalism. It had roots in the ancient text, the *Rig Veda*; and it carried the seeds of exclusion of Muslim Indians from the nationalist project. The absorption of Aryanism in Indo-Guyanese thought, also, was not amenable to empathy with African-Guyanese sensibility. However, Muslim Indians in British Guiana could be accommodated in the narrative of Indo-Guyanese nationalism because it was predicated on the exclusion of African-Guyanese and cohered around it. Ballantyne's argument is instructive in grasping the power of Aryanism to reach even Indians in the diaspora – the assumption of Caucasian provenance, however remote:

> The *Rig Veda*, composed around 1500 BCE [about 3,500 years ago], recorded the incursion of tribes of pastoralists who identified themselves as 'Arya' [literally 'noble'] into India. As these settlers from Central Asia encountered the indigenous populations of north India and developed new polities and religious traditions, 'Arya' continued to function both as a marker of community and as an evaluation of cultural sophistication...As early as 1854...[Max Muller, the German scholar] suggested that when a Briton confronted 'a Greek, a German, or an Indian, we recognise him as one of ourselves'. Because of this shared ancestry, the *Rig Veda* was particularly significant, as it provided the most ancient source, the 'oldest monument of Aryan speech and Aryan thought', for the construction of the shared European and Aryan past...Indians and Europeans shared a common heritage, but for Max Muller their contemporary position was fundamentally different. He believed that Europeans had continued to build upon the high achievements of their Aryan ancestors, while Indian culture had become stagnant, even degenerate.[9]

The light-skinned Aryans in India were a minority in a sea of black or dark people. Therefore, to protect their 'purity', to fortify the 'noble' minority from 'contamination', virtually immutable barriers were constructed. This was the means by which tribals, many with discernibly African features (possibly the original inhabitants of India), were relegated to the bottom. Blackness became the criterion in the Indian imagination for designating the lowest status: the shudras, the untouchables and the tribals. This bred an instinct for hierarchical ordering, sanctioned by ritual. And as Professor Romila Thapar, the eminent historian of ancient India, points out: 'Ritual status meant observing rules of purity and pollution, where the brahmin was regarded as the purest and the others in descending order down to the most impure, who was untouchable...[W]ith the emergence of Vedic [Aryan] culture, the ideological legitimation was encapsulated in *varna* which underlined hierarchy, occupation and purity...The idea of purity and pollution, derived from religious sanction, made it difficult to change the system'.[10]

The late Professor A.L. Basham, another eminent historian of ancient India, has shown how lightness of colour was the motif that shaped this ordering, stemming from the power of the Aryans to define. He argues: 'As they settled among the darker aboriginals the Aryans seemed to have laid greater stress than before to the purity of blood, and class divisions hardened to exclude those Dasas who had found a place on the fringes of Aryan society...The word dasa originally meant a member of the peoples conquered by the Aryans in their first invasion of India. Its later connotation no doubt developed from the reduction to bondage of the many Dasas captured in battle, and here we find the probable origin of Indian slavery...The Dasas are described as dark and ill-favoured, bull-lipped, snub-nosed, worshippers of the phallus, and of hostile speech'.[11]

This attitude to blackness was true of ancient India as it was of subsequent centuries of interminable invasions and subjugation, through to the British conquest and the early years of the nationalist upsurge against British colonialism, from the end of the 19th century. It is no less true of contemporary India as she seeks her place in the sun in a globalised world: lightness of skin, with its roots in Aryanism, is still a tremendous asset. As a Zee TV (India) special on the subject observed in 2006, many women in particular are doomed by the darkness of their skin: 'Despite being revered as goddesses and having our ancient history peppered with women who are great leaders and scholars, it's no secret that in modern times the various biases faced by Indian women are more often ignored than addressed. One of the most baseless yet damning of these biases is the over-riding pre-eminence of fairness, or a fair complexion. By the logic of antonym, dark skin is still considered one of women's biggest disadvantages; *almost a curse* [emphasis added]'. Two women, authorities on the media and advertising in India today, Radhika Parameswaram and Kavitha Cardoza, have documented that the ancient partiality for lightness is being reinforced daily, through advertising of skin-lightening products, aimed primarily at women. It works:

> Advertisements promise women consumers that their investment in these commodities will release them from the chains of their corporeal incarceration within the biological cage of their defective epidermis, a bodily organ whose production of melanin must be controlled in order to belong to the exclusive club of feminine beauty. Secondly, and less obviously, women's light skin colour also operates as a form of cultural capital in a changing India where traditional power relations of colour, caste and class, although still strong influences in shaping institutional and individual policies and practices, are undergoing some shifts and adjustments.[12]

The fact that caste has virtually no place in the Indo-Caribbean universe, save for the retention of Brahmins as priests in orthodox Hinduism or Sanatan Dharma (the path followed by the majority), has reinforced the primacy of lightness and its 'antonym': prejudice against Africans, what Ivan Madray insists on calling 'a hatred of black people'.[13] Brahmins, generally, tend to be lighter and their features more finely chiselled: in some cases discernibly European – desirable; cherished. The fact that the overwhelming majority of Indo-Caribbean people are dark has not invalidated this obsession, neither has it diminished the centrality of fair skin as the ideal worthy of pursuit. In the same way that many successful African or black men pursue the acquisition of a light spouse as integral to their professional ascendancy, many Indian families become engaged in the project, often understated but understood, to procure a light or lighter spouse for their successful sons. This is the case both in India and in the West Indies.

Indeed, as I have argued, Indo-West Indians have looked to the motherland for guidance, even as they sought to become creolised, to be accepted as belonging to the region. Their creolisation is refracted through the lenses of Mother India. With many centuries of partiality for lightness in India, it is difficult, indeed, to eradicate prejudice against the dark or black. It is hard to abjure a predilection for the light. The 'untouchables', among the darkest in India, were virtual slaves to the highest castes: hardly human, these 60,000,000 or one-sixth of India's population, as Peter Ruhomon explained in February 1933: 'These unfortunate people have, for some two thousand years, been held down by their Hindu brethren at the bottom of society in indescribable ignorance, dirt and degradation, on the ground that they are so foul as to be unfit for ordinary human intercourse. According to the orthodox Hindu belief every man born among their people is a soul which in former lives lived so viciously that his present position is the direct consequence of his past misdeeds and is intended as a punishment therefor [*karma*]'.[14]

The eradication of *chamar* and other notions of low caste in British Guiana and Trinidad was manifest early, by the preparedness of Brahmins to minister to all Indians, in their homes, and to partake of their cooked food – a counter to Christian proselytising. The ancient taboos could not be sustained. But this did not mean the acceptance of Africans: in fact, consciously or unconsciously, a sort of outcaste status was transferred to them. Responding to a displacement instinct and a fear of slippage, Indo-Guyanese constructed the African in terms of low caste status with the accompanying rituals of exclusion: virtually the new *chamar*. He was the new *dasa*, with physical features reminiscent of the tribals in India, if not magnified; and having been enslaved, he was soon framed by the old caste paradigms of pollution, avoidance and exclusion. Dale Bisnauth, the historian, observes that African-Guyanese harboured their own stereotypes of Indians; '[b]ut at the core of Indian attitudes to the Afro-Guyanese were the malign vestiges of caste thinking. The Afro-Guyanese were said to belong to the *Kale* (black) caste and were consequently of very low (caste) ranking, or of no ranking at all. They were identified with Rawan, the arch-enemy of the Indian god-hero Rama (in the *Ramayana*), and with the Rakshasa, a demon figure…in the *Mahabharata*…As either Rawan or Rakshasa, the Afro-Guyanese was to be feared and his company shunned'.[15]

Elahi Baksh explores Indo-Guyanese attitudes in his only slightly fictionalised short-story, 'The Propagandist', set largely in 1953 against the backdrop of the first cricket tour by India of the West Indies and the first elections under universal adult suffrage in British Guiana. The latter is often recalled, nostalgically but erroneously, as the golden age of African-Indian unity. The story shows how cricket could resurrect all the ambiguities of belonging for Indo-Guyanese especially when the West Indies play India; how, too, their prejudice towards Africans reproduces vestiges of that older bigotry from the motherland. Baksh's main character is an Indo-Guyanese cane-cutter, an alcoholic, Ramkissoon, 'the Propagandist', but his views on African people in a neighbouring village is not unrepresentative:

> You would think that as a…West Indian by birth he was morally bound to support West Indian cricketers. But the truth is that, as Indo-Guyanese or Indo-West Indians, although we never admitted it, many of us were wracked by guilty ambivalence if not open disloyalty on the subject. We only pretended to be shocked by the Propagandist's partiality towards India while we joined in instinctively with the humour of his racist jokes putting down West Indian cricketers who were mostly Afro-West Indian like the villagers next door [to the plantation]. We cheered and egged him on when he demanded with sneering and conclusive rhetoric: 'Since when yuh hear monkey can play bat and ball?' It was a standard colonial jibe – labelling Africans or people of African descent as less than human.[16]

The eminent Indian psychoanalyst, Sudhir Kakar, observed recently:

> Evidence of the pan-Indian preference for fair skin and a denigration bordering on scorn for the dark-skinned is all around us ... The psychological association of fair skin with everything 'clean', 'regal' and 'desirable', together with memories of being ruled by fair-skinned invaders [Muslim and Christian] and the presumption of wealth associated with fair-skinned visitors makes most Indians fawn over the *goras* ['Whites']. A dark-skinned African, on the other hand, will often be an object of condescension, even ridicule.[17]

The imprint of Mother India, consciously or unconsciously, has not been obliterated; although there are Indians who have been punctilious in embracing their African friends, such as Ivan Madray's relationship with Basil Butcher. The identification of African-Guyanese as 'other' probably hastened the eradication of

The pinnacle of West Indies batting in the 1960s: Kanhai and Sobers, at Bourda, Guyana, March 1968

caste notions, as well as the diminution of the ancient incomprehension between Hindus and Muslims. But the shaping of Indo-Guyanese identity, while rooted in idioms of an imagined India, also fed into strong creole undercurrents: education and cricket – muscular learning. The latter, of course, did help to foster a degree of comprehension between African and Indians: it is often pointed out that behind many successful Indians was an unsung African schoolteacher, man or woman. Consequently many Indians and Africans harboured deep mutual respect. But the political contest after the Second World War, for Independence, with its irrepressible racial trajectory, limited that understanding and distorted the relationship. The instrument itself, cricket and the cricketers, would become enmeshed in the partisan political agendas of Africans and Indians. Players of distinction, such as Rohan Kanhai and Basil Butcher, resented the way their talent was being exploited in the raw contestation of power towards the end of empire. This was how these men from Port Mourant came to epitomise – rather, were saddled with – the uncompromising Indian and African identity projects, by the late 1950s-1960s.

The flip-side of this bifurcated Guyanese identity carries the sectional etchings and prejudices of that mould. Therefore the narratives of belonging are dogged by particularistic validations that exclude the other group. Cricket in British Guiana helped to ease the incomprehension across the African-Indian racial chasm; but it also deepened that divide as representative roles, laden with ethnic agendas as politics became polarised in the 1960s, were thrust upon the top cricketers in British Guiana. Inadvertently, they were imprisoned in the ethnic cocoons of their homeland, in spite of the international recognition of their gifts and their collective endeavour in the making of the great team under Frank Worrell, in the early 1960s.

Dr Tulsi Singh, who has followed West Indies cricket for 50 years, feels that although my argument is correct, it should be noted that the Indo-Guyanese assertion of their Indian identity, through Kanhai, was not counterpoised with Basil Butcher. It was framed often in terms of a Kanhai v. Sobers contest because they were seen as the best, but the racial undercurrent was inescapable. Dr Singh writes:

> When we started to follow cricket, in the late 1950s, Kanhai, Butcher and Solomon were as much of a threesome in Berbice and Guyana cricket as Walcott, Weekes and Worrell were a threesome in earlier West Indian cricket lore. But Kanhai was always the pre-eminent figure even while Butcher was enjoying his highly successful tour of England in 1963. Ethnic congruence had a part in Kanhai's popularity – a big part – among Indo-Guyanese; but, as I recall, the contest was never between Kanhai and Butcher: it was between Kanhai and Sobers. And the ethnic divide was unmistakable.[18]

I agree. There was possibly rivalry between the two best batsmen, Kanhai and Sobers, conducing to jealousy; but it probably stemmed primarily from greater insecurity on the part of Kanhai, juxtaposed with the incomparably gifted Garry Sobers. In any case, as Dr Singh observes, this was rendered as a virtual Jagan-Burnham contest by Indo-Guyanese, in the early 1960s. Sobers seeks to debunk, in a fashion, the allegation of jealousy by Kanhai. But the fact that Frank Worrell, perceptively and tactfully, separated them in the batting order in seven of the last nine Tests he captained – by the first Test in England in 1963 Kanhai was established at no. 3, with Butcher at 4 and Sobers dropping to no. 5 – lends credence to it. Sobers writes:

> When Frank Worrell eventually took over the team in 1960-1 for the tour of Australia, there were many in the Caribbean who felt that there was some sort of ongoing riffle between Rohan Kanhai and myself. It was supposedly caused by a little jealousy on Rohan's part; it was said he was happy only when he had made more runs than me. I never believed this fantasy but this is what people felt...Frank sorted it out in his usual perceptive and diplomatic manner. He said, with tongue-in-cheek, that if Rohan batted at number three and I batted at five or six, Rohan would never know how many runs I was going to make and, to be safe, he would have to make a big total every time he batted. He explained that I had the ability to read the game, to know whether to attack, defend, when to go for quick runs or when to stay there. If the batsmen in front accumulated a lot of runs, I would know to go out and score quickly but if the team were 60 for 4, I could

> go in there and bring the team together by helping the others. He told me I was the only player in his team who could do it and that was why he wanted me at five or six, because they were very important positions.[19]

It is arguable therefore that Butcher, at no. 4, played a crucial role, at a strategic point in Rohan's career, in helping him to find the equanimity to play at his best, unburdened of a measure of inferiority complex occasioned by Garry Sobers's monumental talent. Yet Butcher could not find a place in the Indo-Guyanese narrative because he was enmeshed in a hidden, subliminal transcript that expunged positive images of Africans, even when it is the case of this first-rate Test batsman, born and bred at Plantation Port Mourant. Of African descent, Butcher was captain of the Port Mourant team in the mid-1950s. It is difficult, also, for the sustaining narratives of identity of Indo-Guyanese to accommodate what does not constitute unbridled success. So that although many fine cricketers, such as J.A. Veerasawmy, Chatterpaul Persaud, Johnny Teekasingh, Sonny Baijnauth, Ganesh Persaud and Sonny Moonsammy, contributed much to their self-esteem, which helped to foster a degree of inter-communal understanding, they are almost invisible in the narrative.

It is my contention that the elemental forces of exclusion inherited from Mother India – the stories they tell themselves about who they are – could accommodate Ranji and Rohan, success stories that fit into the narrative of ancient India's magnificent artistic legacy, the 'architect of civilisation', as well as Gandhian India seen to be in revolt against British colonialism; so, too, Naoroji, Tagore and Nehru: all evocative of ascendancy – mastery recognised by the West. While the Indo-Guyanese narrative could not accommodate the real India whence they came, it could, however, celebrate the ushering in of the golden age during the mythical rule of Lord Rama, in the great Hindu text, the *Ramayana*. The Indo-Guyanese narrative could even transcend Mother India's darkness of vision and inscribe Hindu-Muslim unity as integral to their identity. Much of this is admirable and it has made a valuable contribution to the development of the community in the West Indies. But the political evolution of Indians in Guyana seems also to need the African as antithesis in order for the sense of community to cohere. This was true when they fought caste prejudice or religious intolerance, internally. It was exacerbated after the Second World War, as the possibility of Independence loomed for British Guiana, once India had gained hers in 1947.

After this, it became a contest, sometimes bitter as I have shown, between Africans and Indians as to who should inherit the 'kingdom'. Briefly, in 1953, the illusion was created within the People's Progressive Party (PPP) of Cheddi Jagan and Forbes Burnham that Guyanese could co-exist, even unite, in forging a national identity. The split, in 1955, between the two leaders, one Indian the other African, brought to the surface the deep racist attitudes that remained dormant under British rule, yet expressed eloquently within the *cordon sanitaire* of one's own group. Cricket, possibly the most potent instrument for asserting one's claim to belong in creole society, was necessarily contaminable by the wider prejudices and sectional insecurities beyond the boundary. It became an instrument of triumphalism hardening the divide. Because it was essentially charged with sectional responsibilities, the representative roles thrust upon cricketers in British Guiana reflected the colony's bedevilling racial antipathies. Kanhai and Butcher detested it, and probably found it incomprehensible. Although they both emerged from Plantation Port Mourant, and represented Berbice, Guyana and the West Indies, their play was invested with the burdens and anxieties of the African and Indian peoples in Guyana. Because the craft of these men was exercised in probably the most powerful idiom of creole sensibility, a hidden, subliminal transcript unilaterally imposed on them tasks in the making of African and Indian identities at the end of empire. Butcher and Moonsammy, Clyde Walcott, too, played crucial parts in Indo-Guyanese cricket, yet they remain silent in the Indo-Guyanese narrative.

Sonny Moonsammy was born in 1929 at Plantation Skeldon, in Berbice. He was a batsman in the mould of Rohan Kanhai, who should have represented British Guiana before Kanhai, Butcher, Solomon and Madray. He was apparently as technically accomplished as any one of them, although his very aggressive approach often brought a premature end to several of his fine innings. In fact, he only played for British Guiana twice, against Barbados in Bridgetown, in January-February 1959. He was nearly 30 years old; and made the team only because Kanhai, Butcher and Solomon were on tour in India. He scored16 and 1 not out in the drawn first match; in the second, won by Barbados by 121 runs, Moonsammy made 0 and 36.[20]

Ivan Madray knew Moonsammy well and considered him 'a player of outstanding class, a brilliant stroke-player. He had a great cover drive, executed the hook, and was certainly one of the best cover-point fieldsmen I ever came across'. His reputation as a fielder in the cover/cover-point area remains almost mythical, more reflective of contemporary standards. He enjoyed fielding and returned the ball, from the deep, very close to the stumps with monotonous regularity. Madray explains: 'Sonny Moonsammy was the 12th man against Jamaica [probably Barbados] in the Quadrangular Tournament in October 1956. He went on to sub for someone, and I saw him pick up a ball from deep square-point, and he hurled it – you could only see one stump – into Rohan's gloves, above the bails, to run out somebody. Brilliant fieldsman, tremendous arm, any part of the field! But he wasn't a close fielder; it would have been folly to put him in the slips, or silly mid-on'.[21] He believes that Sonny's chance to represent British Guiana, and possibly the West Indies, was squandered because he did a rather irresponsible thing, around 1953, when he was on the verge of playing for British Guiana. During a trial match at Bourda, Moonsammy turned up late because, allegedly, he had gone to the airport to receive a PPP politician, Mohamed Khan, a friend from his own plantation, Skeldon. This was obviously a serious misjudgement, aggravated by the fact that a veteran Guyanese cricketer and influential man in local cricket, Berkeley Gaskin (1908-79), was playing in the trials.[22] Besides, Jagan's PPP was anathema to most of the top brass of the British Guiana Cricket Board of Control. It was seen as a communist party bent on making the colony a Soviet satellite. However, Moonsammy continued to perform well for Berbice, in the inter-county championship, and for Skeldon, in the Davson Cup. He also represented British Guiana Indians on several occasions, with some distinction, in the Kawall Cup, as well as Berbice Indians in the annual Flood Cup tournament between Indians in the three counties. But that misjudgement in the early 1950s was an albatross.

Madray remembers Sonny Moonsammy as a good, humble man, respected by all, on or off the field. Pryor Jonas, an astute cricket observer, reflected many years later on an innings Sonny played at Bourda against the best Guyanese bowlers, probably in the same match when he got into trouble: 'I had seen him make an innings of 40 that could hardly have been surpassed for sheer brilliance. It was his first knock at Bourda against the country's best, [John] Trim and [Berkeley] Gaskin, Hill and Haynes. But he treated them with scant respect. I was amazed at his talent, shining forth like pure gold'.[23] He was only about 24 then, yet he was not forgiven; he was made to wither on the vine. Realising that his chance was slipping by, Moonsammy went into the lumber business at Skeldon; and after his two belated appearances for British Guiana in Barbados in early 1959, he seemed to have retired from all forms of the game; but his many friendships remained unimpaired. Then came a terse item in the *Guiana Graphic* of 28 December 1963; it read:

> A Skeldon, Corentyne, businessman died at the Georgetown Hospital yesterday after he was involved in an accident with a motor lorry in the city. It was reported that Moonsammy, 34, who arrived in the city earlier in the day to do some shopping, was walking along Lombard Street when he was struck down by a motor lorry. He was picked up unconscious and taken to hospital where he died a few minutes after regaining consciousness.

Very few outside of Plantation Skeldon would have taken any notice of this tragedy. The next day, however, the *Graphic* gave the tragedy it had reported the previous day the attention it deserved:

> Sonny Moonsammy, brilliant British Guiana and Berbice cricketer, died at the Georgetown Hospital on Friday [27 December 1963] from injuries suffered in an accident with a motor lorry. He was 34. A brilliant fieldsman in the covers and a delightful batsman, he made several appearances for Berbice in the inter-county championship and also represented British Guiana at home and abroad, particularly in the Kawall Cup of which he was a permanent member for several years.[24]

The *Berbice Times*, published in Moonsammy's county, sought to convey the pain the tragedy evoked in all who knew him. They emphasised his generosity of spirit, while noting that on his home plantation, his death hit the people 'like the sudden eruption of a volcano'. The paper assessed what Sonny had achieved in his short life.

> It is hard to believe that such a brilliant personality, so young, so enterprising, has passed to the great beyond without notice...His life was a shining example – an example which the youths of Berbice should try to emulate. He walked with beggars but was clothed with the garment of a king. His sincerity of purpose, his gentle bearing and dignified manner made him stand out like a lighted torch among his fellow men. He was not only a sportsman and businessman, he was in every sense a gentleman. The 600-odd people who followed his body to its last resting place were evidence of the high esteem in which he was held in the community. One could rightly say that he possessed that enviable quality which made him a friend of all and an enemy of none. In his person there was always that feeling of sympathy for his neighbour. During his cricketing career he performed creditably well in Barbados and Jamaica [I could not verify the latter]. *He could undoubtedly be classified as one of the finest fielders British Guiana has ever produced. He was an artist so to speak and thrilled many with his fine strokes all round the wicket.* Those who are not strangers to him are conscious of the good influence he had among young players at Skeldon on the cricket field. He was their teacher, their inspiration. With head bowed in reverence we say FAREWELL [emphasis added].[25]

Yet Sonny Moonsammy remains a void in the Indo-Guyanese narrative. I dedicated a small book I co-wrote to him: 'the master at cover-point'. That was twenty years ago. Since then I have been trying to find out when he died, recalling vaguely that tragedy from my youth but unable to ascertain when it happened. No one could remember although many spoke of him nostalgically, with discernible respect, as a prodigiously gifted batsman, and as a fielder in the covers *nonpareil*. He has come to epitomise the proverbial seed that lodged on stony ground, somewhat synonymous with that other promising Corentyne man, Ivan

Ivan Madray of Port Mourant during his second and last Test match, Georgetown, March 1958

Madray, with whom Pryor Jonas compared him. He had spoken of 'the forgotten Madray killed by the selectors during the Pakistan tour of 1958'.[26] Both were identified as potential West Indies Test players, but Sonny did not even get a fair chance for British Guiana; and Ivan was selected, precipitately and unwarrantably, for two Tests against Pakistan in 1958, at a time when, out of neglect and despair, he had played no cricket at all for several months. One of the aims of this book has been to traverse the stony ground that led to so many of our outstanding cricketers withering on the vine: unsung although their aborted play gave much pleasure and sustained a modicum of understanding between Africans and Indians.

That is why I wish now, on his 75th birthday, to apologise to Basil Fitzherbert Butcher (he was born on 3 September 1933 at Port Mourant), for the way he has been treated by his Indo-Guyanese compatriots, at Port Mourant and beyond. He is so elemental to that plantation's marvellous cricketing tradition, which is central to Indo-Guyanese cricket and identity, that he deserves a place in the Indo-Guyanese narrative. The fact that Basil is of African descent must no longer exclude him, for he played a crucial role in the development of the game at Port Mourant, when he was its captain, just before he made the West Indies team in 1958-9, on their tour of India and Pakistan. Three Port Mourant men, Basil Butcher, Rohan Kanhai and Joe Solomon, were selected. Although Basil is of full African ancestry, some have erroneously claimed that he is of African/Indian mixture, so-called *dougla*, in the local lexicon. As recently as 2002 a cricket journalist from India, Rahul Bhattacharya, visiting Guyana for the first time, referred to Butcher as 'half-Indian'.[27] This is not true, but it is a consolation of sorts, reflecting a touch of magnanimity, a desire to accommodate an outstanding West Indies cricketer whose roots are as authentically in Port Mourant as any from its overwhelming Indian majority. There were others, however, as Ivan Madray tells me, who, purely for racist reasons, did not even wish Basil to captain Port Mourant. They did not object publicly, asserts Ivan, because Butcher's stature, as batsman and captain, would have demolished whatever spurious arguments the bigots could have mustered. Ivan is categorical that Butcher's absence from the Indo-Guyanese narrative is a consequence of

Indian racism, which he believes has ancient roots in India and with which I concur above.[28] The rise of nationalism in British Guiana after the Second World War, with its bifurcated African/Indian racial promptings, exacerbated those old prejudices.

Ivan Madray says that he grew up three houses away from Basil Butcher, 'near the ball-field' at Port Mourant. They were playmates from as early as he can recall. He would bowl to him for hours, but did not mind because Basil loved to bat whereas he loved to bowl, even in their childhood. That Basil is African and Ivan Indian (of Tamil stock) was immaterial. He saw Basil as a brother; but he became aware early that there lurked a deep prejudice within his own Indian family: lightness of skin was seen as precious, as if it were given by the gods; darkness and blackness were seen as a kind of punishment from the gods. It disturbed him that his aunts treated him better than his sister because he was lighter. One of them would crudely stick her tongue out at his sister, teasing her, because she was black, that she was dark Kali, goddess of destruction, depicted in fearful imagery. He soon recognised that his people considered blackness a defect. Yet it came as a great shock to him, stirring a deep resentment, when his grandfather complained to his mum and dad that 'Ivan too close wid da black bai. Me na like how 'e a bring da bai a de house all de time'. Ivan said that when he learnt of what his grandfather had said about Basil, he was intensely disturbed; he came to 'hate' the old man. He had converted to Catholicism, and was largely responsible for Ivan being baptised as a Catholic. He later located the old man's response within a wider Indian bigotry towards black people.[29]

Ivan himself experienced racism when he played his first Test match in Trinidad in February 1958. He was fielding by the boundary at deep third-man when someone in the crowd shouted: 'We don't want more coolie in this side'. Then a cigarette end was flicked on his back and, an over or so later, a Coca-Cola bottle was hurled in his direction, narrowly missing him.[30] This disturbed him as much as did the prejudice of some towards Basil Butcher that was masked by affectations of camaraderie. Ivan thinks that by not embracing Basil they way they had Rohan Kanhai and Joe Solomon, even himself, Indo-Guyanese had forfeited a golden opportunity to demonstrate what that other man from Port Mourant, Cheddi Jagan, was preaching day in and day out: that race was skin deep; ultimately, it was African and Indian peoples' problems and progress – as a class – that really mattered. They all came from the same roots as far as Ivan is concerned; they all brought pride to Port Mourant; Africans were a tiny minority there; they certainly did not constitute a threat. By not accepting Butcher as their own, in spite of his origin and his immense talent, Indo-Guyanese set race relations back considerably, after the promising tone of the early 1950s.[31]

By the early 1960s Indo-Guyanese were in the ascendancy, economically and politically. They could have taken the initiative to be more magnanimous; they should have made greater overtures to Africans in order to lessen their fears of Indian domination. Eusi Kwayana says that even in the heady days within the PPP, before the Jagan-Burnham split of 1955, Africans were apprehensive of having an Indian leader, Jagan. This was aggravated by the racist behaviour of some Indians at the grassroots, in the villages. Kwayana argues:

> The two major groups have stereotypes of each other. Africans tended to see Indians as clannish, as having more money, having an interest in land. A lot of them were selling out their lands to Indians when they went broke. Although they were doing it voluntarily, it also alarmed them ... A lot of Africans were unable to go beyond that. They would look at the behaviour of Indians near to them in judging the PPP (the PPP does not understand that until now). If there is an aggressive [racist] member of the PPP in their district that is how they see the PPP. Jagan never deals with these things at the subjective level, although he has a lot of rage against Imperialism. That problem was never dealt with; that's one of the reasons why I left the PPP. The psychology of the leader is crucial. *We had to fight to get Africans to accept an Indian leader* [Jagan]. *He didn't have that problem. He never had to accept a leader of another race so he didn't know what it is* [emphasis added].[32]

Moreover, Indo-Guyanese triumphalism reached unconscionable heights after the victory of Jagan's PPP in the general elections of 1961. There was a tawdry display of Indian power, a parade all along the coast: further African humiliation was occasioned by the dragging of the symbol of Burnham's PNC, the broom, behind the cavalcade of Indian cars, trucks and tractors. Kanhai's ascendancy in 1960-1, in Australia, and Jagan's victory in August 1961 made Indo-Guyanese feel invincible. Most thought that Forbes Burnham, the African leader, was vanquished. Butcher, too, was in the wilderness; many believed that his Test career was over. He was not selected to go to Australia; he was not chosen against the weak team from India that lost 0-5 to West Indies in 1962. In fact, having been dropped from the West Indies team after the second Test against England in February 1960, he did not play in another until the first Test in England in June 1963 – an absence of over three years. For African-Guyanese these were bleak times, indeed; but by early 1962, they were aware that President Kennedy was personally committed to getting rid of Cheddi Jagan, obsessed that he would create another Cuba if he were granted Independence, as the British planned to do soon. In league with the rabidly anti-communist United Force (Portuguese and coloured), the Catholic Church and the predominantly African trade unions in the TUC – and crucially, the CIA – Burnham's African supporters resorted to violence in order to make British Guiana ungovernable. Their aim was to delay Independence, get the electoral system changed to proportional representation, and thus remove Jagan from government: he could not get a majority under that system. By late 1963 much of this had been achieved. Cheddi Jagan was tricked by the British Colonial Secretary, Duncan Sandys (Churchill's son-in-law) into signing a document that empowered him to adjudicate on all outstanding issues, including changing the electoral system, while he agreed to abide by Sandys's decisions. The British had succumbed eventually to Kennedy's relentless pressure to remove Jagan.[33]

By early 1964, as I have argued, Indo-Guyanese euphoria and over-confidence of 1961 were dissipated. Cheddi was facing the precipice and there was no way back. African-Guyanese knew that the tide was turning. Butcher was back in the West Indies team and his 133 at Lord's, in June 1963, was a major innings: with his back to the wall, he was largely responsible for saving the Test and possibly the series, while underlining that he was a batsman of high pedigree. Kanhai recognised this and said so: 'I've got a feeling that the world does not fully realise how great this boy Butcher is. His ton was carved out in the true Everton Weekes style – aggressive, decisive, spectacular'.[34] But Butcher's achievement was not seen as a victory for a Port Mourant man. Like the massive obligations thrust upon Kanhai by Indians, Basil was now saddled with the burdens and expectations of his African people. Neither could elude the Guyanese futility.

Meanwhile, Jagan now sought to retaliate, urging Indians to be disruptive to get the British to revoke proportional representation. Violence had worked for Burnham and D'Aguiar, it was Jagan's turn now to use the same instrument, his so-called 'hurricane of protests' strategy. It did not work: the Americans and British saw him as lost to the other side in the Cold War. The Indian futility had bleak repercussions at Port Mourant. Madray told me Butcher informed him that an attempted arson was made on his family home at Port Mourant during the racial violence of the early 1960s: 'We had to run, Ivan. They lit fire in our home. Some people came and tried to burn us in the house. It's not the same, Ivan'.[35] I have spoken to Basil Butcher about this tragic experience. He confirms that there was an attempted arson at their family home at Port Mourant around 1964, when the African-Indian confrontation had degenerated into mutual hatred. He was not there. It pained him to learn of the attempted arson. Apparently two terrorists had hurled a bottle bomb into their window in the night: it was a crude device that brought on a putrid smell of tar and kerosene, but little damage apart from scorching the front of the building. His wife, his father and other members of the family were in the house at the time (his mum had died in 1962). No one was hurt, but the mental damage was severe: his family could not stay any longer in the place that had made him, the place he loved. Basil says that his dad sold the house shortly afterwards – it could not be home any more. He has never spoken publicly about this sad end to his links with his home plantation. But he recalls that one of his friends, who had sought to protect his family rendering support at this difficult time, was Isaac Surienarine, a young Indian cricketer from Port Mourant who later represented Berbice and Guyana. Basil, however, holds no bitterness towards the people of Port Mourant: they, like Africans, had become pawns in the contest for power. But he feels that this question of racial insecurity in Guyana must be faced and not continually papered over.[36]

Butcher, understandably, severed all links with Port Mourant after this. The Indo-Guyanese narrative would already have framed him as being with their enemies: on the African side – Burnham's people. But Madray recalls that as a boy he would visit Basil's home where he was treated like a member of the family. He never encountered any racial prejudice from his parents. His mother was very generous; she baked and sold 'caan pone' and cassava pone for a living and would always put aside a little bit for him and Basil. Madray had left Guyana, but he was in despair when he learnt of the racism meted out to the Butcher family. That racial 'hatred' has since cast a shadow over the rich experiences from his boyhood.[37]

On 25 May 1964 a brutal attack took place at Wismar, opposite the bauxite town of Mackenzie, about 60 miles from Georgetown up the Demerara River. A few Indians were killed; several women raped and the community of about 1,500 fled. Jagan has written about the 'Wismar massacre': 'The whole Indian population which formed a minority was uprooted, and their houses set on fire. A large number was beaten, some of them to death; others had to flee for their lives. Women and even children were raped and otherwise savagely maltreated...Eyewitnesses stated that the police and armed volunteers [Africans] did nothing to help'.[38] The Intelligence Report attributed Wismar to the 'African population's response to events on the coastal strip', where a Jagan-led strike and PPP-fomented violence to force the British to overturn their decision to impose proportional representation had precipitated atrocities on both sides. There was an equally savage retaliation for Wismar: about 40 Africans died when the boat plying between Georgetown and Mackenzie was blasted to bits in early July 1964.

This pattern was entrenched: 'ethnic cleansing' took place in several districts. Wismar became etched in the Indo-Guyanese consciousness as a symbol of African 'savagery' and the signature of Jagan's demise. They therefore put greater pressure on Rohan Kanhai to compensate for the failings of their political leader – their failings in reality. In late 1964 it was announced that Butcher was taking up a job as cricket coach, at Mackenzie (including Wismar), with the Demerara Bauxite Company (Demba). The Indo-Guyanese cricket correspondent of the *Berbice Times,* Shan Razack, hailed it as 'a fine gesture': it ensured that his skills would be passed on to Guyanese.[39] This, however, was the final straw that placed Basil, as far as many Indians were concerned, decisively in the enemy's camp. Not many, apparently, were aware of the treatment his family had received at Port Mourant, or they sought to ignore it. In any case, the mutual racism that claimed the African and Indian people by 1963-4 had become contemptuous of the merits of 'the other', however well earned and irrefutable.

I wish, therefore, as a small atonement to Basil, to write him into the Indo-Guyanese narrative, where he belongs, and I hope, will remain until the last cricket match is played in Guyana. It is important to the future of Guyana that the history of Port Mourant and Berbice is told this way. Butcher says that sharing his boyhood with Ivan Madray shaped him in many ways. They never had any conception of race. The name Cheddi Jagan, of course, would not have meant anything in the Port Mourant of their formative years, in the late 1930s-early 1940s. The politics of race, also, meant nothing to them then. He recalls going often with Ivan to the Port Mourant cricket ground, anxious to be a part of the religion that was cricket on the plantation. That would become almost an obsession when John Trim, the African fast bowler from Port Mourant, played for British Guiana and the West Indies. But he concurs with Ivan that the captain of Port Mourant, Fielda Kempadoo, was not supportive of their boyhood curiosity: he would chase them away. It was when Johnny Teekasingh became captain that windows suddenly opened and they could begin to feel a fresh air that would nourish their seminal gifts. While he recognises the towering presence of Clyde Walcott in getting himself, Kanhai, Solomon and Madray into the British Guiana and West Indies teams by the latter half of the 1950s, he feels that Robert Christiani's presence on the staff at Plantation Port Mourant speeded up the process by which they came to Walcott's attention, benefiting from the latter's knowledge and authority. Madray did come into conflict with Christiani and has tended to minimise his contribution, but Butcher feels that he, too, deserves some credit.

I have already remarked on Butcher's first tour with the West Indies, to India and Pakistan in 1958-9, accompanied by two other Port Mourant men, Kanhai and Solomon. He scored two centuries in India and emerged with an aggregate of 486 runs in the five Tests and an average of 69.42. He made 103 and 142 in Calcutta and Madras respectively, sharing decisive partnerships with Kanhai of 217 and 101. In his two tours of England, Butcher played several crucial innings, particularly a historic one of 133 at Lord's in 1963 (with an average of 47.87), and 209 not out in Nottingham (averaging 60), in 1963 and 1966 respectively. In 44 Tests, between 1958 and 1969, he scored 3,104 runs (including seven centuries and 16 fifties), with an average of 43.11. In 169 first-class matches, between 1955 and 1972, his aggregate was 11,628 (31 hundreds and 54 fifties), at an average of nearly 50. This was an age when West Indies experienced prolonged periods of inaction, so a talented player like Butcher had limited opportunities to perform at the highest level. For instance, after his successful tour of England in 1963, he did not have the opportunity to play a Test for 18 months, between the end of August of that year and the first Test of the Australian tour of the West Indies, in March 1965. As seen earlier, having lost form against England in the West Indies in 1960, Basil was out of Test cricket from 4 February 1960 to 5 June 1963, over three years. He missed the great tour of Australia in 1960-1, Worrell's first as captain, and that of the Indians to the West Indies in 1962. That he was able to accomplish so much in spite of this, speaks of the character of the man. He had a personal resilience that was also at the core of the cricket he played.

How did Butcher cope with the pain of omission from Test cricket? He says that he availed himself of the limited opportunities to play first-class cricket in order to continually remind the selectors that his ability and his commitment were in no way diminished. Shortly after he was dropped by the West Indies in February 1960, he appeared for British Guiana against England, scoring 123; in the Berbice v. England match (as seen earlier), he made 131 not out in an unbroken third wicket partnership of 290 with Joe Solomon. No other first-class matches were played in 1960. Yet he was consigned to the wilderness not only for the rest of the West Indies/England series but well beyond. He was not selected for the tour of Australia scheduled to start shortly. Three batsmen were contesting for two places: himself and two Barbadians, Seymour Nurse and Peter Lashley. Butcher lost. Lashley played two Tests in Australia: his scores were 19 and 0 (the tied Test, Brisbane); and 41 and 18 (the fifth Test, Melbourne). Nurse played in three Tests: 70 and 3 (the second Test, Melbourne); 43 and 11 (the third Test, Sydney); and 49 and 5 (the fourth Test Adelaide). Butcher was a better batsman than either of the two; but he thinks he was a victim of territorial rivalry: the Barbadians had greater influence in West Indies cricket at the time. More woes were to follow.

He played no first class match again until a year later, in March/April 1961, when a Swanton XI toured British Guiana. Basil made 73 in the Berbice v. Swanton match and 113 representing British Guiana. During the latter innings he reached 2,000 runs in first-class cricket. In October 1961 Butcher played in the inter-colonial tournament against the Combined Islands [Leeward and Windward], Barbados and Trinidad. His scores were moderate because of a spate of run outs: 38, 56 (run out), 23 (run out), 46 and 34 (run out). Basil played no first-class cricket in 1962 – there was none on offer in the region! And the touring team from India did not go to British Guiana because of the political riots that engulfed Georgetown in February 1962, marked by looting and burning. Consequently he missed a potentially lucrative series that could have rehabilitated his Test career. West Indies, under Frank Worrell, won all five Tests; Kanhai prospered, with scores of 138, 89 run out, and 139; Solomon made 96 in Barbados.

This must have been a very dark time indeed for Basil. Now two years out of the Test arena, it is arguable that he was rescued from total despair, in the summer of 1962, by a contract with Lowerhouse in the Lancashire League. It provided him with short-term earnings while enabling him to tune his skills to the vagaries of English conditions. He considers the experience a 'great education', a mental and physical toughening that was the 'bottom line' to his re-entry to the West Indies team in 1963. He believes that he became a better player technically; he also developed the mental strength to retain his equanimity under demanding conditions. He adds that most West Indians who played in the Leagues emerged as true professionals. One had to be to retain one's livelihood. A score of over 50 was considered a good one in League matches, all of one day's duration. In 1962 Basil's scores for Lowerhouse were: 13, 27, 61, 70, 87, 85, 40 and 83. Because of his consistency he had won an award; and he believes that Frank Worrell, who was living in Radcliffe, Lancashire, would have followed his resurgence and progress. His development in the Lancashire League, therefore, was decisive to his selection for the tour of England in 1963.[40]

Butcher's innings of 133 (out of 229) at Lord's, 129 of it scored on 22 June 1963, is a pivotal one in the history of West Indies cricket. Without it West Indies would have lost the match. That great series, which West Indies won 3-1, was much more evenly contested than the final results suggest. They won the first Test at Manchester by 10 wickets; England came within six runs of winning the drawn second – Butcher's Test; and they won the third, at Birmingham, by 217 runs. If England had won the Lord's Test, they would have been virtually unconquerable going into the fourth, at Leeds. Butcher says the 133 at Lord's is the innings he will take with him wherever he finally ends up. Joe Solomon agrees that it was a crucial innings in terms of the series, and one of high pedigree, a personal tribute to the maturity of Butcher, combining technical kills with the capacity to punish any delivery that was even minimally flawed.[41]

In the first innings West Indies made 301, Kanhai's 73 and Solomon's 56 being the best scores. Butcher made 14, having scored only 22 in his only innings at Manchester. He had fallen to Fred Trueman again, who got 6 for 100. It was not an auspicious return to Test cricket after over three years in the wilderness. England's response was very robust: 297, with Dexter's famously imperious 70 ('one of the greatest I have ever seen', says fast-bowler Charlie Griffith) and Barrington's 80 being the top scores. West Indies did not start well in their second innings, losing both Conrad Hunte and Easton McMorris with the score at 15. Kanhai and Butcher were at the wicket, but Kanhai fell with the score at 64. By the time it reached 104, Sobers and Solomon were also out. This is the context, then, in which Butcher's innings must be assessed. West Indies were, in fact, 108 for 5, when Frank Worrell joined Butcher. The former made 33 but they shared a sixth wicket partnership of 110. Worrell was out at 214; West Indies were all out for 229: the last five wickets had subsided for 15 runs (Trueman got 11 wickets in the match for 152; Shackleton 7 for 165). Set 233 for victory, England reached 203 for 5 because of two innings of sterling doggedness, from Barrington (60) and Close (70) – true heroism with which Test cricket is infused from time to time, thus expanding our own conception of possibilities. But, mirroring the West Indies precipitous decline earlier, four England wickets fell for 25 runs: 228 for 9. With two balls remaining in the match, Colin Cowdrey, his left arm in plaster broken by Hall earlier, joined David Allen to save the Test. They had needed 8 from the last over, but Shackleton was run out with six runs still needed for victory from two balls. Allen, facing both, opted for survival. J.S. Barker watched and recorded the final over of that memorable Test:

> Hall walked thoughtfully up from third man to bowl the last over of the match, to Shackleton, with eight runs needed. Shackleton drove hard at the first and missed; stabbed the second down in front of him and Allen came in like a greyhound for the single. Allen took a single to fine-leg off the third ball. Six to win, three balls to go. Shackleton repeated his dabbing stroke and missed, but Allen rushed again down the pitch for a single. Murray coolly tossed the ball to Worrell and Worrell, with a flying start, sprinted to the stumps just ahead of Shackleton to break the wicket, ball in hand. There were two balls left in the match and, thank heaven, it was Allen who had to face them, not Cowdrey who had made his way to the wicket, twiddling his bat in his right hand, while awkwardly and gingerly keeping his plaster-encased left arm by his side. Hall could still win the match. Even after three and a half hours he was scarcely less formidable than he had been at the beginning. Worrell reminded Hall that a no-ball at this stage would be disastrous. Wesley banged them both straight at the stumps. Allen stunned the fifth, got his bat somehow to the sixth – and the great match was over, with Cowdrey a wryly smiling hero at the non-striker's end.[42]

Hall and Griffith accounted for 70 of 91 overs bowled by the West Indies in their second innings. Alan Ross, the poet and cricket writer, has memorialised Wes Hall's bowling on the last day of this absorbing Test, one of the truly historic matches that reminds us from time to time – always timely – that rumours of the death of Test cricket are necessarily exaggerated: 'It had been a day almost without precedent; but not only a day, for the whole match had swung this way and that, unpredictably and absorbingly. There were no dull stretches, not even a momentary let-up. Hall, for three hours twenty minutes, broken only by the tea-interval, had bowled without rest. It had been a spectacular demonstration of stamina, attack and endurance, probably unrivalled by any bowler of comparable pace in this century. His last over was as ferocious as his first, and there had been no slackening in between. His immense run, while it may have rested him on the way back, would have long since exhausted a lesser man. Griffith, who bowled only five overs less, had the wind to contend with, and his accuracy allowed Hall to give everything to speed. His 30 overs had cost less than two runs apiece; Hall's 40 overs cost 93 runs'.[43]

V.S. Naipaul saw all five days of the Test. It was not easy: 'Day after day I have left Lord's emotionally drained. What other game could have stretched hope and anxiety over six days [Sunday was a rest day]...[T]here were moments when it was torment to watch, when I joined those others, equally exhausted, sitting on the grass behind the stands'.[44]

All these rich ingredients are admirable, indeed, and deserve to be memorialised; but it is my conviction that this was Basil Butcher's Test because without his 133 the West Indies would have lost: the second highest score in their second innings was Worrell's 33. Michael Manley puts the innings in perspective: 'When the West Indies set out with their tiny lead of 4 runs, Trueman was again irresistible, taking 5 for 52 in 26 overs. Indeed, were it not for Basil Butcher, it would have been a rout. The young British Guianese, batting at no. 5 [no. 4], was beginning the first of several great rescue operations in which he seemed ready at last to take over the mantle of Collie Smith [1933-59] as the man in the middle of the batting order who rises to occasions that might otherwise be lost. His 133 will not rank among the great innings for elegance. On the other hand, it was courageous, full of aggression against deliveries that were the least bit wayward and completely dominant in its surroundings, for the rest of the side,

Basil Butcher of Port Mourant: the end of his historic innings, Lord's, 24 June 1963

including extras, only managed 96 other runs between them, 33 of which came from Worrell'.[45]

Alan Ross points out that Butcher's 133 commenced with the score at 15 for 2, and ended 4 hours and 22 minutes later, at 228 for 9: he was at the wicket for all but 16 of West Indies score of 229. The innings was made off 261 balls and comprised two sixes, 17 fours, fourteen two's and 25 singles. Basil's boundaries were struck off the following bowlers: five 4's off Fred Trueman; eight off Derek Shackleton; two off Fred Titmus; and two 6's and two 4's off David Allen. The 133 runs were made off 58 scoring shots, thus 203 deliveries were 'dot' balls. It was a true reflection of sound defence and judgment, coupled with controlled aggression against deliveries that were fractionally loose. The skills Basil gained in the Lancashire League, especially against the moving ball, of which Trueman and Shackleton were among the finest exponents, proved a priceless asset in constructing this invaluable innings. Speaking sarcastically, and meant as a compliment, of course, in order to emphasise that a daring dimension was not missing from Butcher's play, Worrell's caution notwithstanding, C.L.R. James said at the end of the tour: 'I don't know that anyone was more astonished than I was at some of the things that Butcher did at Lord's in his century. That ill-educated young man had 92 and went to 100 by hitting two fours down to the pavilion. You just don't do that sort of thing! In addition to that, when slow bowlers were bowling to him he kept on jumping out and driving for six. You remember the stroke when he had made 50 or 60. The average batsman does not do that'.[46]

The following excerpts from Alan Ross's description of Butcher's dominance of the crucial sixth wicket partnership of 110 with Worrell, with the benefit of hindsight, is illustrative of the fact that he was now a mature professional, and that this innings marked the watershed in his Test career. Ross writes:

> The last and crucial session began with Trueman, from the pavilion end, and Allen [from the nursery]…[Solomon was soon out to the latter.]…Worrell…was all but caught in the same over, during which Butcher made a second, dancing assault on Allen, taking six to long-off. Next Butcher turned his attention to Trueman, on-driving and swinging him to leg for two fours in the

> same over…After a subdued twenty minutes, Butcher, like one suddenly released from imprisonment, raced out to Allen, the flimsiest snick standing between four runs and being stumped by yards. Shackleton returned and Butcher pulled him unceremoniously to the Tavern, a stroke of pure relish. That meant 50 for the partnership with Butcher, getting out of hand, being quieted by Worrell. But two more thumping leg-side hits followed, the second taking Butcher to his hundred, flamboyantly made out of only 154 scored since he had come in. Predominantly an on-side innings, it had a West Indian lavishness to it, a branch-to-branch swinging from the studious to the impulsive. Latterly, Worrell's restraining calm had kept it within limits…[47]

As soon as the new ball was due Cowdrey gave it to Trueman. Ross says that this was an incentive for Basil to get even better:

> Seeing it even better, Butcher, during the six overs remaining, played stroke after stroke of a dreamy softness timed to perfection. It was as if he had kept them on ice all his life, reserved for this moment. Together with Worrell he had taken West Indies from 104 for 5 to 214, waving away England's chances…Cowdrey had done everything possible but Butcher, savaging the spinners on quick feet, had forced back the tiring Shackleton and Trueman. These he had in turn plundered, clipping the leg stump half-volley with the minimum of back lift. In defence he was scrupulously correct, didactic to a degree.[48]

This innings was crucial to the West Indies; it was also of great import to Butcher. If he had failed here again, after over three years in the wilderness, this could well have ended his career; his prodigious talent might have been silenced. As it happened, this innings at Lord's epitomised the new spirit of West Indies cricket, ushered in by Frank Worrell's captaincy and congruent with his belief that with the death of the West Indies Federation, it was imperative for the region's cricketers to demonstrate unimpeachable collective will. Indeed, as Butcher told me, Frank was able to meld players – new and seasoned, black, brown or white – in a manner inconceivable under his predecessor, Gerry Alexander (under whom Basil played ten Tests). The sense of being a unit was so powerful now that the fact they had 18 players on tour in England (several did not get the chance to play regularly), in no way detracted from their single-minded pursuit of victory. Basil recalls that even young Deryck Murray, just 20 (nearly 19 years younger than his captain), was quickly made to feel a part of the unit – and the endeavour.[49]

Charlie Griffith has remarked on Worrell's conviction that the insularity that had routinely dogged several West Indies tours must be eliminated: 'He was a true West Indian. From the moment we had our first team meeting in London, he and Berkeley Gaskin, the manager, made it clear that we were a representative West Indian team and sectional or personal desires had to be forfeited in the interest of unity. We were told to realise that we did not represent ourselves but three million West Indians at home and abroad. The West Indies Federation had just collapsed and there was a spirit of nationalism and separatism developing in the islands. We realised that cricket, of all the other institutions in the West Indies, was the one unifying force in the area which really touched the souls of our people. Throughout the tour the spirit of unity prevailed…'[50]

Frank Worrell had a knack for reason and reasonableness, as James recalls. He pointed out what had to be done and left his players to get on with it; but he never asked of them what he himself could not do. Moreover, there was a social/sociological attribute that James discerned in the first black captain of the West Indies team: 'As a result of his previous training (as a member of the black West Indian middle class of Barbados…) Frank had certain other qualities which expressed themselves in his captaincy…[H]e was always calm and unruffled even in times of crisis…'[51] Alan Ross offered a most astute judgment on Worrell's captaincy at the end of the tour of 1963. I have seen no finer verdict on the leadership of this fine West Indian: '[H]is presence, on or off the field, was as pervasive as the most lingering of scents. It might have appeared to the undiscerning, judging only by the casualness of his approach, that he was merely the figurehead, the father-figure dispensing soothing advice from behind the lines. Nothing could have been further from the truth. On the field, as captain, he kept gesture to a minimum, but his control, authority and astuteness were never in doubt. He had, it is true, all the

Basil Butcher at 75: on his left are Guyanese compatriots, politician/lawyer, Moses Nagamootoo, and cricket commentator, 'Reds' Perreira, Providence, Guyana, March 2009

weapons, but he deployed them with a single-mindedness and psychological subtlety that ensured they were never blunted'.[52]

In an interview with Frank Birbalsingh in Toronto in 1998, Butcher gave an example of Worrell's powers of discernment and his uncanny gift for timely intervention. He guided him to the famous century at Lord's and to the resurrection of his international career:

> In the first Test at Old Trafford I had made 22 and got out lbw trying to hook Trueman. In the first innings of the second Test [at Lord's], I was caught for 14 on the square-leg boundary again hooking Trueman. So Frank said something during the second innings: 'Butch, if you want to beat the bowling it's not one ball you have to hit: you have to beat the ball the whole day'. Most people knew that, in 1960, during the English tour of the West Indies, Trueman had a lot of negative things to say about some West Indian players, including myself, and Frank understood that I wanted to punish Trueman. But Trueman had got me out twice already on the 1963 tour, so Frank said if I wanted to beat Trueman it had to be for hours. When I was on 92 Shackleton bowled me a half-volley and I hit it straight over his head first bounce for four. Frank said: 'You, son of a bitch! I've known that man for twenty years, and he has never bowled me a half-volley'. When I got to a hundred he said: 'You've just finished batting for Butcher. Look at the score. Now you have to bat for West Indies'.[53]

Charlie Griffith appreciates what that innings meant not only to that Test but the series. He also drew attention to the character of the man, the author of that masterly performance: 'Basil Butcher played a superb knock of 133 at a time when we were struggling. He not only got a hundred in his first Test at Lord's but he made his runs at a time when he was undergoing great personal stress. The fact that he was able to concentrate to get a hundred, to my mind, was clear proof of his class and pedigree'.[54]

I asked Butcher about the nature of his stress and he said that he had just received a letter prior to the Test in which he learnt of his wife's miscarriage. It was a difficult situation, but it seemed to have drawn out of him the resolve to concentrate, to do well – to give his people in British Guiana something to celebrate, to be proud of, amidst the political gloom. It was a Herculean effort and, therefore, this innings must be seen not only as significant in the history of West Indies cricket; but potentially valuable, too, for Guyana in future: a symbol of something of resolve, flexibility and hope.

The English cricket writer, Clayton Goodwin, watched Basil's innings on the Saturday at Lord's. It has left an indelibly pleasant image in his mind: 'Basil Butcher was the quiet, methodical run-scorer in the great team. He was not flamboyant either as player or as man, but opponents rated him the most difficult batman to get out...[A]t Lord's in 1963...[he] played one of the most enjoyable knocks I have ever seen. While Worrell defended his wicket with mature authority, the young Guyanese drove and cut with growing confidence. His enterprise was never rash and he waited for the bad ball. He drove the fast bowlers straight into the shadows of the pavilion as the Saturday evening sun went down. This was cricket as it should be, hard but entertaining'.[55]

That the men from Port Mourant, Rohan Kanhai, Basil Butcher and Joe Solomon had, by 1963, reached the top was due initially to a man from the black Barbadian middle class that James spoke about: a people with a sense of decency and responsibility that bred ambition and gave them honour. That man was Clyde Walcott; he had led them to the foothills. By 1960 Clyde had retired from Test cricket, but another man of similar background and outlook, Frank Worrell, made it possible for the men from Port Mourant to reach the summit. Walcott and Worrell had no time for race or petty prejudices. Like Basil Butcher, therefore, they must have a place in the Indo-Guyanese narrative. Because however powerful the continuing resonance of Mother India in the making of Indo-Guyanese identity, there is also a deeply rooted creole component that is just as valid as that which comes from ancestral sources.

Indo-Guyanese have made remarkable strides in all areas of West Indian life, and the ultimate quest to belong, through mastery of the instrument of greatest validity in West Indian societies, cricket, has been achieved. This has been a long process, commencing with their appropriation of Ranji from the 1890s, through the acquired competence of Veerasawmy, 'Doosha' Persaud, Ganesh Persaud, Sonny 'Sugar Boy' Baijnauth, Sonny Moonsammy and others, culminating in the 'comfortable intractability' of Joe Solomon and the crowning mastery of Rohan Kanhai. Yet because the game was made to carry their social and political insecurities, Indo-Guyanese saddled their few top-class cricketers with huge racial obligations. In the process the game that had helped to build bridges, however tenuous, towards the African community became contaminated by their prejudices, their hopes and aspirations. The fact, however, is that they have been in the region for 170 years; they have reached the summit in every sphere of endeavour – they do belong. But they also have multiple identities (religious and ethnic), and Mother India (as I have discovered after many visits there since 2000) still has the power to influence her descendants in the diaspora, although there is no equivocation with regard to their loyalty to places like Guyana and Trinidad.

A palpable defensiveness on the part of Indo-Guyanese became eloquent after the fall of Jagan in 1964 and the remorseless rigging of elections by the African PNC, between 1968 and 1985. As I have argued, to partially counter their powerlessness, they had imposed unconscionable burdens on Rohan Kanhai. But their problem was compounded in the mid-1980s-early 1990s, when, for the first time since 1950, no Indian represented the West Indies. Cricket is an instrument of politics; and when the latter was seen to be completely shut off because of the chronic rigging of elections, Indo-Guyanese used the instrument of cricket to articulate their grievances as they sought to compensate for their exclusion. But with the end of the careers of Kanhai, then Alvin Kallicharran (66 Tests between 1972 and 1981) and Faoud Bacchus (19 Tests between 1978 and 1982), no Indian represented the West Indies in Tests for another 12 years, from 4 February 1982 until the appearance of Shivnarine Chanderpaul on 17 March1994, appropriately, at Bourda in Georgetown. Even the cricketing weapon they had used so vigorously since the 1950s had become blunted: double exclusion. The futility showed: they supported not only India and Pakistan against the West Indies, but every other opponent, even Australia, England and New Zealand.

In 1990 Viv Richards, the West Indies captain, made a tactless comment to *Outlet*, an Antiguan newspaper, which really underlined the marginalisation at the time of Indo-Guyanese, not only in cricket but also in politics. He said that 'the West Indies cricket team…is the only sporting team of African descent that has been able to win repeatedly against all international opposition, bringing joy and recognition to our people'.[56] Viv did try to 'clarify' what he meant but the damage was done. This aggravated the alienation of Indians in the region. There had been no Indian in the team for eight years, so Viv was factually correct and as an Antiguan he probably could not see the implications of his statement underlining the African provenance of his team.

Hubert Devonish, the Guyanese linguistics scholar, has empathised with the perceived exclusion encountered by Indo-West Indians at the time. And he suggested that the region must come to terms with its cultural pluralism and the reality of its peoples having multiple identities. This should not be perceived as sectional and impoverishing; rather it should be embraced as a potentially enriching component of West Indian identity:

> Up to at least the end of the 1970s in Guyana, it was the norm for Indian Guyanese to support the West Indies against any team except those from the sub-continent. The principle of multiple identities was at play here. Depending on which was the opposing team, their Indianness or West Indianness would be the one that receives particular emphasis. With the increased alienation of Indian Guyanese from the political process and West Indian cricket, they swung to the position of supporting any team against the West Indies [even New Zealand, in 1985, to the consternation of the Kiwis]. In 1990 many of them turned out to support England ...at Bourda. In the 1991 Test match against Australia at Bourda, the Indian section of the crowd is reported to have strongly supported Australia and booed members of the West Indies team. In the light of his description of the West Indies team as a sporting team of African descent, the captain, Vivian Richards, was singled out for special treatment.[57]

Devonish makes his case for greater tolerance of cultural diversity and for magnanimity in cricket: 'The arrogance of African West Indians in trying to dictate to their compatriots who they should support at a cricket match, clearly shows up the pitfalls of nationalism. Nationalism requires the suppression of all other identities in favour of that defined as national by those with the power to make such a definition. When large crowds of West

Indian origin throng the cricket grounds in England to support the West Indies against the land of their residence and very often citizenship, their right to do so is firmly supported by African West Indians...The view that any group of people could be made to express themselves by way of a single common identity is both contrary to good sense and everyday life in the Caribbean'.[58]

It may be a good thing if in Guyana, for instance, the principle of multiple identities, shaped by an imagined Africa and India, is encouraged. But this must be combined with a resolve to foster an understanding of, and respect for, the ethnic foundations of identity (as enriching, not as racist), coupled with a determination to create a political process that does not simply revolve around the arithmetic of race: winner cannot take all in elections. In the context of greater cultural and political security cricket may eventually lose the ethnic foundation of its articulation. Guyana and Trinidad must celebrate their diversity and genuinely begin to draw from the immense wealth that remains dormant in this legacy. It is not conducive to the making of a regional sensibility to seek to impose one creole culture, comprehensive and immutable. The more one challenges minority groups, such as Indians in the Caribbean, to confirm to a procrustean creole mould, the more they will dig their hells in and seek inspiration from ancestral sources. As Professor Brinsley Samaroo argues, the creole sensibility must be inclusive, even more opened to a greater measure of hybridity if an authentic West Indian nationhood is ever to become a reality:

> [T]he Indo-Caribbean person feels increasingly beleaguered in a larger Caribbean society which makes little effort to try to understand the different socio-cultural perspectives of Islam and Hinduism. For this reason, culture becomes a tool of survival, where people hold on to what they have and are reluctant to adapt to the new norms which must, inexorably, be the bases for our West Indian nationhood...Part of the solution must surely be an acceptance of difference to be followed by an effort to appreciate the richness of our diversified civilisation. In the longer term we must seek to build a civilisation in the Caribbean which could draw from the wealth of the East and would merge this richness with that of Africa, the Middle East and Europe.[59]

It is one of the enviable strengths of the Anglophone Caribbean that, save for pockets of Amerindians, all the peoples of the Caribbean are 'immigrants'. No great indigenous civilisations, with ancient roots in ancestral space, hinder the path to flexibility and imagination in the continual aggregation of creole culture. Indo-Guyanese still look, periodically, to Mother India for inspiration but they are now a Caribbean people. They have had political power since 1992 when, with the collapse of the Soviet empire and the personal intervention of Jimmy Carter, the predominantly African People's National Congress was persuaded to hold the first free and fair elections since 1964. Two years later, in 1994, the first Indo-West Indian in twelve years made his debut for the West Indies cricket team: Shivnarine Chanderpaul (born 1974). He is now the most dependable batsman in the team; but since the late 1990s it has become common for three or four Indians to play in each Test match. Besides, since Rohan Kanhai and Alvin Kallicharran in the 1970s, several Indians have captained the West Indies: Chanderpaul, Ramnaresh Sarwan and Darren Ganga. Politically, economically, educationally and in regional cricket Indo-Guyanese have arrived at centre-stage – in no way inferior to other groups. But it is imperative that this does not breed triumphalism and the disregard of the feelings of African-Guyanese. They must not repeat the grave errors of the early 1960s: the triumphalism towards black people after Jagan's victory in August 1961, and the lack of magnanimity towards Basil Butcher of Port Mourant, for example. Now is the time for Indo-Guyanese to do something really generous with potentially lasting benefits for Guyana and the region as a whole. They must seek to include African-Guyanese in the political process while accommodating and endeavouring to comprehend their curiosity in, and pursuit of, their African heritage. Hybridity is necessarily germane to the building of a West Indian identity. Indo-Guyanese could be at the core of this project. Cricket is politics by other means. In the past they have thrust upon their cricketers their ethnic fears, despair, hopes and aspirations. Indo-Guyanese players, such as Chanderpaul and Sarwan, could now be an example, as the team shows possibilities of resurgence, pointing the way for the politicians towards genuine regional integration, based on our diversity, not some imagined creole procrustean mould.

Indo-Caribbean people are a vital strand in this region of rich diversity. Their solid achievements in diverse spheres of endeavour have already gained recognition from all peoples of the region. This offers hope for greater integration. But it is important to remember that the 'Tiger of Port Mourant', possibly more than any other West Indian (Cheddi Jagan, V.S. Naipaul and Sonny Ramphal included), paved the way with his imperious bat not only for Indians to belong but also for them to be seen to belong. John Woodcock has said that 'his cricket was all about self-expression…Such was Rohan Kanhai's genius for batting that, had he been so minded, he might well have averaged not 47 in Test matches for West Indies but 77 or even 87. But he would not have been the great attraction that he was'.[60] Ernest Eytle, the biographer of Frank Worrell, wrote the entry on Kanhai in *Wisden* of 1964, when he was one of their five cricketers of the year: 'Quick of eye and foot, he times the ball almost perfectly when executing a wide variety of strokes, some of which border upon the audacious, and at his best he can master the most formidable of bowlers'.[61] One could argue that something of the spirit, originality and genius of Ranji was passed down to Rohan, for the gist of the portrait of Ranji in *Wisden* of 1897, when he was one of their five cricketers of the season, could easily be applied to him:

> As a batsman Ranjitsinhji is himself alone, being quite individual and distinctive in his style of play. He can scarcely be pointed to as a safe model for young and aspiring batsmen, his peculiar and almost unique skill depending in large measure on extreme keenness of eye, combined with great power and flexibility of wrist. For any ordinary player to attempt to turn good length balls off the middle stump as he does, would be futile and disastrous. To Ranjitsinhji on a fast wicket, however, everything seems possible, and if the somewhat too-freely-used word genius can with any propriety be employed in connection with cricket, it surely applies to the young Indian's batting.[62]

I wish now to give the last reflection – economical but resonant – on what Rohan Kanhai meant to Indo-Guyanese (Indo-West Indians as a whole) to Dr Tulsi Singh, a distinguished doctor of medicine, entrepreneur and philanthropist, of the town of Midland, in west Texas. He was born in 1949 and grew up in Palmyra Village in Berbice, British Guiana, about nine miles from

Port Mourant. Rohan's years of glory on the world stage of cricket in the late 1950s-early 1960s were Tulsi's formative ones:

> Rohan launched my most enduring passion: Test cricket. And for the first 15 years [ca 1958-73], he was the anchor that kept that passion firm and fast. I grew up at the boundary between the Corentyne and Canje [districts], and from there this world-class cricketer from Port Mourant seemed larger than life. While we were surrounded by an enlarging group of Indo-Guyanese stars in the professions and politics, they were of local repute; Rohan's star shone around the world. He was our *bhai* [brother]. Each time he bisected the gap between cover and extra-cover he severed another link in the chain that restricted our imagination. His panache flowed to us. We turned our collars up and strutted a little higher. He was truly *abby bai* [our boy].[63]

By claiming Rohan as our '*bhai*' ('brother' in Hindi), Dr Singh is alluding to the common ancestral link to Mother India; while his recourse to the Indo-Guyanese creole expression, 'abby bai' (our boy), suggests his iconic stature in the making of Indo-Guyanese identity: suggestive of the son of the immigrant who had made good, thus creating a niche – the example – for all his people. This is symbolic of the full journey: the arrival and ultimate affirmation of belonging. 'From Ranji to Rohan' encapsulates, therefore, the validation of Indo-Guyaneseness as an authentic strand of creole (West Indian) sensibility.

NOTES

1. See Birbalsingh and Seecharan, *Indo-West Indian Cricket*, (London: Hansib 1988), p.124
2. Interview with Ivan Madray, London, 11 June 2008.
3. This is developed in several of my writings, especially *Mother India's Shadow over El Dorado: Indo-Guyanese Politics and Identity, 1890s-1930s* (Kingston, Jamaica: Ian Randle Publishers, [forthcoming, 2009].
4. The *Daily Chronicle*, 24 April 1932.
5. The *Daily Chronicle*, 13 November 1932.
6. The *Daily Chronicle*, 30 August 1936.
7. The *Daily Chronicle*, 22 March 1936.

8. Leader, the *Daily Chronicle*, 1 May 1938.
9. Tony Ballantyne, *Orientalism and Race: Aryanism in the British Empire* (Basingstoke: Palgrave, 2002), pp. 5, 42-3.
10. Romila Thapar, *Early India: From the Origins to A.D. 1300* (New Delhi: Penguin Books, 2002), pp. 65-6.
11. A.L. Basham, *The Wonder that was India* [3rd ed.] (New Delhi: Rupa and Co.), pp. 32, 35, 152.
12. See *http//www.allacademic.com/meta/p169882_index.html.*
13. Interview with Ivan Madray, London, 11 June 2008.
14. The *Daily Chronicle*, 19 February 1933.
15. Dale Bisnauth, *The Settlement of Indians in Guyana, 1890-1930* (Leeds: Peepal Tree Press, 2000), pp. 222-3.
16. Elahi Baksh, 'The Propagandist', in Frank Birbalsingh, *Jahaji: An Anthology of Indo-Caribbean Fiction* (Toronto: TSAR, 2000), pp. 19-20.
17. Sudhir Kakar and Katharina Kakar, *The Indians: Portrait of a People* (New Delhi: Penguin Books, 2007), pp.36-7.
18. Personal communication, Dr Tulsi Singh, Midland, Texas, 10 July 2008.
19. Garry Sobers, *My Autobiography* (London: Headline, 2002), pp. 77-8.
20. See *cricketarchive.com.*
21. See note 1, p. 125.
22. Interview with Ivan Madray, London, 11 June 2008.
23 *Guiana Graphic*, 25 January 1964.
24 *Guiana Graphic*, 29 December 1963.
25 *Berbice Times*, 4 January 1964.
26. See note 23.
27. Rahul Bhattacharya, 'Ancestral Sentiment or National Loyalty?', Wisden Asia Cricket Online (2002).
28. Interview with Ivan Madray, 11 June 2008.
29. *Ibid.*
30. See note 1, p. 118.
31. Interview with Ivan Madray, London, 11 June 2008..
32. See my *Sweetening 'Bitter Sugar', op. cit.* [2005], p. 590.
33. *Ibid.*, Chapters 31-2.
34. Kanhai, *op. cit.* [1966], p. 97.
35. Interview with Ivan Madray, 11 June 2008..
36. Interview (by phone) with Basil Butcher, 25 July 2008.
37. See note 31.
38. Cheddi Jagan, *The West on Trial: My Fight for Guyana's Freedom* (London: Michael

Joseph, 1966), p. 358.
39. *Berbice Times*, 28 November 1964.
40. Interview (by phone) with Basil Butcher, 27 July 2008
41. Interview (by phone) with Joe Solomon, 30 July 2008.
42. J.S. Barker, *op. cit.* [1965]), pp. 58-9.
43. Alan Ross, *West Indies at Lord's* (London: Constable, 1986 [1963]), pp. 59-60.
44. V.S. Naipaul, 'England v. West Indies (1963)', in Michael Davie and Simon Davie (eds.), *The Faber Book of Cricket* (London: Faber and Faber, 1987), p. 194.
45. Michael Manley, *A History of West Indies Cricket* [rev. ed.] ([Kingston], Jamaica: West Indies Publishing Ltd.), pp. 165-6.
46. C.L.R. James, 'The 1963 West Indians', in Anna Grimshaw (ed.), *Cricket: C.L.R. James* (London: Allison and Busby, 1986), p. 138.
47. See note 43, pp. 40-1.
48. *Ibid.*, p. 41.
49. Interview (by phone) with Basil Butcher, 27 July 2008.
50. Charlie Griffith, *Chucked Around* (London: Pelham Books, 1970), pp. 57-8.
51. C.L.R. James, 'Sir Frank Worrell', in Anna Grimshaw (ed.), *op. cit.* [1986], p. 261.
52. See note 43, p. 85.
53. 'Basil Butcher: Interview', in Frank Birbalsingh, *Guyana and the Caribbean: Reviews, Essays and Interviews* (Chichester, West Sussex: Dido Press, 2004), p. 137.
54. See note 50, p. 64.
55. Clayton Goodwin, *Caribbean Cricketers: From the Pioneers to Packer* (London: George G. Harrap, 1980), p. 138.
56. Hubert Devonish, 'African and Indian Consciousness at Play: A Study in West Indies Cricket and Nationalism', in Hilary McD. Beckles and Brian Stoddart (eds.), *Liberation Cricket: West Indies Cricket Culture* (Kingston, Jamaica: Ian Randle Publishers, 1995), p. 187. This article is reproduced as Appendix IV.
57. *Ibid.*, p. 188.
58. *Ibid.*, pp. 189-90.
59. Brinsley Samaroo, 'Asian Identity and Culture in the Caribbean', in George Lamming (ed.), *Enterprise of the Indies* (Port of Spain: The Trinidad and Tobago Institute of the West Indies, 1999), p. 45.
60. John Woodcock, *The 'Times' One Hundred Greatest Cricketers* (London: Macmillan, 1998), p. 52.
61. Ernest Eytle [E.E.], 'Rohan Kanhai', *Wisden 1964*, p. 85.
62. 'Kumar Shri Ranjitsinhji' [Five Cricketers of the Season], *Wisden 1897*, pp. xlix-l.
63. Personal communication, Dr. Tulsi Singh, Midland, Texas, 12 October 2006.

APPENDIX I

SELECT CAREER STATISTICS

RANJI

Full name: Kumar Shri Ranjitsinhji
Born: 10 September 1872, Sarodar, Kathiawar, India
Died: 2 April 1933, Jamnagar Palace, Gujarat, India
Batting: Right-hand batsman
Biography: Made first-class debut for Cambridge University, Fenner's, 8 May 1893; made Test debut, 16 July 1896, England v. Australia, Manchester, with scores of 62 and 154; became Maharajah Jam Sahib of Nawanagar in 1907; *Wisden* cricketer of the year, 1897.
Teams: England (Test: 1896-1902); Cambridge University (1893-4); Sussex (1895-1920)

[*Test Career Batting and Fielding (1896-1902)*]
England:

Matches	*Innings*	*Not Out*	*Runs*	*Highest Score*	*Average*	*100*	*50*	*Catches*
15	26	4	989	175	44.95	2	6	13

[*First-Class Career Batting and Fielding (1893-1920)*]

307	500	62	24,692	285 no	56.37	72	109	234

Ten or More Centuries in a Season

1896 10 centuries
1900 11 centuries

Three Thousand Runs in a Season

1899 3,159 runs (average 63.18)
1900 3,065 runs (average 87.57)

Sources: *cricketarchive.com*; Alan Ross, *Ranji: Prince of Cricketers* (London: Collins, 1983)

ROHAN KANHAI

Full name: Rohan Bholalall Kanhai
Born: 26 December 1935, Port Mourant, Berbice, British Guiana [Guyana]
Batting: Right-hand batsman
Teams West Indies (Test: 1957-74); British Guiana [Guyana] (1955-1974); Western Australia (1961-2); Trinidad (1965); Warwickshire (1968-77); Tasmania (1969-70)
Biography: Made first-class debut, 5 February, 1955, v. Barbados; made Test debut, 30 June 1957, v. England (Birmingham); married Brenda Hague, 11 September 1963; *Wisden* cricketer of the year, 1964; his book, *Blasting for Runs*, published in 1966; captain of the West Indies, 1973-4 (13 Tests)

[*Test Career Batting and Fielding (1957-1974)*]
West Indies:

Matches	*Innings*	*Not Out*	*Runs*	*Highest Score*	*Average*	*100*	*50*	*Catches*
79	137	6	6,227	256	47.53	15	28	50

[*First-Class Career Batting and Fielding*]

421	675	83	29,250	256	49.40	86	120	325

Sources: *cricketarchive.com*; Rohan Kanhai, *Blasting for Runs* (London: Souvenir Press, 1966)

BASIL BUTCHER

Full name: Basil Fitzherbert Butcher
Born: 3 September 1933, Port Mourant, Berbice, British Guiana [Guyana]
Batting: Right-hand batsman
Teams: West Indies (Test: 1958-1969); British Guiana [Guyana] (1955-1971)
Biography: First of trio of West Indies batsmen from Plantation Port Mourant to represent British Guiana, 29 January 1955, v. Barbados; made Test debut, 28 November 1958, v. India, Bombay; *Wisden* cricketer of the year, 1970

[*Test Career Batting and Fielding (1958-1969)*]
West Indies:

Matches	*Innings*	*Not Out*	*Runs*	*Highest Score*	*Average*	*100*	*50*	*Catches*
44	78	6	3,104	209 no	43.11	7	16	15

[*First-Class Career Batting and Fielding (1955-1971)*]

169	262	29	11,628	209 no	49.90	31	54	67

Source: *cricketarchive.com*

JOE SOLOMON

Full name: Joseph Stanislaus Solomon
Born: 26 August 1930, Port Mourant, Berbice, British Guiana [Guyana]
Batting: Right-hand batsman
Teams: West Indies (Test: 1958-65); British Guiana (1956-1969)
Biography: Made first-class debut, 11 October 1956, v. Jamaica; made Test debut, 12 December 1958, v. India, Kanpur; ran out Ian Meckiff [with direct hit, side-on from square-leg] to produce the first tied Test in cricket, Brisbane, Australia, 14 December 1960

[*Test Career Batting and Fielding (1958-1965)*]
West Indies:

Matches	*Innings*	*Not Out*	*Runs*	*Highest Score*	*Average*	*100*	*50*	*Catches*
27	46	7	1,326	100 no	34.00	1	9	13

[*First-Class Career Batting and Fielding (1956-1969)*]

104	156	28	5,318	201 no	41.54	12	27	46

Source: *cricketarchive.com*

APPENDIX II

WORRELL ON THE TOUR OF AUSTRALIA, 1960-1

In 1963 Ernest Eytle published a biography of Frank Worrell. He caught the essence of the man, the source of his *presence*, on and off the field: 'Frank Worrell possesses neither the ferocity of Walcott nor the pocket-sized explosiveness of Weekes. Worrell – tall, lithe and graceful – strokes the ball persuasively and with perfect timing. A man for the big occasion he seems to flow into his strokes the moment he arrives at the wicket. There is neither dawn nor sunset to a Worrell innings: it begins at high noon...[He was] a tower of strength to the side he led in Australia, both as batsman and captain. He moulded a new combination of young players and made them stars. He was firm with them yet gentle. He set the example and they followed. On the field he was never demonstrative. They knew what he expected and were happy to go along with him. He remained calm in all the crises the team faced'. [(*Frank Worrell: The Career of a Great Cricketer* (London: Hodder and Stoughton, 1963), p. 13].

Worrell was asked to respond to each chapter of the book by way of a brief summary. The following excerpts help us to comprehend his *modus operandi* on his first tour as captain, in Australia in 1960-1. It was a triumph of leadership (a rare gift) and sportsmanship [see pp. 134-5; 151-3]:

The 1957 tour of England was very disappointing [they lost 0-3]...Players like Sobers and Kanhai, who had got a stack of runs behind them, were expected to do really well...But the tour proved a failure because of...lack of good administration...The unity of purpose we had in 1950 was sadly lacking. There were factions in the 1957 team...Although we all wanted to win there was a lack of advice to young players unfamiliar with English conditions...It was most unfortunate that our administrators on that tour [,also,] were so unfamiliar with English conditions...There was little tact employed in dealing with the younger members, and it was depressing to see them struggling in unfamiliar conditions without proper advice and assistance. We had the sort of team that should never have been beaten in three days. We might have lost the series. But the kind of fight we put up was shabby. It seemed we had developed a kind of inferiority complex that left us denuded of the strength we really possessed...It was clearly time for a new policy, and the experience of the 1957 tour served us in good stead on future tours...

We decided on our Australian tour, after the experience of 1957, there should be a rota in which each player was given a fair crack of the whip. We were influenced by the belief that each individual selected to represent the West Indies was a potential Test player, and there was no reason for us to establish a first team within the team for what were considered important matches, thereby giving the less experienced players an inferiority complex. Each player had been selected to represent the West Indies and should be capable of holding his own against the best the Australians could produce. This was our policy in Australia, and with this in mind we selected the first team. The others just evolved.

The teams were selected on form and throughout the tour the results were gratifying, and I am sure the factor responsible for this was that the...[players] all realised they were having a fair crack. The tour ended on a very happy note. We found that in virtually every spot we went to and every party we attended there were within the team no suggestions of factions and no show of insularity. *Our players were living in absolute harmony no matter what islands they came from, something we had never experienced before. On previous tours Barbadians seem to stick together, and so with players from Trinidad, Jamaica and British Guiana. We cut across all that. We were a team* [emphasis added].

It was a pleasure to see that when a party was arranged by any one player, that member never thought in terms of inviting only players from his own island to the exclusion of others. He would come into the dressing-room or hotel lobby and ask the first half-dozen players he saw whether they were interested in a party, and all went off fabulously well. So much for the off the field experiences.

The tour...was the most enjoyable one we have ever played in. Benaud as opposing captain was quite willing to accept any challenge that was thrown at him, and vice versa. The most pleasing thing was that there never was a defensive field set at any stage of the tour. The accent was on positive cricket. This is what I mean by positive cricket. Take field-placing, for instance: there is a kind of field-placing in which, if the batsman wants to see a blade of grass, he has got to look over a fieldsman's shoulder. This is attacking cricket, if you like.

The defensive type of field-placing has players dotted around the boundary. But there is a stage between attacking and defensive field-placing where a batsman thinks he sees a gap in the field. This is the sort of challenge by the bowler and the opposing captain that induces a batsman to attempt to pierce the field and gives the bowler a chance of getting him out. You lure the batsman by this challenge into attempting to pierce the field, and make sure that the batsman does not become despondent by seeing half a dozen men on the boundary and knowing that every powerfully executed shot is merely a possible single. You induce the batsman to pierce the field, and if in the course of time he gets a bit casual about it he soon finds himself back in the pavilion.

This was the case throughout the Australian tour. The Australians are punishing, aggressive batsmen. The West Indians go for their shots, and here we had two teams who enjoyed the idea of making shots. It is now history that in the first Test we achieved a tie at Brisbane. The second at Melbourne we lost. Then in Sydney we won. The fourth at Adelaide was a [controversial] draw. The final Test went to Australia by the narrow margin of two wickets, and some say that West Indies achieved a moral victory.

It was a wonderful tour. At no stage did we hear any one player say he would be glad to get back home. Such was the hospitality showered upon us that at the end of the tour many of the players were seen with tears in their eyes, myself included. Our fabulous send-off was so much in keeping with the spirit of the tour, and I am sure many of us regret that we shall never see Australia again as players.

APPENDIX III

JOHN ARLOTT ON WORRELL'S LEADERSHIP

The following are excerpts from John Arlott's reflections on the West Indies tour of England in 1963, when they won the Test series 3-1. He explores the source of the achievement, particularly the astute leadership of the captain, Frank Worrell (1924-1967), a marvellously subtle and discerning man, with a gift for humour – an inspiration, stirring a plenitude of pride in West Indian peoples at home and abroad. The article, 'The 1963 West Indian Tour: A New Appraisal', appeared in *The Cricketer* (Winter Edition), 1963, pp.4-6.

We live in deeds, not years; in thoughts
Not breaths;
In feelings, not in figures on a dial.

It is not easy to give Frank Worrell's 1963 West Indian team the depth of examination and understanding they deserve: only someone who shared closely in the life of the side on the field as well as off, fully appreciates *all** the influences that moulded them. Indeed, Worrell himself has said that the foundations of this team were laid in Australia in 1960-1, and certainly the team had qualities not always apparent on the surface, but which contributed to its dual success, in play and in public interest.

The usual assessment of a touring side deals, from the start, with technical aspects. But the success of the side was more than technical. Before it came, some hoped it might provide the same stimulus to cricket in England as it did in Australia in 1960-1 [Worrell's first series as captain]. But there were few who dared do more than hope. Yet the highest of those hopes were realised.

The England-West Indies rubber of 1963 was more than simply another Test series; it lifted English cricket back to a pinnacle of public esteem it had not known for years, and, also, altered the history of the game. That alteration is something which the body of English cricket, at the moment, accepts with unmixed delight. But it is not merely a change – it is also a challenge.

The effect of these cricketers on Australia in 1960-1, and England in 1963 was magnificent. But, between these two tours, England and Australia met each other twice, once in each country [in 1961 and in 1962-3], with more or less the same players yet neither of those series had a comparable impact or atmosphere…[But] [i]t was not the West Indies alone that made their tours so successful. What is the quality that enables them to strike from English and Australian cricketers a spark those two teams cannot kindle in one another?...

It is not simply a question of technique, definable, capable of cold transition into words. It is a question of *'feelings, not the figures on the dial'*;* and the imponderables can be annoyingly imponderable. The atmosphere in which the side lived grew slowly over some three years; created in Australia, it absorbed the newcomers of 1963 with no trouble.

*Importantly, the colour prejudice which in the past has impaired many aspects of West Indian life was never apparent.**

The first factor to be considered is Frank Worrell, outwardly relaxed – and certainly never hurried – but highly astute, and quite ruthless, as a playing captain. He had the experience of some 14 years of first-class play, of Test cricket all over the world (except, of course, South Africa). He was, too, still a capable player: he produced some of the most graceful strokes of the Test series, could turn his arm at a pinch [as a left-arm medium-pacer], did not hesitate to field dangerously close to the bat, and held some useful catches. But, above all, he never missed a tactical trick, kept his players full bore, knew when to press them, when to give them free rein.

Away from play he kept them a happy side: they could joke – and he could joke with them. We may note, too, the subtle part played by the team manager, Berkeley Gaskin [1908-79]. Unlike some touring managers, he was content to accept the leadership of the captain, happy to defer to Worrell, but also constantly co-operating with him: their mutual respect and liking was as valuable as it is rare. Gaskin, a former Test cricketer [from Guyana], was at ease with the players and they with him; though it was noticeable that respect was maintained – to the players he was always 'Mister Manager' as Worrell was 'Skipper'. The discipline was unmistakable but unforced, but none resented it.

The domestic atmosphere was one of gaiety. It was never possible to distinguish, by their manner, between those who achieved Test selection and those who did not [five in a party of 18: David Allan, Lester King, Seymour Nurse, Alf Valentine and Tony White]; and, when the team was faced with crisis, those who remained in the dressing room were completely identified with those on the field.

Of course, the Tests were important to them, but they were important aspects of a summer, not the be-all and end-all of the tour. It is relevant, too, that they laughed more, and louder, than any other cricket touring side of my experience. Happy, with a family spirit, much humour, firm discipline and a genuine devotion to cricket, this was close indeed to the ideal touring team.

The West Indian players themselves were fully conscious of the effect of their supporters, who brought a fresh approach to cricket in England. For the first time in the history of the game...there were truly bi-partisan crowds at Test matches. For many English followers it was a refreshing experience. The West Indian spectators, well informed and deeply involved, *lived** the game.

They did not demand fast scoring; they appreciated, as so many English spectators do not, when a batsman was in trouble, and were prepared to applaud him for runless survival. Of course, they were partisan: the fall of an important English wicket roused them to immense and capering delight. But their applause could burst out for a good stroke and, in a fraction of a second, change to salute a brilliant stop in the field.

Though it may be an over-simplification, it is fair to say that the West Indian players and supporters were unique in English experience because of their absolute determination to enjoy themselves. This attitude, rather than the details of play, produced the new spirit which inspired the English cricket season of 1963...

[T]his was not only a strong team, but a magnificently balanced one...There have been good West Indian sides before – if never one quite so balanced in pace and spin – and some whose batting was as strong. But the 1963 team was the first to play in England with genuine resolution when the game was going against them. It is not hard to believe that the side of 1957 [when West Indies lost the series 0-3], faced with the situation at Lord's, or even at the Oval – or after the defeat at Edgbaston – might have crumpled and lost: this team, thanks largely to Worrell's captaincy, met every challenge.

Outside the Tests, the touring side made all reasonable efforts to entertain, despite some unfriendly weather...Unlike some Australian teams, this West Indies side never gave the impression of being embattled. Its members went out and about in provincial towns meeting old friends, making new ones: their public relations were excellent.

The over-riding impression of the tour must be that the West Indies, players and spectators, demonstrated that the most toughly-fought cricket match can be a happy occasion.

* denotes emphasis in the original.

NOTES

The following were the members of Frank Worrell's team to Australia in 1960-1:

Frank Worrell (1924-67) (captain), Conrad Hunte (1932-99), Garry Sobers, Wes Hall, Cammie Smith, Seymour Nurse, Peter Lashley [Barbados]; Rohan Kanhai, Lance Gibbs, Joe Solomon [British Guiana]; Gerry Alexander, Jackie Hendriks, Chester Watson, Tom Dewdney, Alf Valentine (1930-2004) [Jamaica]; Sonny Ramadhin [Trinidad].

Nine of those who toured Australia were in Worrell's victorious team to England in 1963: Worrell, Hunte, Kanhai, Sobers, Solomon, Nurse, Gibbs, Valentine and Hall. These were augmented – formidably – by Basil Butcher [British Guiana], Charlie Griffith [Barbados] and Deryck Murray [Trinidad]. The other members of that touring team were: David Allan, Tony White [Barbados]; Lester King (1939-98), Easton McMorris [Jamaica]; Joey Carew and Willie Rodriguez [Trinidad]. Ten of these played in all five Tests: Worrell, Hunte, Kanhai, Butcher, Sobers, Solomon, Murray, Hall, Griffith and Gibbs. The only weakness was the lack of a reliable opening partner for Conrad Hunte: McMorris (two Tests), Carew (two Tests), Rodriguez (one Test).

APPENDIX IV

African and Indian Consciousness at Play: A Study in West Indies Cricket and Nationalism

by
Hubert Devonish
Professor of Linguistics, University of the West Indies, Mona, Kingston, Jamaica

Introduction

Nationalism has two ultimate objectives. One is to secure a state for those who consider themselves to share a common identity. The other is to promote the interests of that state over all others. Every other identity, whether within the national group or outside it, is a competitor. A competing identity either has to be made to submit to the overarching dominance of the national identity or be deemed to be anti-national and treated accordingly. Ethnic cleansers, their gas chambers and killing fields, are the constant companions of nationalism.

In the cricket playing Caribbean, imperial nationalism stamped a British identity on all its subjects. No other identity was allowed. As an act of resistance, the nationalists of the various anti-colonial movements proceeded to create images of alternative national identities. These new images were equally monochrome, simply black where they were previously white. The nationalist struggle aimed at changing the relationship between the colours within a totally European view of the nation and the state. The colour palette borrowed from the European original did not allow the shades of competing identities to blur the new vision which was taking shape. This was true of the individual national identities created in each emerging newly independent state and the larger and more diffuse West Indian identity of which the West Indies cricket team is a symbol.

Communities are organised into overlapping units made up of people sharing common identities. Any single individual is a composite of a multiplicity of identities. These may involve gender, age group, language group(s), community of origin, occupation and religious persuasion to name but a few. Social life for a person is, therefore, a game of drama in which the players constantly switch roles. When, in the name of nationalism, however defined, people are prevented from playing out any of their identities, their social rights are violated. West Indian nationalism created in the image of its European counterparts, is as prone as any other to having such censorship imposed in its name.

The cricket field is a screen against which the drama of West Indian society is often starkly projected. The cricketers do not simply play with a ball. Whether or not they are aware of it and do so willingly, they play roles which are assigned them by the spectators. These roles reflect the various identities which spectators have to take on in the course of everyday life. In Guyana and Trinidad, Indian people in the Caribbean make up a significant portion of the spectators at cricket matches. The way in which they interpret the acts performed by the players on the field provide an important insight into the way they interpret their own roles outside the ground. Equally important is how other members of the community respond to the Indian Caribbean interpretation of play. This provides a good guide to their responses to identities assumed by Indian Caribbean people as they are played out away from the cricket field.

Play seen through Indian Caribbean eyes

Indian Caribbean people and their relationship to a West Indian national identity and cricket first became a public issue in 1953. This was the year the Indian cricket team first toured the West Indies. Seecharan (1988: 54) relates an incident told to him by his grandfather who had made his first trip to Georgetown in that year. The trip was to see the Indian team play the West Indies at Bourda. 'An ebullient Hindu priest of considerable repute, unleashed a string of popular Hindi curse words, punched the air, uncoiled his sacred turban, turned to the crowd and waved it triumphantly...All this, because the Indian bowler, Ramchand, had bowled Bruce Pairaudeau, the West Indies opening batsman, a white Guyanese from Georgetown'.

Note the identities highlighted in the anecdote, i.e., that the bowler, Ramchand, was Indian, that the batsman was playing for the West Indies, was white, was Guyanese, and was from Georgetown. The Hindu priest was Indian as was the grandfather relating the incident. There is a good chance that both of them would have been born in India though they would have spent the bulk of their lives in Guyana. Most certainly his grandfather and the Hindu priest were from rural Guyana. They are likely to have both worked in the ranks of the rural proletariat on the sugar plantations. Almost the only thing they shared in common with the batsman was country of residence. Given the role of Europeans as owners, managers and overseers on the Guyana sugar plantations, the class rift was wide enough to rule out any desire by these two men to identify with him. They chose instead to emphasise the common core of an Indian identity which they shared with the bowler. The bowler was playing the role of the warrior from the motherland avenging the wrongs heaped upon the heads of her children exiled in Guyana.

Seecharan (1988: 54) indicates that the Indian Guyanese community was thrilled by the fielding of the Indian tourists and the quality bowling of the leg-spinner, Subhash Gupte. The fact that the Indian team drew four Tests with the West Indies, losing only one, was a matter of great pride. There was enormous support for the Indian team amongst the Indian Guyanese community. Like Seecharan's grandfather, Indian Guyanese travelled long distances to see the Indian cricket team. That the visitors were from India was as important as the fact that they were accomplished cricketers. Oral tradition has it that one Indian man arrived at the cricket ground having journeyed the whole of the previous day. When the Indian team took the field, he asked a spectator to identify by name the players on the Indian team, Ramchand, Mankad, Subhash Gupte, etc. This done, he nodded in satisfaction and left the ground heading for the train station to begin his journey back home.

The attitude of African Guyanese to this outpouring of support for the Indian team was one of tolerant amusement. The year 1953 was the one in which the mass of Guyanese, Africans and Indians, rallied behind the non-sectarian anti-colonial movement headed by the People's Progressive Party (PPP) led by Cheddi Jagan and Forbes Burnham. In that year the PPP was voted into power. In the space of a few months, however, the British had suspended the constitution and jailed many of the PPP leaders. Notions of nationalism whether at the level of Guyana and the wider West Indies, had yet to gel. Like their Indian Guyanese counterparts, the claims of African Guyanese to either Guyanese or West Indian identity were circumscribed by European power both outside the field of play and within. The accession by an African Caribbean cricketer to the permanent captaincy of the West Indies team was some seven years in the future. It was the general feeling that African cricketers within the West Indies team were discriminated against by a European dominated cricket hierarchy. In relation to the anecdote related by Seecharan, African Guyanese cricket fans would hardly have been upset by the dismissal of a European Guyanese by a bowler in the Indian team, nor the attendant celebration by the Hindu priest. In fact, some African Guyanese may well have been inclined to have joined in the celebration.

A second reason for African Guyanese tolerance was their awareness of the ambivalent position which the Indian Guyanese found themselves in when dealing with Indians from India. Seecharan (1988:63) refers to the experiences which returning migrants to India suffered. They were often discriminated against on grounds that they had lost caste through the act of having crossed the ocean. As a result, many of these had remigrated to Guyana bringing with them accounts of their unpleasant experiences in India. In addition, according to stories circulating within the African Guyanese population at the time, Indian Guyanese had been trying to use what they considered to be Hindi to talk to the visitors. Unfortunately, however, communication was difficult. This is, however, not surprising. The vast majority of Indian immigrants to the Caribbean came from North-east India, mainly from around the area outside of the Hindi heartland and in which Bhojpuri, a related but quite distinct language, is spoken. The use of Guyanese Bhojpuri to speakers of Hindi, therefore, was bound to cause a great deal of communication problems.

A third reason for the tolerant African Guyanese response was the fact that up to this point the Indian Guyanese population was not perceived to be making a serious bid for political and economic power. It was to be two years later, in 1955, that the last ship sailed from Guyana for Calcutta taking repatriated former indentured servants back to India. This may have signalled an important change in the way the Indian Guyanese population saw itself and was seen by others. Now the mother country has been severed, a new identity began to gel. Indian Guyanese as a group were no longer a marginal immigrant group. They had clearly now become full competitors in the local arena.

With the divergence between the identities of Indian Guyanese and Indians from the sub-continent, the former needed their own champions. The conditions for this were being laid since 1950. Seecharan (1988: 52-5) neatly sums these up. Firstly, there were the conditions external to the Indian community. In 1948, malaria which had been endemic to Guyana was eradicated. This was achieved through the malariologist, George Giglioli, who had been employed by the Sugar Producers' Association. In 1950 [1952], Jock Campbell, a Fabian socialist was appointed to the chairmanship of Bookers, the British company which dominated the sugar industry in the country. His appointment seemed to have triggered a number of social reforms on the sugar estates. Health centres, community centres and sports facilities were constructed and maintained on the sugar estates. One feature of the sporting facilities provided was excellent cricket grounds. Robert Christiani, a Guyanese batsman in the West Indies team, was sent to Port Mourant estate as a cricket coach. In 1954, Clyde Walcott, the Barbadian batsman on the West Indies team, was employed by the Sugar Producers' Association as a sports organiser.

There were also conditions internal to the community. In 1955 the African-Indian anti-colonial alliance broke apart into Jaganite and Burnhamite factions of the PPP. The split was originally ideological but, in due course, African support rallied around the Burnhamite-PPP eventually renamed the People's National Congress (PNC). Indian mass support swung solidly behind the Jaganite-PPP. Even though Jagan as a good socialist never presented himself in this light, the Indian community had found in him its political champion. The Indian Guyanese community had begun to see itself as a serious challenger for political and economic power in society.

At the same time, the talent spotting and coaching of Clyde Walcott had begun to bear fruit. A string of four players were about to make their way first into the Berbice, British Guiana and the West Indies team. They were all from the sugar estate of Port Mourant in Berbice, the same estate from which Cheddi Jagan had come. The first and greatest of these was Rohan Kanhai who entered the West Indies team for the 1957 tour of England. This was also the year in which the PPP under Jagan won the general elections, defeating the PNC led by Burnham. Kanhai and to a lesser extent the other two Indian players from Port Mourant, Joe Solomon and Ivan Madray, had very difficult roles to play. They had to act as symbols of the newly emerging Indian Caribbean identity.

Seecharan (1988:59) refers to the insecurity within the Indian Guyanese community. My comment would be that this was coming from three different sources. There was, of course, the feeling of inferiority in the face of Europeans and European Caribbean people who dominated the society. There was also a sense of insecurity when dealing with Indians from the sub-continent. Finally, there was the feeling of inferiority brought on by the scant respect paid them by the African Guyanese population alongside whom they lived. The goal was to grab for the community the attention, respect and acceptance from these three groups. Seecharan (1988: 59-60) suggests that the Indian Guyanese community felt that one way to achieve this was to produce a truly great Indian Guyanese cricketer.

Kanhai was chosen for this role, to parallel the success of Jagan in politics. At first Kanhai failed to live up to expectations. In the Test series of the 1957 tour of England, the West Indies lost 3-nil. Kanhai's performances were barely better, totalling 206 runs at an average of 22.88. The interests of the Indian Guyanese community and those of the West Indies team coincided. Cricket is a team game. It would, therefore, have been difficult for their champion to excel in the midst of the total disaster which his team faced. The mood amongst Indian Guyanese was gloomy as they listened to the radio commentary on the Test series. 'The victory of Cheddi Jagan in the elections of August 1957 transported us out of the blankness of the summer (Seecharan 1988: 58).'

During the 1958 Pakistan tour of the West Indies, Kanhai's performance improved with a batting average of 37.37. Seecharan (1988: 59) again presents the Indian Guyanese perspective when he states: 'This was slight in the midst of the Olympian effort of Garry Sobers whose average was 137.33'. Kanhai's performance could not impress African Caribbean people when viewed alongside that of the equally young and promising African Barbadian, Sobers.

The 1958-9 West Indies tour of India was a special occasion. Two Indian Guyanese, Kanhai and Joe Solomon, were travelling to the land of their fore-parents for the first time, and were doing so as players on the West Indies cricket team. In the meantime, Ivan Madray, another player from Port Mourant, had played for the West Indies in two Tests against Pakistan in 1958. One must add to this the consistent presence of Sonny Ramadhin, the Indian Trinidadian off-spinner, on the side over the previous several years. It was becoming clear to Indian Caribbean people that membership of the cast of the West Indies cricket team was opening to them. This was becoming equally clear to non-Indians who saw these new identities as challenging theirs. In the second Test match between the West Indies and Pakistan in Trinidad, a country with a sizeable Indian population, Ivan Madray was playing his first Test match. He reports fielding at deep third-man and someone shouting from the crowd: 'We don't want more coolie in this side'. This was followed up with a cigarette end flicked on to his back and a bottle thrown at him (Madray 1988: 118).

The Indian team was no longer perceived as playing the role of champions of the Indian Guyanese population. Subhash Gupte, the same leg-spinner on the Indian team who was their hero in 1953, had been transformed into their arch-enemy. In the first two Test matches, Gupte seemed able to capture the wicket of Kanhai at will. For the Indian Guyanese population, 'with Kanhai seemingly a possession of Gupte, to us this now inspired shame, a reassertion of patriarchal authority, snuffing out tentative autonomy (Seecharan 1988: 61)'. In the third Test at Calcutta, Kanhai proceeded to demolish the Indian bowling attack including that of Gupte. Kanhai made a score of 256 in what was the first Test innings in which he scored a century. Joe Solomon made 69 not out. Basil Butcher, an African Guyanese also from Port Mourant, made 103. This conquest of the Indian bowling was filled with symbolism for the Indian Guyanese community. Seecharan (1988: 63) suggests that Kanhai's performance was revenge for Indian returnees from the Caribbean humiliated through loss of caste. This was particularly satisfying since Calcutta was the port from which the vast majority of the Indian immigrants to the Caribbean sailed and to which the returnees were repatriated.

The involvement of Butcher in the triumph introduces an additional dimension. The success of Kanhai, Butcher and Solomon was seen as a triumph for rural Guyanese over their urban counterparts. The county of Berbice and in particular the Corentyne Coast and Port Mourant had prevailed over the county of Demerara and the capital, Georgetown. According to Ivan Madray (1988: 108), John Trim, an African fast bowler from Port Mourant who played for the West Indies in the late 1940s [-early 1950s], was viewed by Indians in Berbice as one of their own. He blazed the trail for the string of West Indian Test players, Kanhai, Butcher, Solomon, Madray, Alvin Kallicharran and Roy Fredericks, all coming out of the Berbice sugar estates cricket system.

The excitement of the Hindu priest during the 1953 Test match was partly because Pairaudeau was a symbol of urban dominance over the rural population. The image of a rural identity which transcended the African-Indian divide was not confined to the minds of those who watched cricket or listened to it on the radio. This was also how the players saw the situation. Seecharan (1988: 55) quotes Butcher as crediting Clyde Walcott with 'advancing their [those of Butcher and fellow Port Mourant players] claims to the czars of Georgetown'.

The rural, regional and Caribbean identities played out by Kanhai's brilliant performances as a batsman tended to be overlooked by African Guyanese. The Indian identity as expressed in his play was the image which usually overshadowed all others in their minds. The PPP won another electoral victory in 1961. Between 1962 and 1964, the government was challenged strongly by the local African community and big business, aided and abetted by the colonial authorities and the Central Intelligence Agency (CIA) of the USA. This took the form of civil disobedience, industrial action, riots and inter-communal terrorism. Against this background, Seecharan (1988: 70) suggests that 'the fact that Kanhai's work was infused with a profoundly West Indian spirit the character of his art recognised and appropriated by all West Indians, save we suspected by most Afro-Guyanese fired by a black messianism, made it possible for it to carry our massive racial burdens'. The suspicions of Seecharan and the Indian community were correct. The first name 'Rohan' is fairly common amongst African Jamaicans born during or after

Kanhai's international cricket career. Amongst African Guyanese, the name occurring with equivalent frequency is 'Gary' after Garfield Sobers. 'Rohan' is so rare amongst African Guyanese that one is tempted to speculate that it is never used.

In the midst of the destabilisation of the PPP government under Jagan the February 1964 match between Guyana and Barbados took place in Bridgetown. The game meant one thing for most African Guyanese, many of them descended from African Barbadians. For them, the game would play out the assertion of African Guyanese identity vis-à-vis that of African Barbadians. In the eyes of the former, the latter were seen as immigrants with strange speech habits who had come in to Guyana over the years to weaken the bargaining power of local labour. For Indian Guyanese, a totally different plot was unfolding. Remarkably, the feared Barbadian fast bowling pair of Wesley Hall and Charlie Griffith were being assigned the part of African Guyanese terrorists. Guyana are down 13 for 3. Kanhai and Solomon come to the rescue. Kanhai scores 108, Solomon 63. 'And through the three hours that he (Kanhai) ruled, in our nervous jubilation, we saw each boundary hit as a blow against Burnhamite terror (Seecharan 1988: 73)'.

The British impose a change in the electoral system in Guyana. Fresh general elections are held in Guyana in [December] 1964 and the PNC under Burnham in alliance with a small party [the United Force] supported by the business class, manages to snatch political power from the PPP. The Indian Guyanese community is devastated and haunted by a sense of defeat. In the Test match at Bourda a few months later in April 1965, Kanhai receives massive support from the Indian Guyanese crowd as he scores 85 [89] in the first innings. His role was, as the saying goes, 'to take shame out of their eyes'. Cheered lustily to the wicket in the second innings, he scored 0. He was booed back to the pavilion by people 'haunted and shamed by Cheddi's fall…we were booing ourselves to pre-empt the blacks from booing us (Seecharan 1988: 73)'.

The new game in town

After the change in government, the new game in town was consolidating with the aid of state power an African Guyanese community imbued with a sense of its right to rule. In 1968, two years after the country received political independence from Britain, this right to rule became institutionalised. During that year, the first of a series of brazenly rigged elections took place. Rigging elections became an amusement for the PNC and the African elite who dominated it. National elections, while made to look like a game which either side could win, became a play which, with minor script variations, was enacted every five years or so. The ending of the play was always the same, of course. African Guyanese as a group either played active parts in the farce, applauded it or looked the other way and pretended it was not happening. This was to continue until the 1992 elections when the presence of neutral umpires in the form of international observers helped restore the process to that of an electoral game played according to established rules.

State power was, however, only a means to an end. The power and influence which the Indian Guyanese community had accumulated had to be destroyed. Race was not an acceptable basis for publicly rationalising or justifying moves by the Guyana government. Therefore, measures had to be adopted which were not explicitly directed at Indians. The strategy was to target those sectors of the society and economy in which Indians were dominant. Since the rural agricultural population was predominantly Indian, this sector was singled out for special attention. Resources would be transferred from a rural agricultural sector composed mainly of Indians to a state dominated by Africans.

Though comparable tactics were employed in the rice industry, we will focus on the sugar industry, the area of agriculture which had the most relevance for cricket. In 1974 the PNC government slapped a sugar levy on the profits of the sugar industry. This was done on the pretext that the earnings from sugar should be used to benefit the entire nation rather than just sugar workers (Debiprashad and Budhram 1987: 152). Then there was the master-stroke. The sugar industry was nationalised in 1976, placing it and its work force directly at the mercy of the state. The African dominated state ran down the industry through lack of investment and while transferring surpluses to itself. All of this reduced the share of the revenue available to sugar workers either directly through profit sharing or indirectly through estate expenditure on health, housing and social amenities.

The sporting facilities developed by the sugar industry from the beginning of the 1950s were poorly maintained after nationalisation. Many of the estate cricket grounds were allowed to revert to pasture. By 1976 Alvin Kallicharran and Roy Fredericks, the last of the products of the sugar estate cricket programme to appear with any frequency for the West Indies, were already in the team. Since the late 1970s, the only new Guyanese entrants to the West Indies Test team have been Roger Harper and Carl Hooper, both urban Africans. No Guyanese Indians have played on the West Indies team for over a decade. [Shivnarine Chanderpaul was the next, in March 1994, the first in 12 years since Faoud Bacchus in February 1982.] The mission had been accomplished. This has, however, been at the expense of Africans on or near the sugar estates who, like their Indian counterparts, have also been denied access to cricket playing opportunities.

We have so far examined moves which were made to limit the ability of Indian Guyanese to use local and West Indies cricket to act out roles which express and strengthen their group identity. There was as well a programme to have the symbols of African Guyanese, PNC and Burnhamite dominance projected into the arena of West Indies cricket. This took the form of seeking to have African Guyanese players promoted to positions of power and influence in the West Indies team. The major power play by the PNC regime was the efforts it made to ensure that African Guyanese Clive Lloyd became captain of the West Indies team.

Ever since the struggle to have Frank Worrell appointed captain of the West Indies team, the captaincy has acquired an enormous symbolic importance. In 1973, Gary Sobers distinguished [relinquished] the captaincy of the West Indies team. The candidate of the Burnham government in Guyana for the post was Clive Lloyd. The problem was that, due to poor batting performances, Clive Lloyd had not even been named to the original squad to play against the Australians during their Caribbean tour of that year. In fact, it was Kanhai who was appointed as Sobers's successor. Given the kind of symbolic role which Kanhai played for the Guyanese population, this was not as bad news for Burnham and the PNC as it might at first seem. Kanhai [aged 37] was almost at the end of his career as an international cricketer. He was therefore merely warming the seat for a successor. Burnham was determined that Lloyd would be that successor.

When the West Indies Cricket Board realised that Gary Sobers might be unable to play during the series because of injury, it cabled Lloyd requesting that he put himself on standby. According to [Trevor] McDonald (1985: 58), at this point Prime Minister Forbes Burnham intervened personally 'by asking his friend, the Australian Prime Minister, Gough Whitlam, to make sure that there would be no problem getting Lloyd's release from his commitment to club cricket in Australia'. In Manchester in the UK where Lloyd resided, he was informed through the Guyana High Commission in London that the Guyana government was paying his fare back to the Caribbean. Burnham preferred that he wait on standby in the Caribbean. Lloyd's response was that: '…my Prime Minister made a request that I come back home and I found it impossible to refuse and certainly, I wanted to be near the action (McDonald 1985: 58)'.

Lloyd distinguished himself in the match between Australia and the Guyana team. As a result, he forced himself back into the West Indies team, scoring 178 on the first day of the fourth Test. McDonald (1985: 60) cites [Tony] Cozier's description of Burnham as 'basking in reflected glory'. Lloyd went on to secure his place in the team and eventually the captaincy. The image which Indians saw within West Indies cricket of a Caribbean identity in which they had no presence became even more sharply defined with the 1990 statement by Lloyd's successor as captain, Vivian Richards. In an interview with the *Outlet* newspaper in Antigua, he is reported to have stated that 'the West Indies cricket team…is the only team of African descent that has been able to win repeatedly against all international opposition, bringing joy and recognition to our people (*West Indies Cricket Annual, 1990*: 33)'. Subsequent efforts by Richards to 'clarify' would have done little to change the original impression.

This is the background against which one needs to understand the evolution in the behaviour of Indian cricket spectators in Guyana. They know instinctively that the absence of any Indians from Guyana on the West Indies team is probably not a matter of chance. The captaining of the team by Clive Lloyd, otherwise known as 'Burnham Magic', made the entire team a symbol of everything hated by the oppressed Indian majority in the country. The team in its conquest of the cricketing world for over a decade, was for Indian Guyanese an acting out of the trampling of their rights by the African dominated state.

From the visit of the first Indian touring team to the Caribbean in 1953, there has been a tendency for Indian Trinidadians and Indian Guyanese to support visiting Indian and Pakistani teams. As was pointed out earlier, however, this support became rather ambivalent at least amongst Indian Guyanese, as long as there were prominent Guyanese Indian players such as Kanhai in the West Indian team. In spite of these nuances, however, Africans have become increasingly hostile to expressions of support for visiting teams from the Indian sub-continent. In Guyana, when such behaviour occurred during the 1980s, articles and letters appeared in the PNC controlled government press accusing those involved of being disloyal and unpatriotic. The typical response in the *Mirror* newspaper of the opposition PPP was that Indian Guyanese at cricket matches were paying patrons and had the right to cheer who they please.

African Trinidadians and Guyanese who see themselves as being besieged by an expanding and increasingly self-confident Indian community stubbornly refused to recognise this right, however. One typical example of this attitude occurred during the 1976 Indian tour of the Caribbean. The support of Indian Trinidadians for the Indian team in the Test matches played in Trinidad was overwhelming. Africans in the crowd regularly threw orange skins at groups of Indians cheering for the visitors.

To add insult to injury, India won the third Test at Queen's Park in Trinidad by scoring 406 runs. The celebrating Indian Trinidadians in the ground on the final day of the match serenaded each boundary hit by the Indian batsmen with the carnival road-march tune for that year, 'La La' by Nelson. One African Trinidadian remarked that what hurt him most of all is that they chose this tune rather than some much more appropriate properly Indian melody. Interestingly enough, here again we see the tendency to assume that symbols of collective identity such as the calypso belong to Africans and them alone.

Up to the end of the 1970s in Guyana, it was the norm for Indian Guyanese to support the West Indies team against any team except those from the sub-continent. The principle of multiple identities was at play here. Depending on which was the opposing team, their Indianness or West Indianness would be the one which receives particular emphasis. With the increased alienation of Indian Guyanese from the political process and West Indian cricket, they swung to a position of supporting any team against the West Indies. In 1990, many of them turned out to support the MCC [England] in the one-day matches against the West Indies played at Bourda. In the 1991 Test Match against Australia at Bourda, the Indian section of the crowd is reported to have strongly supported Australia and booed members of the West Indies team. In the light of his description of the West Indies team as a sporting team of African descent, the captain, Vivian Richards, was singled out for special treatment. The then Prime Minister, Hamilton Green, quickly apologised to the West Indies team for the behaviour of the crowd. This indicates the extent to which support for the West Indies had become a matter of state policy rather than an expression of individual personal preference.

With the entrenchment of rigging within the electoral process of Guyana, Indian Guyanese along with many others of their countrymen despaired of being able to change their government by the casting of a ballot. The very word 'ballot' owes its origin to the casting of votes or lots using balls. The electoral game had been turned into a farce, in effect into 'lots of balls'. The early 1980s was a period during which pressure built up for electoral reform. Indian Guyanese therefore chose symbolically to cast their lots in another ball game, that of cricket. Here at last, rules were still followed, umpiring still impartial and the outcome not prescribed by an already written script

At the beginning of the 1990s, the nationalised sugar industry was in poor shape. The sugar conglomerate, Booker Tate of the UK, was brought in on a management contract to run the sugar industry. The new British chief executive of the industry, Neville Hilary, announced significant increases in wages for sugar workers. Steps were also taken to improve the various facilities provided to workers by the industry. Sport, and cricket in particular, was to benefit by the reappearance of this welfare oriented approach to managing the industry. In 1992 it was announced that Joe Solomon, himself a product of an earlier period of investment in cricket on the sugar estates, had been contracted to train sugar estate cricket coaches and to develop young talent on the sugar estates (Razack 1992 b: 14). All of this was taking place amidst the build up of the campaign for free and fair elections and eventually the defeat of the PNC in the October 1992 elections.

This situation had created a surge of public expectation concerning sport on the Guyana sugar estates. This is clearly expressed in a series of articles on sport on the sugar estates published in the PPP organ, the *Mirror*, in the course of which Razack (1992 a: 12) states: 'With the present re-organising of the sugar estate community centres by Guysuco [the Guyana Sugar Corporation], hopes run high for a return of the glory days that this estate [Port Mourant] once enjoyed'.

On the pitfalls of nationalism: the cricket test

The arrogance of African West Indians to try to dictate to their compatriots who they should support at a cricket match, clearly shows up the pitfalls of nationalism. Nationalism requires the suppression of all other identities in favour of that defined as national by those with the power to make such a definition. When large crowds of people of West Indian origin throng the cricket grounds in England to support the West Indies against the land of their residence and very often citizenship, their right to do so is firmly supported by African West Indians. African West Indian public opinion was very loud in its condemnation of the British Conservative Member of Parliament, Norman Tebbit, who proposed the application of the cricket test. According to this test, when England played the West Indies or India in England, a test of loyalty should be applied to the spectators. Those who supported the opposing team against England would be deemed to have failed the test. They would therefore be deported from England to their countries of origin.

The test has been applied in the Caribbean to people other than Indian West Indians. It was the 1975 Shell Shield match between Trinidad and Tobago and the Combined Islands. Large numbers of people from the Leeward and Windward Islands residing in Trinidad turned out to cheer the visitors on to their first ever victory over Trinidad and Tobago. This was immortalised in the Paul Keens-Douglas short story, 'Tantie Merle at the Oval'. Trinidad public opinion was scandalised. These 'small island people', enjoying milk and honey purchased with Trinidad oil, had bitten the hand which fed them. The only appropriate measure was to banish them back to the barren little rocks whence they came. That this was more than mere rhetoric can be seen by a subsequent incident.. The mid-1980s represented the peak of Guyanese migration, both legal and illegal, to Trinidad. A crowd of Guyanese turned up to support the visiting Guyana team in a Shell Shield match. Immigration officers surrounded the stand occupied by Guyanese. Some fled. Others were arrested and presumably subsequently deported as illegal immigrants. This was certainly not cricket. It was nationalism pure and simple.

Ethnic cleansing, the constant companion of nationalism, may take the form of the application of the cricket test in relation to Leeward islanders, Windward islanders, or Guyanese resident in Trinidad and Tobago. It may be applied to people of Caribbean origin in the UK or Indian Caribbean people in Guyana and Trinidad and Tobago. If it can be justified in one case, it can be in any other.

Nationalism and all with which it is associated are the natural enemies of any notion of genuine unity amongst people, either within individual Caribbean states or across these states. The view that any group pf people could be made to express themselves by way of a single common identity is both contrary to good sense and the experience of everyday life in the Caribbean. Such a scenario is essentially Afro-Saxon in nature. This is true whether its players are of conservative demeanour and bear the title of knights, in the style of the West Indian cricket captains of the 1960s and early 1970s, or are of more radical comportment and wear the red, green and gold symbols of the Rastafari as did the captain who retired in 1991 [Viv Richards]. More importantly, the scenario represents a violation of social rights of Caribbean people. The challenge, both within and beyond the boundary, is to create an atmosphere which tolerates and encourages the interplay between the multiple identities which exist within Caribbean societies.

References

Debiprashad, Sahadeo and Dowlat Ram Budhram, 1987, 'Participation of East Indians in the Transformation of Guyanese Society, 1966-79', in David Dabydeen and Brinsley Samaroo (eds.), *India in the Caribbean* (London: Hansib), pp. 145-71.

McDonald, Trevor, 1985, *Clive Lloyd* (London: Granada).

Razack, Shan, 1992 a, 'Port Mourant – Home of Outstanding Sportsmen', *Mirror*, 29 November 1992, pp. 7,12.

— 1992 b, 'Clyde Walcott's Contribution to Cricket in Guyana', *Mirror*, 6 December 1992, pp12, 14.

Clem Seecharan, 1988, 'The Tiger of Port Mourant: Rohan Bholalall Kanhai', in Frank Birbalsingh and Clem Seecharan, *Indo-Westindian Cricket* (London: Hansib), pp. 41-88.

— 1988, 'Clem Seecharan in Conversation with Ivan Madray: "Da Coolie Ga Mek Abi Hunt Ledda"', in Birbalsingh and Seecharan (1988), pp. 89-128.

Source: This article was published in Hilary McD Beckles and Brian Stoddart (eds), *Liberation Cricket: West Indies Cricket Culture* (Kingston, Jamaica: Ian Randle Publishers, 1995), pp. 179-91. I am grateful to Christine Randle and Hubert Devonish for allowing me to reproduce it here.

BIBLIOGRAPHY

PRIMARY SOURCES:

Newspapers

The *Age* [Melbourne]
The *Argosy* [British Guiana]
Barbados Advocate
The *Berbice Times* [British Guiana]
The *Cricketer* [England]
The *Daily Argosy* [British Guiana]
The *Daily Chronicle* [British Guiana]
Guiana Graphic
The *Guiana Sunday Graphic*
The *Herald* [Melbourne]
The *Hindu* [India]
The *Hindustan Times* [India]
The *Indian Opinion* [British Guiana]
The *Nation* [Trinidad]
The *New Daily Chronicle* [British Guiana]
Pakistan Times
The *Sun-Herald* [Sydney]
The *Times* [London]
The *Trinidad Guardian*

SECONDARY SOURCES:

Articles and Books

Altham, H.S., *A History of Cricket: From the Beginnings to the First World War* (London:George Allen and Unwin, 1962 [1926]).

— 'Ranji, Fry and Jessop – The Golden Age of Batting', in Alan Ross (ed.), *The Penguin Cricketers' Companion* (Harmondsworth: Penguin Books, 1981 [1960]).

Andrews, C.F., 'Impressions of British Guiana', (mimeo.), enclosure in the following file at the National Archives (Kew, London): CO111/689/75141 [1930]. (See Mangru [2007])

Arlott, John, *Days at the Cricket* (London: Longman's, Green and Co., 1951).

Bailey, Trevor, 'Rohan Kanhai: The Magician from Guyana', in his *The Greatest of my Time* (London: The Sportsmans Book Club, 1970 [1968]).

Baksh, Elahi, 'The Propagandist', in F. Birbalsingh (ed.), *Jahaji: An Anthology of Indo-Caribbean Writing* (Toronto: TSAR, 2000).

Ballantyne, Tony, *Orientalism and Race: Aryanism in the British Empire* (Basingstoke: Palgrave, 2002).

Barker, J.S., *Summer Spectacular: The West Indies v. England, 1963* (London: The Sportsmans Book Club, 1965 [1963]).

— *In the Main: West Indies v. M.C.C.* (London: The Sportsmans Book Club, 1969 [1968]).

Basham, A.L., *The Wonder that was India* [3rd ed.] (New Delhi: Rupa and Co., 1981).

Beckles, Hilary McD, 'The Political Ideology of West Indies Cricket Culture', in Beckles and Brian Stoddart (eds.), *Liberation Cricket: West Indies Cricket Culture* (Kingston, Jamaica: Ian Randle Publishers, 1995).

Benaud, Richie, *A Tale of Two Tests* (With Some Thoughts on Captaincy) (London: The Sportsman Book Club, 1963 [1962]).

— *The New Champions: Australia in the West Indies, 1965* (London: The Sportsmans Book Club, 1966 [1965]).

— *Willow Patterns* (London: The Sportsmans Book Club, 1970 [1969]).

— *Anything but...an Autobiography* (London: Hodder and Stoughton, 1998).

— *My Spin on Cricket* (London: Hodder and Stoughton, 2005).

Birbalsingh, Frank, *The Rise of Westindian Cricket: From Colony to Nation* (London: Hansib, 1997 [1996]).

— 'Robert Christiani: Interview', in Frank Birbalsingh, *Guyana and the Caribbean: Reviews, Essays and Interviews* (Chichester, West Sussex: Dido Press, 2004).

— 'Basil Butcher: Interview', in *Guyana and the Caribbean*

— and Clem Seecharan, *Indo-Westindian Cricket* (London: Hansib, 1988).

Bose, Mihir, *A History of Indian Cricket* (London: Andre Deutsch, 1990).

Bowen, Rowland, *Cricket: A History of its Growth and Development throughout the World* (London: Eyre and Spottiswoode, 1970).

Buruma, Ian, *Playing the Game* (London: Vintage, 1992 [1991]).

Butcher, Basil, 'Guyana', in Garfield Sobers and J.S. Barker (eds.), *Cricket in the Sun: A History of West Indies Cricket* (London: Arthur Barker Ltd., 1967).

Cardus, Neville, *A Fourth Innings with Cardus* (London: Souvenir Press, 1981).

Cashman, Richard, *Patrons, Players and the Crowd: The Phenomenon of Indian Cricket* (New Delhi: Orient Longman, 1980).

Clarke, John, *Cricket with a Swing: the West Indies Tour, 1963* (London: Stanley Paul, 1963).

Davidson, Alan, *Fifteen Paces* (London: The Sportsmans Book Club, 1965 [1963]).

Devonish, Hubert, 'African and Indian Consciousness at Play: A Study in West Indies Cricket and Nationalism', in Hilary Beckles and Brian Stoddart (eds.), *Liberation Cricket: West Indies Cricket Culture* (Kingston, Jamaica: Ian Randle Publishers, 1995).

Eytle, Ernest, *Frank Worrell: The Career of a Great Cricketer* (London: Hodder and Stoughton, 1963).

— [E.E.], 'Rohan Kanhai' [Five Cricketers of the Year], *Wisden 1964*.

Fingleton, J.H., *The Greatest Test of All* (London: Collins, 1961).

Fraser, Cary, *Ambivalent Anti-Colonialism: The United States and the Genesis of West Indian Independence, 1940-64* (Westport, Ct: Greenwood Press, 1994).

Frewin, Leslie (ed.), *The Poetry of Cricket: An Anthology* (London: Macdonald, 1964).

Gavaskar, Sunil, *Idols* (London: George Allen and Unwin, 1984).

Gibbes, Michael, 'Rohan Kanhai: the Peter Pan of West Indian Cricket', in Gordon Rohlehr, *Kanhai/Gibbs 1974: Tribute to Two Outstanding West Indians* [a benefit brochure for Kanhai and Gibbs] (Port of Spain: Self-published, 1974).

Gilchrist, Roy, *Hit me for Six* (London: Stanley Paul, 1963).

Goble, Ray and Keith A.P. Sandiford, *75 Years of West Indies Cricket, 1928-2003* (London: Hansib, 2004).

Goodwin, Clayton, *Caribbean Cricket: From the Pioneers to Packer* (London: George G. Harrap, 1980).

Griffith, Charlie, *Chucked Around* (London: Pelham Books, 1970).

Grimshaw, Anna, (ed.), *Cricket: C.L.R. James* (London: Allison and Busby, 1986).

Hall, Stuart, *Myths of Caribbean Identity* [The Walter Rodney Memorial Lecture, October 1991] (Coventry: Centre for Caribbean Studies, University of Warwick, 1991).

Hall, Wes, *Pace like Fire* (London: The Sportsman Book Club, 1966 [1965]).

Hardy, W.A.S. (ed.), *They Live for Cricket: A Souvenir Programme Featuring the West Indies Cricket Tour, 1957* (London: the Author, 1957).

Harris, Bruce, *West Indies Cricket Challenge, 1957* (London: Stanley Paul, 1957).

Hunte, Conrad, *Playing to Win* (London: Hodder and Stoughton, 1971).

Jagan, Cheddi, *The West on Trial: My Fight for Guyana's Freedom* (London: Michael Joseph, 1966).

James, C.L.R., *Beyond a Boundary* (London: Serpent's Tail, 1994 [1963]).
— 'Kanhai: A Study in Confidence', *New World Quarterly*, Guyana Independence Issue (1966).
Kakar, Sudhir and Katharina Kakar, *The Indians: Portrait of a People,* (New Delhi: Penguin Books, 2007).
Kanhai, Rohan, *Blasting for Runs* (London: Souvenir Press, 1966).
Mangru, Basdeo, (ed.), *C.F. Andrews, Impressions of British Guiana, 1930: An Emissary's Assessment.* (Chicago: Adams Press, 2007).
Manley, Michael, *A History of West Indies Cricket* [rev. ed.] ([Kingston], Jamaica: West Indies Publishing Ltd, 1995 [1988]).
Marshall, Tevor, 'Ethnicity, Class and the Democratisation of West Indies Cricket Culture', in Hilary Beckles (ed.) *An Area of Conquest: Popular Democracy and West Indies Cricket Supremacy* (Kingston, Jamaica: Ian Randle Publishers, 1994).
McDonald, Ian, 'Rohan Kanhai – Batsman Extraordinary', 'Viewpoint', Broadcast on the Guyana Broadcasting Service, Georgetown, Guyana, 5 February, 1983 (mimeo).
— 'Five Great Berbician Cricketers', in Susil Dharry (ed.), *West Indies v. India (Souvenir Programme)*, (Hampshire, Berbice, Guyana: The Central Corentyne Lions Club, 1983).
— 'Tiger in the Stars', in Joel Benjamin, Lakshmi Kallicharan, Ian McDonald and Lloyd Searwar (eds.), *They Came in Ships: An Anthology of Indo-Guyanese Prose and Poetry* (Leeds: Peepal Tree Press, 1998).
— 'Vote for Kanhai', *Stabroek News* [Guyana], 26 November 2006.
Moyes, A.G., *A Century of Cricketers* (London: George G. Harrap and Co. Ltd., 1950).
— *With the West Indies in Australia*, 1951-52 (London: George G. Harrap and Co. Ltd., 1952).
— *With the West Indies in Australia*, 1960-61 (London: The Sportsman Book Club, 1963 [1961]).
Naipaul, V.S., *The Middle Passage: The Caribbean Revisited* (London: Andre Deutsch, 1962).
— 'Cricket', in his *The Overcrowded Barracoon* (London: Andre Deutsch, 1972).
— 'England v. West Indies (1963)', in Michael Davie and Simon Davie (eds.), *The Faber Book of Cricket* (London: Faber and Faber, 1987).
Richards, Jimmy and Mervyn Wong, *Statistics of West Indies Cricket, 1865-1989* (Kingston, Jamaica: Heinemann, 1990).
Rodney, Walter (ed.), *Guyanese Sugar Plantations in the Late Nineteenth Century:*

A Contemporary Description from the 'Argosy' (Georgetown: Release Publishers, 1979).
Rohlehr, Gordon, *Kanhai/Gibbs: Tribute to Two Outstanding West Indians* (Port of Spain: Self-published, 1974).
Ross, Alan, *Ranji: Prince of Cricketers* (London: Collins, 1983).
— *West Indies at Lord's* (London: Constable, 1986 [1963]).
— *Through the Caribbean: England in the West Indies, 1960* (London: Pavilion Books, 1986 [1960]).
Ruhomon, Peter, *Centenary History of the East Indians in British Guiana, 1838-1938* (Georgetown, Guyana: the East Indians 150th Anniversary Committee, 1988 [1947]).
Samaroo, Brinsley, 'Asian Identity and Culture in the Caribbean', in George Lamming (ed.), *Enterprise of the Indies* (Port of Spain: The Trinidad and Tobago Institute of the West Indies, 1999).
Sandiford, Keith A.P., 'Indo-Caribbean Contributions to West Indian Cricket', *Cricket Lore*, Vol. Five, Issue Two (November, 2002).
Seecharan, Clem, *'Tiger in the Stars': The Anatomy of Indian Achievement in British Guiana, 1919-29* (London: Macmillan, 1997).
— *Joseph Ruhomon's India: The Progress of her People at Home and Abroad and how those in British Guiana may Improve Themselves* (Kingston, Jamaica: The University of the West Indies Press, 2001).
— *Sweetening 'Bitter Sugar': Jock Campbell, the Booker Reformer in British Guiana*, 1934-66 (Kingston, Jamaica: Ian Randle Publishers, 2005).
— 'The Anatomy of Cheddi Jagan's Marxism', in John Gaffar La Guerre and Ann Marie Bissessar (eds.), *Calcutta to Caroni and the Indian Diaspora* (St. Augustine, Trinidad: School of Continuing Studies, University of the West Indies, 2005).
— *Muscular Learning: Cricket and Education in the Making of the British West Indies at the End of the 19th Century* (Kingston, Jamaica: Ian Randle Publishers, 2006).
— *Mother India's Shadow over El Dorado: Indo-Guyanese Politics and Identity, 1890s-1930s* (Kingston, Jamaica: Ian Randle Publishers [forthcoming, 2009]).
Shils, Edward, *The Intellectual between Tradition and Modernity: The Indian Situation* (The Hague: Mouton, 1961).
Sobers, Garry, *My Autobiography* (London: Headline, 2002).
Swan, Michael, *British Guiana: The Land of Six Peoples* (London: Her Majesty's Stationery Office, 1957).
Swanton, E.W., *West Indies Revisited: The M.C.C. Tour, 1959-60* (London:

Heinemann, 1960).
Thapar, Romila, *The Penguin History of Early India: From the Origins to A D 1300* (New Delhi: Penguin Books, 2002)
Trautmann, Thomas R., *Aryans and British India* (Berkeley: University of California Press, 1997).
Walcott, Clyde, *Island Cricketers* (London: Hodder and Stoughton, 1958),
— *Sixty Years on the Back Foot: The Cricketing Life of Sir Clyde Walcott* (London: Orion Books, 1999).
Wilde, Simon, *Ranji: A Genius Rich and Strange* (London: The Kingswood Press, 1990).
Williams, Jack, *Cricket and Race* (Oxford: Berg, 2001).
Woodcock, John, *The 'Times' One Hundred Greatest Cricketers* (London: Macmillan, 1998).
Woodward, Ian, *Aussies versus Windies: A History of Australia-West Indies Cricket* (Petersham, New South Wales: Walla Walla Press, 1998).
Wooldridge, Ian, *Cricket, Lovely Cricket: the West Indies Tour, 1963* (London: Robert Hale, 1963).

Interviews

Basil Butcher (by phone), New Jersey, USA, 25 July 2008; 27 July 2008.
Dr Cheddi Jagan (1918-97), Coventry, England, 10 May 1992; Georgetown, Guyana, 8 September 1992.
Ivy Jailall, Sea Well, Berbice, Guyana, 10 February 2003.
Eusi Kwayana, Georgetown, Guyana, 22 September 1992.
Ivan Madray, London, 2-3 November 1987; 11 June 2008.
Joe Solomon, L.B.I., Guyana, 27 August 1997; (by phone), New York, USA, 30 July 2008.

Web Sources

I have relied heavily on *cricketarchive.com* for much of the statistical information in the text. It is an excellent source. So, too, is the book compiled by Jimmy Richards and Mervyn Wong, *Statistics of West Indies Cricket* (Kingston, Jamaica: Heinemann, 1990).

INDEX